Palgrave Studies in Masculinity, Sport and Exercise

Series Editors
Rory Magrath
Solent University
Southampton, UK

Jamie Cleland
University of South Australia
Adelaide, Australia

Eric Anderson
University of Winchester
Winchester, UK

Recent years have seen the emergence of a considerable body of research investigating the complex nature of masculinity, and how it impacts on a wide-range of sporting (and exercise) cultures. Palgrave Studies in Masculinity, Sport and Exercise is the first series solely dedicated to providing innovative and high-quality scholarship within this area of study. The series welcomes proposals for research monographs, Palgrave Pivots and edited collections examining critical, empirical and theoretical issues related to the study of masculinity, sport and exercise. The series has an international focus – both in terms of its authorship and readership – and welcomes relevant scholarship by established and emerging scholars in the field from any country.

Jack Hardwicke

Masculinities and the Culture of Competitive Cycling

palgrave
macmillan

Jack Hardwicke
University of Northampton
Centre for Physical Activity and Life Sciences
Faculty of Arts, Science and Technology
Northampton, UK

ISSN 2662-740X ISSN 2662-7418 (electronic)
Palgrave Studies in Masculinity, Sport and Exercise
ISBN 978-3-031-26974-5 ISBN 978-3-031-26975-2 (eBook)
https://doi.org/10.1007/978-3-031-26975-2

© The Editor(s) (if applicable) and The Author(s), under exclusive licence to Springer
Nature Switzerland AG 2023
This work is subject to copyright. All rights are solely and exclusively licensed by the
Publisher, whether the whole or part of the material is concerned, specifically the rights of
translation, reprinting, reuse of illustrations, recitation, broadcasting, reproduction on
microfilms or in any other physical way, and transmission or information storage and retrieval,
electronic adaptation, computer software, or by similar or dissimilar methodology now
known or hereafter developed.
The use of general descriptive names, registered names, trademarks, service marks, etc. in this
publication does not imply, even in the absence of a specific statement, that such names are
exempt from the relevant protective laws and regulations and therefore free for general use.
The publisher, the authors, and the editors are safe to assume that the advice and information
in this book are believed to be true and accurate at the date of publication. Neither the publisher nor the authors or the editors give a warranty, expressed or implied, with respect to the
material contained herein or for any errors or omissions that may have been made. The
publisher remains neutral with regard to jurisdictional claims in published maps and institutional affiliations.

Cover illustration: MANUEL PUGA CASTILLO/Alamy

This Palgrave Macmillan imprint is published by the registered company Springer Nature
Switzerland AG.
The registered company address is: Gewerbestrasse 11, 6330 Cham, Switzerland

CONTENTS

1 Rolling Out: Introduction   1

2 Theorising Sporting Masculinities   21

3 The Gentlemen's Club: Cycling and Masculinity in Victorian Britain   41

4 'Don't be soft': Cycling and Masculinity in the Twenty-First Century   61

5 Joining the Peloton: The Cult(ure) of Competitive Road Cycling   77

6 Getting Back on the Bike: Debating Injury and Masculinity   103

7 Winning at All Costs: The Intersects of Doping, Hypercompetition and Masculinity in Cycling   123

8 Out in the Peloton: Sexual Minorities in Road Cycling   141

9 Women on Wheels: Orthodox Masculinity and the Marginalisation of Women in Competitive Cycling   159

10 Crossing the Finish Line: Conclusions   173

References   181

Index   209

LIST OF TABLES

Table 1.1	Interview participant characteristics	10
Table 8.1	Demographic breakdown of survey respondents (N = 359)	149
Table 8.2	Frequency of Likert survey responses (n =148)	150
Table 8.3	Frequency of responses to experiences anti-LGBTQ+ discourse (n = 148)	151
Table 8.4	Frequency of Likert survey responses (n =211)	152

CHAPTER 1

Rolling Out: Introduction

It was early on a warm summer's morning and a sea of lycra-clad cyclists gathered around the community hall that was serving as the race headquarters for this particular race. There was a nervous atmosphere present as the race was the Regional Road Race championship, a target event for many of the serious cyclists in the local area. The chatter, joking and laughing was silenced by the blow of a whistle as the race commissaire signalled to the riders that the race debriefing was about to take place. The standard pre-race information was recited to the racers, and the reminder that the roads were still open to the public, and any riders crossing the central white line to oncoming traffic would be disqualified. With that completed, the commissaires car rolled out of the village hall car park with a trail of keen cyclists closely following. After about 5 km of a neutralised 'roll out' through sleepy country roads, the whistle blew, the lead car pulled away and it was 'go time'; the first kilometre of a 140 km road race began.

There was no hanging around for things to get kicked off, as the first 40kms of racing saw several attacks and a high pace maintained—averaging just over 43kph. Despite numerous attempts, no attacks were successful and as the first hour of the race passed the peloton remained all together. But as the bunch hit the most significant climb on the circuit, a small group of 8–10 riders managed to break clear from the rest and quickly established a significant gap from the peloton, all working well together and sharing the workload. This group was to be joined by another 4 riders, forming a strong 'breakaway' that kept the pace high.

© The Author(s), under exclusive license to Springer Nature
Switzerland AG 2023
J. Hardwicke, *Masculinities and the Culture of Competitive Cycling*,
Palgrave Studies in Masculinity, Sport and Exercise,
https://doi.org/10.1007/978-3-031-26975-2_1

This breakaway continued working well and building a gap between themselves and the peloton. As the group came off a fast descent, disaster struck. The tranquillity of the local countryside setting was disrupted with sounds of screeching, carbon fibre snapping and bodies hitting concrete. Seconds before, the group was 'lined out' as the pace was increased, and about the 6th rider in this line had touched wheels with the rider in front leading to them losing control and falling to the ground at 45kph. With nowhere else to go, and the speed the group was travelling at taking away any opportunity to slow down or react quick enough to avoid the inevitable, a subsequent bunch of riders collided into the fallen rider as bodies and bikes flew everywhere.

From the spectators' view, the following few minutes could be likened to a battle ground as bloodied bodies in differing states of pain staggered around trying to find their bikes and assess the damage done (to themselves and their machine). One body, however, remained motionless on the floor. It would be a few moments before this rider gained consciousness and followed suit with the other riders of picking himself up, checking down his bike and considering getting back on to try re-join the race. Then the initial adrenaline rush wore off and the pain set in. This rider was going nowhere and returned to laying on the floor at the side of the road. He was soon to find out he had suffered a traumatic brain injury, broken jaw, elbow and left significant amounts of skin on the tarmac.

Competitive road cyclists are often a strange group of people. I should know, I competed in the sport for over ten years. The above vignette was a recollection from one of the more severe crashes, of the many, I experienced in my time as a racing cyclist. The unconscious rider described was me. Being involved in a bicycle crash is an experience that is hard to describe until you experience it first-hand. The sounds and bodily sensations of crashing are unique, terrifying and often times can be traumatic for the victim. Of particular interest is the almost automatic response of the racing cyclist to 'get back on the bike' following a crash and try to re-join whatever the race is. This happens at the very top level of the sport right down to regional-level races.

Road cycling is a curious and nuanced sport. Who willingly gets up at 5 am on a Sunday to essentially go torture themselves? Well, a significant, and increasing, number of the British population do. There is a largely hidden social world of racing cyclists, who dedicate themselves to strict training regimes, financial commitments and put their bodies on the line to compete in races at the weekend, and weekday evenings, from February through to October around the UK. In 2019, British Cycling (the national governing body for the sport) had 150,000 active members, which represents a three-fold increase since 2012 and the largest recorded membership base since its establishment (British Cycling, 2019). It is a sport that has seen significant increase in participation over recent years.

The sport has a long and rich history in Britain dating back to the 1880s. It is also a sport which is steeped in risk and involves significant material and bodily sacrifice. I have been privy to these as the above vignette detailed. Having suffered several serious injuries from participating in the sport, as well as conditioning my body for performance over a number of years, I am well accustomed to the nuances of competitive road cycling. With my academic training in the social sciences, I am also acutely aware of the wider socio-cultural factors that influenced many of my experiences in the sport. For example, why I was back training a week after the crash detailed above and returned to racing within a month.

One such influence, amongst others, is that of masculinity. When masculinity and sport is considered, images of the rugged muscular rugby player, boxer or American football player is often conjured up and not the slim, lycra-clad road cyclist with shaved legs. Yet, as this book will go on to detail, the sport of road cycling has historically been deeply tied to notions of masculinity which has shaped the culture of the sport and continues to influence the attitudes, behaviours and practices of racing cyclists today.

What follows is the introduction to this monograph, *Masculinities and the Culture of Competitive Cycling*. The book aims to provide a comprehensive investigation into the sport of road cycling, using the lens of masculinity and subcultural theorising. A range of topics are covered such as risk taking, injury, doping and experiences of sexual minorities and women to provide a theoretical and empirical exploration of the culture of competitive cycling and its relation to masculinity. In doing so, it is hoped a significant gap in the literature is addressed as well as advancements in understandings for contemporary health concerns in the sport, such as the often-harmful injury management behaviours of racing cyclists. Before beginning this analysis, this introductory chapter outlines the context of the book, the context of researching cycling, the research the book is based upon and some of the research problems associated with the work.

This chapter concludes with brief overviews of each chapter allowing the reader to know the *'parcours'* ahead.

OVERVIEW

The aim of this book is to provide a novel account, and socio-cultural analysis, of masculinities and the culture of an individual sport: competitive road cycling. This is particularly germane as much of the literature on masculinity and sporting cultures in the sports studies field is predicated on organised team sports, such as rugby and football, with limited work on individual sports. The book is based on extensive auto-ethnographic, qualitative and quantitative research into this field which has shown competitive cycling presents unique challenges and is lagging behind wider cultural changes. For example, the sport has a problematic injury culture, there are currently no openly gay male professional cyclists, evidence of high levels of homophobia, limited support from governing bodies for LGBTQ+ inclusion; and my research shows hypermasculinity remains idolised within the sport.

Sport, more broadly, offers a rich social context for analysis in Western societies. This is because we (Western society) are obsessed with sport. It is a prevailing collective belief that sport is a socially valuable enterprise with much positive functions for society (Anderson & White, 2018). Indeed, this obsession with sport led Burstyn (1999) to call sport 'a great secular masculine religion', arguing that it maintains such a privileged position in our society that critical scrutiny of it is often overlooked.

This book is grounded in a critical approach to sport studies, in which the institution does not escape critical analysis and scrutiny. Drawing on socio-cultural research, and sociological theory, the book offers a detailed and extensive exploration into the culture of competitive road cycling and uses the lens of masculinity to examine a range of issues. As such, the book approaches the issues from a sociological perspective in that I focus, and am interested in, individual experiences, but these are examined against the backdrop of collective experiences and socio-cultural influences.

In understanding where this book is situated in the wider literature, a brief overview is required. Firstly, the past two decades has seen a significant transformation of Western masculinities. The scholarship on the relationship between sport and masculinity in the twentieth century highlighted how heterosexual men and boys were regulated by an orthodox form of masculinity, commonly referred to as hegemonic masculinity (e.g. Connell, 1995). This regulation was achieved through the high levels of homophobia associated with this epoch (Pronger, 1990) and has been retrospectively conceptualised using Anderson's (2009a, 2009b) concept of 'homohysteria'—the fear of being culturally perceived as gay (this is discussed in more detail in the following chapters).

In the last few decades, however, a paradigm shift has occurred. A new generation of masculinity scholars have documented that athletes have significantly redefined their version of normative masculinity. Housed mostly in the disciplines of sociology (e.g. Anderson, 2009a, 2009b; McCormack, 2012, 2014; Roberts, 2020), the primary finding is that decreasing homophobia has a positive impact on the promotion of more inclusive forms of masculinity. This has been theorised as Inclusive Masculinity Theory by Anderson (Anderson, 2009a, 2009b), which outlines the theoretical framework for this book. This is discussed in the following chapter.

This shift has been particularly evident in men's team sport culture, which has seen a significant decline in stigma against gay men (Anderson et al., 2016). As this has diminished, heterosexual men have been able to engage in a wider range of gendered behaviours than previously permitted. However, much of the previous research has been done on organised team sports, such as rugby and football. Anderson (2009a, 2009b) has described these sports as primary domains for studying shifts in masculinity because they have been theorised to be social locations of men steeped in orthodox understandings of gender.

To date, only two studies have examined inclusive masculinity among individual sport athletes in modern times, one on American high-school runners (Morales & Caffyn-Parsons, 2017) and one on high-school wrestlers (Michael, 2015); both report findings consistent with inclusive masculinity. It is important to examine masculinities in specific sporting contexts as not all sports promote the same forms of masculinity to the same degrees. This is particularly the case with a nuanced sport such as competitive road cycling. As McDonald (2014, p. 484) notes 'there are specificities to the form that masculinity takes in competitive cycling. Each sport has to be understood on its own terms' (McDonald, 2014, p. 484). As such, the context of this book is to understand and theorise masculinity within competitive road cycling.

To achieve this, research from around the world is used in citation, but the specific focus is within the UK, and this is where most of the original empirical data reported on was collected. Furthermore, the context of this book, and the research data, is concerned with men and masculinities. As such, the overarching focus is on male cyclists throughout. However, my research has included women and discussions are provided throughout for how notions of masculinity influence and intersect with women's experiences in the sport. This is discussed further in Chap. 9.

Contextualising Competitive Cycling

It is important to explicitly set the parameters of this book, and situate the research, regarding what I mean when I say, 'competitive cycling'. This is a surprisingly difficult task. Competitive cycling differs from other sports in that it is made up of numerous subdisciplines, non-conventional competition structures and varied team and training structures (Ayala et al., 2021). Popular competitive cycling disciplines include road and criterium racing, track racing, mountain biking and, more recently, gravel racing. Many cyclists compete in multiple disciplines. The sport is also nuanced in that it shifts between being an individual and a team sport depending on discipline and context. This is explored further in Chap. 4 with a consideration for the competing ideologies of individualism and collectivism in road cycling. Of interest to this book is that competitive cyclists will also train with cyclists from other clubs/teams as well as with recreational cyclists who do not race but may be considered 'serious leisure cyclists' (Ayala et al., 2021; Hardwicke, 2022a, 2022b, 2022c).

The primary focus of this book is on competitive road cycling, from amateur up to professional levels. Whilst other disciplines, and research from other disciplines, will be used, this is only done so to provide greater context to the discussions. Road cycling typically, with the exception of Stage Races and Time Trials, involves group racing where there is a mass-start in which riders then compete on a fixed route for a set distance, with the first across the line being deemed the winner. The racing system in the UK works by cyclists paying for membership to the main governing body, British Cycling. New members that have never raced are designated as 'Fourth category'. An individual enters a race equal to their category (e.g. a 'Fourth category' only race) and earns points through placing in the top 10 (or top 20 for a national-level race) of a British Cycling sanctioned race. These points accumulate and allow riders to move through categories from Fourth, Third, Second, First and Elite. This categorisation system is used throughout the book to describe research participants, indicating the level of competition they engage with.

With the complexity of the sport noted above, being clear about exactly *who* and *what* is meant by 'cyclists' in research is paramount. This is problematic in the academic literature, across different academic fields, as there is little uniformity or consensus in how researchers describe and define competitive cyclists (Roberts et al., 2022). To avoid this, competitive cyclists in this book are understood as cyclists that compete in sanctioned cycle events and engage with cycling as sport. Various terms may be used throughout to describe cyclists, but the purpose of this section is to provide clarity on the overarching parameters of the book. The most commonly used phrase will be competitive road cyclists, to denote I am talking about competitive cyclists competing in road-based disciplines.

However, there is further complexity here in that many 'blurred' lines exist when researching road cycling participants, and social research on cycling as serious leisure and/or as sport is limited (Falcous, 2017). Cox (2005, p. 1) notes that 'cycling has very different meanings and connotations for those who cycle' and the social construction of cycling must be acknowledged. Expanding on this, Cox (2005) suggests that the meanings and interpretations cycling participants place on their activity must be considered and that there is a wide spectrum in which we can consider someone a 'road cyclist'. Germane here is the rise in the 'serious' leisure road cyclist that mirrors much of the culture of the competitive sport (following the sport media, buying the equipment, adhering to training regimes) but do not formally 'compete' in sanctioned events (O'Connor & Brown, 2007). Yet that is not to say they are not competitive, these cyclists often self-organise into groups and 'compete' on public roads outside of the formal competitive races governed by sporting bodies (Brown et al., 2009). This has led to the popular culture, and academic, reference of 'Weekend Warriors' that engage in competitive cycling culture but do not race (O'Connor & Brown, 2007). It is important this group is not overlooked in socio-cultural research into cycling, and considerations for this group are provided throughout this book. The data reported on throughout the book is based on competitive road cyclists (unless specified otherwise) but applies to serious leisure cyclists also.

Building on this, the reason this group is important not to overlook is because many cycling practices for serious leisure purposes are reflective and influenced by the competitive sport. The sport of road cycling has a long and rich history as a codified sport which emerged in the 1880s in Victorian Britain against the backdrop of large social changes attributed to the transition from an agrarian to an industrial society. Emerging as a sport in this period, it holds the traits seen in modern sports such as being highly competitive, codified with rules and regulations and being technology driven. Furthermore, sports that emerged from this era have also been theorised as being part of a political project to instil orthodox masculinity into boys and men to combat the perceived trends of feminised boys who were growing up without father figures for the first time (Anderson, 2014). Chapter 3 discusses how cycling practices were shaped by gender relations in this environment leading to competitive road cycling being developed as a sport steeped in notions of orthodox masculinity.

To contextualise this book, it is important to highlight that contemporary road cycling (competitive and recreationally) is regularly described as a sport dominated by middle-class males (Falcous, 2017; Jones, 2022). Indeed, the gender disparity of participation across cycling contexts has been an ongoing concern (Heesch et al., 2012; Aldred et al., 2016), which is discussed in more detail in Chap. 9. Furthermore, the sport has been described as having a 'conservative culture' in regard to diversity and inclusion (Cycling News, 2017). As will be explicated throughout the book, the sport was developed by men and this demographic remains the most represented within the contemporary sport.

Moving to a more theoretical discussion of the context of this book, there has been very little written on socio-cultural aspects of competitive road cycling (Falcous, 2017; Hardwicke, 2022a, 2022b, 2022c). There was a flurry of early work from Williams (1989) and Albert (1990, 1991, 1997, 1999) from an interactionist perspective that examined the subcultural dynamics of competitive road cycling. Recent years have seen other scholars consider the subcultural aspects of competitive cycling (O'Connor & Brown, 2007; Rees et al., 2014; Falcous, 2017; Glackin & Beale, 2018). This body of work is discussed in depth in Chap. 4.

Much of the socio-cultural research into competitive cycling has been influenced by the interactionist perspective, focusing on the micro-level experiences of cyclists and symbolic meanings attached to engaging in their activity. The theoretical frame of this book (explained further in the following chapter) builds on this work by examining the sport from a meso-level perspective in which individual everyday experiences are examined and connected to wider social-cultural influences, mainly gender. Further, there have been very limited socio-cultural gendered analysis of competitive road cycling and none that use the lens of masculinity. O'Connor and Brown's (2007) ethnographic work suggested road cycling was a central feature in the social construction of gender amongst cyclists.

1 ROLLING OUT: INTRODUCTION   9

Subcultural membership of informal road cycling groups were argued to be social locations in which cyclists aligned behaviours and produced gendered ideology of the 'weekend warrior'. But, to my knowledge, there has not been a detailed exploration into the construction of gender amongst competitive cyclists and very little research into masculinity and its influence on the sport of road cycling. This outlines a key rationale for this book.

THE STUDY

This book offers both theoretical and empirical insights to the research area outlined above. The empirical work has developed out of my PhD, as well as a range of research I have subsequently conducted. Both qualitative and quantitative research is drawn on throughout the book, and this reflects my research philosophy. As a mixed-methods researcher, I see value in all research methods and use a range within my own work. The book also uses a range of relevant theory to support the wider implications of the discussions and understand the data reported on, and, as will be discussed in the following chapter, the book is situated in the theoretical framework of Inclusive Masculinity Theory (Anderson, 2009a, 2009b).

As such, this work provides empirical-theoretical insights and explanations of the development of competitive road cycling from its emergence in the late nineteenth century through to the present day. Being concerned with a sociological analysis of the sport, the main focus of the study is understanding how masculinity and cycling intersect, historically and contemporarily, as well as providing a detailed insight to the culture of the sport more broadly. The topics used to discuss this include injury, risk taking, doping, hypercompetition and sexual minority and women's experiences in the sport.

All original studies reported on in this book have received institutional ethical approval, and the works are referenced where appropriate so greater detail on the methods can be read in the original research articles. All ethical guidelines of the British Sociological Association were adhered to throughout the body of research associated with this project. For my qualitative interview work, to protect the identity of participants, each has been allocated a number and are simply referred to by this throughout the book (e.g. 'Participant 1'). Research participants are mostly referred to by their relevant characteristics, for example, racing category, age and sex. Table 1.1 provides an overview of the participants interviewed. Other empirical studies reported on involved self-report cross-sectional surveys,

Table 1.1 Interview participant characteristics

Participant No.	Sex	Age	Racing category	Years competing
1	M	26	Second	6
2	M	27	First	5
3	M	39	Second	25
4	M	50	Fourth	13
5	F	34	Second	13
6	M	37	Third	10
7	M	45	Fourth	11
8	M	20	Elite	8
9	M	29	Elite	10
10	M	54	Third	10
11	M	32	Elite	9
12	M	29	Elite	10
13	F	43	Elite	15
14	M	19	First	4
15	M	19	First	12
16	M	26	Elite	10
17	M	30	Third	5
18	F	25	Second	3

Abbreviations *M* = male; *F* = female.

with a combined sample of over 900 competitive cyclists across a range of studies (Hardwicke & Hurst, 2020; Hardwicke, 2022a, 2022b, 2022c; Hardwicke et al., 2022). Whilst not published as secondary data, the book also draws on detailed socio-historical analysis of publicly available cycling material as well as contemporary cycling literature and journalism. The benefit of this for the study of sport is justified in the following chapter.

In addition to the surveys, semi-structured interviews and media discourse analysis conducted, I draw upon a reflexive auto-ethnography and participant observation via my extensive experience as a competitive road cyclist for over ten years. This has included competing in over 150 regional, national and international road races. And over 1000 hours (this is a conservative estimate) spent training and socialising with competitive cyclists around the UK. Using past training diaries, retrospective accounts, self-reflection and conversation with peers I have applied principles of auto-ethnography to enrich the insights provided throughout this book (Chang, 2016).

Further to this, I have used my status as a 'road cyclist' to have numerous unstructured conversations with competitive road cyclists that has helped refine my theorising and the arguments made throughout this work. This experience has provided me with detailed knowledge of the social world of the racing cyclist which is used to compliment the empirical data reported on and the available literature used throughout this book. This use of personal experience, hyper-subjectivity and my deep involvement with the research area will set off alarm bells for some scientists. Indeed, it does bring significant problems to the research that must be considered. This is addressed in the following section.

RESEARCH PROBLEMS

Cycling has always been a part of my life in various forms. From a young age I was on a bike, and weekends regularly consisted of family bike rides. I raced intermittently throughout my childhood but took up competitive road cycling in earnest from the age of 16. Every former athlete has stories of their competitive past that are of great interest to themselves and that is usually the extent of the captive audience. I will not depict my cycling 'career' as it is not important, nor is it of interest to anyone but myself (or that impressive). But the important point here is that I was completely invested in the sport; I lived and breathed cycling for a significant period of my life. This has provided me with wide-ranging experiences in the sport and interactions with racing cyclists. Sharing a biography with the area of study (cycling culture) and subjects of study (racing cyclists) brings unique benefits and challenges to this book that must be attended to.

Firstly, Hamdan (2009) writes that, as researchers, we do not approach a topic in a value-free vacuum but have distinctive agendas in seeking answers to research questions. As a result, a somewhat common-sensical observation is that most researchers research topics they are interested in or have a background in. This is particularly true within sport studies. Hill and Dao (2021) comment on this, stating that accompanying many researchers is an attraction towards studying topics that they have a personal connection to. As such, 'those who undertake research that stems from personal histories and biographies, a space of subjectivity is constantly present, underlying the entire project' (Hill & Dao, 2021, p. 521). This can become problematic if not addressed and acted on. Hamdan (2009) argues we must apply reflexive scrutiny to unpack the researcher identities and how biography may guide and shape the entire research process. This is the task of the remainder of this section.

A key idea to first consider is the insider/outsider relationship of the researcher and the data. I have outlined my close relationship and experiences in the research area, highlighting my 'insider' status. Merton (1972) has described the 'insider' as someone who holds a substantial amount of knowledge of a community and its members. This is true of my position, as I have significant knowledge of the UK competitive cycling 'community' and an understanding of the intricacies and nuances of the sport that would not be available to someone that has not participated in competitive cycling. Further, Gair (2012) suggests insider status in the field is developed when shared and common experiences are discussed and materialise throughout the research process. This ability to share common experiences enriched the interviews undertaken for this work, as well as the associated participant observation and discourse analysis of secondary data.

There are, however, problems with being close to the object of study. Hill and Dao (2021) outline two key disadvantages being hyper-subjectivity and the inability to remove the researcher from the research. Resultantly, this poses the risk that personal biases will steer the research based on previous assumptions and beliefs about the object/subjects of study (Chavez, 2008). This is an ongoing issue in social science research which positions the importance of 'reflexivity'. Reflexivity can be defined as 'the process or faculty by which the mind observes and examines its own experiences and emotions, intelligent self-awareness, introspection' (Sherry, 2013, p. 283). It is a process which enables researchers to acknowledge their influence on the research and plan to limit and mitigate issues of subjectivity where possible. It also brings into question researcher biography and identity in how it may benefit or limit the collection and interpretation of data (Kidd & Kral, 2005; Denzin et al., 2005).

The above discussion relates to the concept of 'objectivity'. The term has a long history in the social sciences and specifically sociology. Much common-sense approaches in sociology, largely from interpretivists, is that objectivity is a myth (Jenkins, 2002). An argument goes that it cannot be obtained when you have humans researching humans, within the human world. We are the objects of our study, and this brings with it a can of worms that must be considered. However, I argue we should not abandon attempts to obtain objectivity when researching the human world.

Objectivity can be thought of on two levels in how it impacts research. These are (1) politics and personal values and (2) the production of knowledge. Firstly, I believe that sociology is a tool to understand the world, and the ability to critically examine social issues is a strength of the discipline

(McCormack et al., 2021). As such, I do not desire a value-free approach to social research, nor do I think it is possible. Politics, personal values and ethics will always be present in social science research but, as Jenkins (2002) argues, this need not prevent us from striving towards the second level of objectivity. Our subjectivities as researchers of the human world should be acknowledged and grappled with, not ignored as if they do not exist or viewed as an unavoidable flaw of social research.

To achieve the above desire, a plan and a process is required. Jenkins' (2002) discussion of this process is useful here with his comments on objectivity meaning 'working hard to prevent politics and values getting in the way of finding out as much as we can, as honestly as we can, and as systematically as we can' (p. 10). I believe this to be a worthwhile pursuit to produce good social science research. Whilst we cannot achieve complete objectivity, as researchers we can work towards it, even if it is only ever achieved partially. Without doing so, claims of knowledge about the human world will often not be taken seriously (Jenkins, 2002).

The above discussion will now be applied to the process taken for the research conducted for the book to ensure rigour. I have discussed the concept of 'reflexivity', acknowledging my shared biography and experiences with the object and subjects of study for this project. Importantly, this has been engaged with before, during and after the entire research process. In designing the methodological approach to examine various areas of competitive road cycling, I have used methods in which I have been distanced from the data, such as self-report surveys, and methods in which I am more involved, such as the semi-structured interviews and auto-ethnography. The purpose of this was to use my experiences as a research tool, but also to triangulate any findings with alternative methodologies in which I was removed from the process of data collection and analysis.

Due to my experiences in the sport, my ability to be entirely critically distanced from the data is somewhat compromised (Chavez, 2008). This is pertinent for the studies using qualitative methodologies, as well as the auto-ethnographic accounts. This must be acknowledged as a potential limitation of the research and the steps taken to mitigate my personal biases steering the research will be outlined. The primary method used here was a network of 'critical friends' (see Smith & McGannon, 2018, for a detailed discussion on the utility of this process and its relationship to qualitative research traditions).

Throughout the associated work with this project and research studies used, I have used a network of colleagues in which I have been in continuous critical dialogue. This has involved the presentation of alternative interpretations of the data and critical questioning of the arguments presented and evidence they are grounded in. Importantly, I have sought to engage in this critical dialogue with academic colleagues from a range of different disciplines and interests, inside and outside of the social sciences. Even more important is I have had this critical dialogue with competitive cyclists to ensure I am not working within an academic echo chamber. This diversity has resulted in wide-ranging interpretations and discussions of the research and data that afforded me the space to reflect on my own assumptions and biases throughout the research process and writing of this book.

In engaging in this practice, reflexivity was encouraged by the challenging of my construction of knowledge (Cowan & Taylor, 2016). Through this process, I have been able to obtain detailed insider knowledge of competitive road cycling culture but also pursue a deeper critical interpretation and analysis of the data gained. Furthermore, this systematic process aided me in pursuing the need to keep a critical distance from the data to then attempt to provide the best possible honest view of it (Jenkins, 2002). This is the hope of this book.

CHAPTER OUTLINES

Chapter 2 lays the theoretical foundations for discussing the relationship between sport and masculinity. The study of masculinity more broadly is examined before being considered within the sporting context. The reader is familiarised with the relevant literature on the topic and the chapter outlines the theoretical framework the book works within and the terms used throughout. The general groundwork of the book is also further explained, with some consideration for the research approach taken.

Chapter 3 illustrates the importance of history in understanding contemporary social settings. Namely, the historical development of competitive cycling during the nineteenth century is explored and its relationship to masculinity. Masculinities in Victorian British society are first discussed before this foundation is used to discuss the development of competitive sport and how road cycling maps onto this historical process. It is explained that masculinity has had a deep and enduring influence on the development of competitive road cycling.

Chapter 4 examines the current social environment of competitive cycling as it relates to masculinity. The notion of competitive road cycling having a 'macho culture', which is commonly referred to in popular press, is examined and interrogated in line with the available academic evidence on the topic. Research on male cyclists' identity with masculinity is presented, with findings suggesting male cyclists identify with a stricter notion of masculinity compared to the general population. From this, the argument is made that competitive road cycling presents a cultural lag behind the broader culture in its understanding and relationship to masculinity.

Chapter 5 discusses the culture of competitive cycling more broadly by building on the previous chapters that outline the orthodox masculine foundations in which much of the sports culture has been built on. The sociology of sporting subcultures is discussed and then applied to the sport of road cycling. Then the everyday experiences of the competitive road cyclist within a sport with a strong, often cult-like, subculture associated with it is considered as well as the process of identity formation in the sport. The chapter shows the power of sporting subcultures to direct and influence behaviours and attitudes. The chapter concludes with an argument put forward that competitive road cycling is a sport that operates within a 'culture of risk', and this theoretical framing provides the starting point of analysis for the following two chapters.

Chapter 6 examines the injury culture and management practices of competitive cyclists framed through the notion of performance being favoured over health in cycling culture and cyclists' behaviours. The chapter shows how participating in the sport of road cycling carries a high risk of physical injury, with crashing and injury being normalised aspects of competing in road cycling. A problem of cyclists competing whilst injured and 'getting back on the bike' before it would be medically advised to do so is discussed. The chapter discusses the utility of examining such practices through the lens of masculinity.

Chapter 7 addresses the issue of doping in cycling. The chapter shows the importance of moving away from considering doping in sport as an individual act of moral failing and towards an understanding of doping as an expected outcome of hypercompetitive sport in the West. The foundations of competitive sport within a capitalist society and how this led to an emphasis on competition and winning are explained to the reader. The relationship between sport, masculinities and doping is then examined before being applied specifically to cycling. The chapter concludes with the argument that the orthodox masculine foundations on which competitive road cycling was developed is a significant factor, amongst others discussed, leading to the environment in which doping became a logical option for cyclists and thus was consumed into the culture of the sport.

Chapter 8 turns the attention away from health and towards different experiences of individuals in the sport with an examination of sexual minorities in competitive cycling. After demonstrating the link between masculinities, sexualities and sport, the chapter considers why there are no openly gay male professional cyclists, at the time of writing, and what available data suggests the experiences of sexual minorities, namely, gay males, are like in the sport.

Chapter 10 continues this discussion through an examination of women's experiences in competitive cycling, and how orthodox masculinities may influence this. The chapter reminds readers of the influences of gender relations on the development of sport and on the sport of road cycling specifically. The chapter discusses how the culture of competitive road cycling, in which orthodox masculinity is idolised, may lead to women being marginalised in the sport.

The final chapter brings the arguments made throughout the book together. The thesis is put forward that competitive road cycling culture presents a cultural lag behind broader society in its relationship to masculinity, and theorising of this is explicated. This can manifest in numerous ways as will be demonstrated throughout preceding chapters. The implications of the book and contributions to the literature are outlined. The book concludes with a discussion on what the future of the sport might look like (or what it is hoped to look like) as well as departure points for future research being highlighted.

REFERENCES

Albert, E. (1990). Constructing the order of finish in the sport of bicycle racing. *Journal of Popular Culture, 23*(4), 145–154.

Albert, E. (1991). Riding a line: Competition and cooperation in the sport of bicycle racing. *Sociology of Sport Journal, 8*(4), 341–361.

Albert, E. (1997). Bicycle racing and the social construction of place. In P. De Nardis, A. Mussino, & N. Porro (Eds.), *Sport: Social problems, social movements*. Edizioni Seam.

Albert, E. (1999). Dealing with danger: The normalization of risk in cycling. *International Review for the Sociology of Sport, 34*(2), 157–171.

Aldred, R., Woodcock, J., & Goodman, A. (2016). Does more cycling mean more diversity in cycling? *Transport Reviews, 36*(1), 28–44.

Anderson, E. (2009a). *Inclusive masculinity: The changing nature of masculinities (Routledge research in gender and society)* (1st ed.). Routledge.

Anderson, E. D. (2009b). The maintenance of masculinity among the stakeholders of sport. *Sport Management Review, 12*(1), 3–14.

Anderson, E. (2014). *21st century jocks: Sporting men and contemporary heterosexuality*. Palgrave Macmillan.

Anderson, E., Magrath, R., & Bullingham, R. (2016). *Out in sport* (1st ed.). Routledge.

Anderson, E., & White, A. (2018). *Sport, theory and social problems*. Routledge Taylor & Francis Group.

Ayala, E. E., Riley-Schmida, A., Faulkner, K. P., & Maleski, K. (2021). Microaggressions experienced by women and gender diverse athletes in competitive cycling. *Women in Sport and Physical Activity Journal, 29*(1), 59–67.

British Cycling. (2019). British Cycling reaches 150,000 members milestone for first time. Available at: https://www.britishcycling.org.uk/campaigning/article/20190502-campaigning-BRITISH-CYCLING-REACHES-150-000-MEMBERS-MILESTONE-FOR-FIRST-TIME-0

Brown, T. D., O'Connor, J. P., & Barkatsas, A. N. (2009). Instrumentation and motivations for organised cycling: The development of the Cyclist Motivation Instrument (CMI). *Journal of Sports Science & Medicine, 8*(2), 211.

Burstyn, V. (1999). *The rites of men: Manhood, politics and the culture of sport*. University of Toronto Press.

Chang, H. (2016). *Autoethnography as method*. Routledge.

Chavez, C. (2008). Conceptualizing from the inside: Advantages, complications, and demands on insider positionality. *The Qualitative Report, 13*(3), 474–494.

Connell, R. W. (1995). *Masculinities*. University of California Press.

Cowan, D., & Taylor, I. M. (2016). 'I'm proud of what I achieved; I'm also ashamed of what I done': A soccer coach's tale of sport, status, and criminal behaviour. *Qualitative Research in Sport, Exercise and Health, 8*(5), 505–518.

Cox, P. (2005, May). Conflicting agendas in selling cycling. In *Proceedings of the Velo-City 2005 Conference*, Dublin, UK.

Cycling News. (2017, December 12). Philippa York: Cycling's conservative culture suppresses LGBT issues. Cyclingnews.Com. https://www.cyclingnews.com/news/philippa-york-cyclings-conservative-culture-suppresses-lgbt-issues/

Denzin, N. K., Lincoln, Y. S., & Guba, E. G. (2005). *Paradigmatic controversies, contradictions, and emerging confluences. The sage handbook of qualitative research* (pp. 163–188). Sage Publications.

Falcous, M. (2017). Why we ride: Road cyclists, meaning, and lifestyles. *Journal of Sport and Social Issues, 41*(3), 239–255.

18   J. HARDWICKE

Gair, S. (2012). Feeling their stories: Contemplating empathy, insider/outsider positionings, and enriching qualitative research. *Qualitative Health Research, 22*(1), 134–143.

Glackin, O. F., & Beale, J. T. (2018). 'The world is best experienced at 18 mph'. The psychological wellbeing effects of cycling in the countryside: An interpretative phenomenological analysis. *Qualitative Research in Sport, Exercise and Health, 10*(1), 32–46.

Hamdan, A. (2009). Reflexivity of discomfort in insider-outsider educational research. *McGill Journal of Education/Revue des sciences de l'éducation de McGill, 44*(3), 377–404.

Hardwicke, J. (2022a). *An investigation into attitudes towards, and experiences of, sexual minorities in cycling.* University of Northampton. https://doi.org/1 0.24339/5011a1d2-7adb-4584-9373-de911f4d91cb

Hardwicke, J. (2022b). An investigation into masculinity among competitive road cyclists. *Journal of Emerging Sport Studies, 7.*

Hardwicke, J. (2022c). *Inside the peloton: An exploration into the culture of competitive road cycling with reference to masculinity, risk and injury, with a principle focus on concussion* (Doctoral dissertation, University of Winchester).

Hardwicke, J., & Hurst, H. T. (2020). Concussion knowledge and attitudes amongst competitive cyclists. *Journal of Science and Cycling, 9,* 53–66.

Hardwicke, J., Baxter, B. A., Gamble, T., & Hurst, H. T. (2022). An investigation into helmet use, perceptions of sports-related concussion, and seeking medical care for head injury amongst competitive cyclists. International Journal of Environmental research and public health, 19(5), 2861.

Heesch, K. C., Sahlqvist, S., & Garrard, J. (2012). Gender differences in recreational and transport cycling: A cross-sectional mixed-methods comparison of cycling patterns, motivators, and constraints. *International Journal of Behavioral Nutrition and Physical Activity, 9*(1), 1–12.

Hill, T., & Dao, M. (2021). Personal pasts become academic presents: Engaging reflexivity and considering dual insider/outsider roles in physical cultural fieldwork. *Qualitative Research in Sport, Exercise and Health, 13*(3), 521–535.

Jenkins, R. (2002). Foundations of sociology. In *Foundations of sociology* (pp. 1–14). Palgrave.

Jones, T. (2022). Amateur sport cycling: The rise of the MAMIL. In *Routledge companion to Cycling* (pp. 287–297). Routledge.

Kidd, S. A., & Kral, M. J. (2005). Practicing participatory action research. *Journal of Counseling Psychology, 52*(2), 187.

McCormack, M. (2012). *The declining significance of homophobia.* Oxford University Press.

McCormack, M. (2014). The intersection of youth masculinities, decreasing homophobia and class: An ethnography. *The British Journal of Sociology, 65*(1), 130–149.

McCormack, M., Anderson, E., Jamie, K., & David, M. (2021). *Discovering sociology*. Bloomsbury Publishing.

McDonald, I. (2014). Portraying Sporting masculinity through film: Reflections on Jorgen Leth's A Sunday in hell. In *Routledge handbook of sport, gender and sexuality* (pp. 480–487). Routledge.

Merton, R. K. (1972). Insiders and outsiders: A chapter in the sociology of knowledge. *American Journal of Sociology, 78*(1), 9–47.

Michael, B. (2015). 'Just don't hit on me and I'm fine': Mapping high school wrestlers' relationship to inclusive masculinity and heterosexual recuperation. *International Review for the Sociology of Sport, 50*(8), 912–928. https://doi. org/10.1177/1012690213501168

Morales, L., & Caffyn-Parsons, E. (2017). "I love you, guys" : A study of inclusive masculinities among high school cross-country runners. *Boyhood Studies, 10*(1), 66–87. https://doi.org/10.3167/bhs.2017.100105

O'Connor, J. P., & Brown, T. D. (2007). Real cyclists don't race: Informal affiliations of the weekend warrior. *International Review for the Sociology of Sport, 42*(1), 83–97.

Pronger, B. (1990). *The arena of masculinity: Sports, homosexuality, and the meaning of sex*. Macmillan.

Rees, A., Gibbons, T., & Dixon, K. (2014). The surveillance of racing cyclists in training: A bourdieusian perspective. *Surveillance & Society, 11*(4), 466–480.

Roberts, S. (2020). *Young working-class men in transition (critical studies of men and masculinities)* (1st ed.). Routledge.

Roberts, C. J., Hurst, H. T., & Hardwicke, J. (2022). Eating disorders and disordered eating in competitive Cycling: A scoping review. *Behavioral Sciences, 12*(12), 490.

Sherry, E. (2013). The vulnerable researcher: Facing the challenges of sensitive research. *Qualitative Research Journal, 13*(3), 278–288.

Smith, B., & McGannon, K. R. (2018). Developing rigor in qualitative research: Problems and opportunities within sport and exercise psychology. *International Review of Sport and Exercise Psychology, 11*(1), 101–121.

Williams, T. (1989). Sport, hegemony and subcultural reproduction: The process of accommodation in bicycle road racing. *International Review for the Sociology of Sport, 24*(4), 315–333.

CHAPTER 2

Theorising Sporting Masculinities

INTRODUCTION

Sport provides a useful social context in which we can examine gender. Since its structuring as an institution in the Western world during the late nineteenth and early twentieth centuries, it has been significantly shaped by gender relations, in particular, masculinity, which has been deeply tied to the development of sport. Sport was organised as a male preserve, which served the interest of men and was built on an ideology of gender that ascribed different natures, abilities and interests to men and women (Theberge, 2000, p. 321). In doing so, it was structured to produce and reproduce a rigid form of masculinity that was culturally esteemed and at the top of a masculine hierarchy. In the socio-cultural environment of the Victorian era, Anderson and White (2018, p. 110) suggest sport offered a 'perfect venue for the establishment of this sort of hierarchy. Sport is an arena in which men can literally battle for supremacy'.

This chapter considers this complex relationship between sport and the social construction of masculinities. To do so, the study of masculinities more broadly is discussed before being applied to the sporting context with a consideration for the historical development and function of sport. From this discussion, the context of this book and its location in the literature are outlined. This chapter concludes with a discussion of the

© The Author(s), under exclusive license to Springer Nature   21
Switzerland AG 2023
J. Hardwicke, *Masculinities and the Culture of Competitive Cycling*,
Palgrave Studies in Masculinity, Sport and Exercise,
https://doi.org/10.1007/978-3-031-26975-2_2

22   J. HARDWICKE

theoretical framework the book works within, which is directed by Anderson's (2009a, 2009b) Inclusive Masculinity Theory (IMT).

THEORETICAL OVERVIEW OF MASCULINITY SCHOLARSHIP

The scholarship on men and masculinities developed during the twentieth century was largely problem orientated. Research focused on social problems associated with masculinity through privileges gained by men due to their gender (Lorber, 1994), the social costs of dominant masculinities on others, particularly related to the subordination and exclusion of gay men (Connell, 1995; Kimmel, 1994a, 1994b; Plummer, 2001), and the social costs to girls and women (Borkowska, 2020).

The culturally esteemed form of masculinity of the late twentieth century was characterised through notions of being tough and stoic and it was framed in opposition to femininity. This archetype of masculinity consisted of 'no sissy stuff; be a big wheel; be sturdy as an oak; and boys were to give (other boys) 'em hell' (Brannon & David, 1976). This led to social expectations that boys would not show fear or weakness and would withhold many natural emotions. These masculine attributes are labelled by Anderson (2005a, 2005b) as aspects of 'orthodox masculinity' and are described as maintaining negative social values in many, but not all, social contexts. Men who adhered to this orthodox archetype were thought to gain privilege and prestige, both among men and collectively over women (Anderson, 2009a, 2009b).

However, men also paid a price for this privilege, something rarely acknowledged in the academy and wider Western culture (Anderson & Magrath, 2019). Social norms related to orthodox forms of masculinities encouraged men to put their health at risk (Courtenay, 2000) and also caused damage by avoiding and stigmatising behaviours that have been associated with positive mental and emotional health (Way et al., 2014). Plummer (2001) posits that emotional expressionism, intellectual endeavours, physical tactility and exhibiting caring behaviours were all stigmatised due to their association with femininity. The rejection of homosocial intimacy was evident in Western cultures throughout the 1980s and 1990s and likely influenced internalised desires for how men perceived themselves (Floyd & Morman, 2000; McCreary, 1994). The hypermasculine standards of the epoch saw very different homosocial behaviours than we are seeing among young men in contemporary research (Adams, 2011; Anderson & McGuire, 2010; Morris & Anderson, 2015).

In this environment, the concept of hegemonic masculinity and subsequent Hegemonic Masculinity Theory (HMT) became the dominant approach to understand the masculinity of the late twentieth century (Connell, 1995; Connell & Messerschmidt, 2005). One important component to this theorising was how Connell recognised that masculinities were multiple, fragmented and contested. Perhaps the most successful part of the theorising was understanding the stratification of men. Connell's (1995) theorising of masculinities presented that the different forms of masculinities operated within a hierarchy in which the orthodox (read hegemonic) archetype was located at the top, being the most esteemed and outlining the 'gold standard' in which men would aspire to. Connell (1987) designated three categories of masculinities that, by definition, were thought to emerge 'under' the hegemonic form: complicit, subordinated and marginalised. This conceptualisation held that boys and men who most closely embody hegemonic masculinity rise up the hierarchy and are afforded the most social status and capital, relative to other boys and men.

Some of the characteristics of hegemonic masculinity concern variables which are earned, such as attitudinal depositions (including the disposition of homophobia), while other variables concern static traits (i.e. whiteness, heterosexuality and youth). Connell first argued that regardless of body mass, age or even sporting accomplishments, gay men were at the bottom of this hierarchy, in a category of marginalised masculinity. This was later revised, however, to suggest that gay men might be accepted as masculine and thus part of the patriarchy (Connell & Messerschmidt, 2005).

Connell also argued that heterosexual men who behaved in ways that conflict with the dominant form of masculinity are also marginalised. This thus not only raised an issue of oppression, subordination and exclusion of gay men (Connell, 1995; Kimmel, 1995; Plummer, 2001), but it meant that heterosexual men who did not conform to tenets of hegemonic masculinity were also adversely affected. Essentially, Connell argued that men were attempting to distance themselves from subordinate status by promoting their attitudes about homosexuality and masculinity in line with orthodox notions of masculinity. This then creates a fraternal system which reproduces hegemonic masculinity through an institutionalised, gender-segregated, racially exclusive, sexist and highly homophobic masculine peer culture (Martin & Hummer, 1989; Sanday, 1992).

HMT undoubtedly helped scholars understand, and explain, masculinities in the late 1980s and 1990s. Indeed, the stratification of men and a hierarchy of esteemed masculinities was evident, particularly in youth cultures, during this period. However, the diversification of men's gender presentation and increasing inclusion of gay men in young men's peer groups in the twenty-first century is beyond what hegemonic masculinity scholars were documenting in the decades earlier (Anderson, 2002, 2009a, 2009b; McCormack, 2012). HMT lost explanatory power in light of these new findings and therefore also failed to properly conceptualise these new forms of masculinity increasingly being documented since the turn of the twenty-first century (Anderson, 2009a, 2009b). To address this theoretical gap and offer a more contextualised understanding of the relationship between homophobia and masculinity, Anderson (2009a, 2009b) devised Inclusive Masculinity Theory (IMT), which has recently been described as the third and most recent wave of masculinity scholarship (Borkowska, 2020).

According to Anderson and McCormack (2018, p. 2) '(IMT) was developed to explain sport and fraternity settings where the social dynamics were not predicated on homophobia, stoicism or a rejection of the feminine'. The theory was developed based on empirical findings which reported more inclusive behaviours of heterosexual men and the changing dynamics of male peer group cultures in the US and UK. In short, many young heterosexual males include gay peers in friendship networks, are more emotionally intimate with friends, are physically tactile with other men, recognise bisexuality as a legitimate sexual orientation, embrace activities and artefacts once coded feminine and eschew violence and bullying (see McCormack and Anderson, 2014a for a detailed overview of these findings). In short, boys and men's presentation of gender in the twenty-first century is inclusive of a range of masculinities.

Therefore, research suggests that masculinity in British and American, as well as other Anglo-American, societies (Clements & Field, 2014; Twenge et al., 2016) are shifting from orthodox to more inclusive forms (Anderson, 2009a, 2009b, 2014; McCormack, 2012; Roberts, 2018). However, masculinity is not shifting only in Western countries. Research has found evidence of shifts from hegemonic to inclusive masculinities in Spain (Vilanova et al., 2020), Bangladesh (Hasan et al., 2018), India (Philip, 2018), China (Hu, 2018) and Czechia (Chvatík et al., 2022).

Masculinities are changing across the world as cultures shift either towards or away from antipathy towards male homosexuality. The shifts in masculinity evidenced in the latter part of the first decade of the twenty-first century in Anglo-Western cultures appear to be both profound and enduring. Of course, changes in masculinity are not homogenous across cultures and contexts, as different areas develop at different rates. However, the net shift in masculinity is now widely recognised in many cultures. There exists a growing body of empirical research demonstrating this shift, which has been conceptualised through a response to increased awareness of homosexuality and decreasing antipathy towards it (McCormack & Anderson, 2014a, 2014b). This refers to IMT's underpinning concept of homohysteria (Anderson & McCormack, 2018).

Homohysteria is the fear of the social ostracisation of being perceived as homosexual by peers. IMT architects Anderson and McCormack suggest that homophobia serves as the primary policing mechanism of polarised gendered identities due to heterosexual men's inability to definitively prove their heterosexuality to others (Anderson, 2009a, 2009b, Anderson, 2011; McCormack & Anderson, 2014a; Anderson & McCormack, 2018). As a consequence, men must closely adhere to behaviours and attitudes socially coded as masculine to avoid homosexual suspicion within cultures where antipathy towards homosexuality is high.

For a culture to be considered homohysteric, Anderson (2009a, 2009b) and later McCormack (McCormack & Anderson, 2014a) propose that three parameters must exist. These are the acceptance of homosexuality as a legitimate sexual orientation, a cultural antipathy towards homosexuality and a conflation that femininity is a predictor of homosexuality. Each variable can fluctuate in line with different socio-cultural contexts, impacting male gender performances and sexual identities.

Applying this theory within a culture where cultural awareness of homosexuality is high, but antipathy towards homosexuals is low, such as in the UK, then we see how a culture of inclusivity is proliferated (Anderson, 2009a, 2009b, 2014; McCormack, 2012). As homosexuality is not a socially ostracised practice, boys can more freely engage with behaviours previously coded as synonymous with homosexuality. These include behaviours such as cuddling, being more emotionally open and bromances (Robinson et al., 2019; Robinson & Anderson, 2022). Here, we see the erosion of the previous power of homophobia to regulate and police boys' behaviours and interactions with each other. Being thought of as gay is no longer a concern for most millennial, white and university attending males. And increasingly so in other demographics.

Homohysteria is a crucial factor for understanding IMT because it is a concept that explains social change. Essentially, the term homohysteria describes the social conditions in which homophobia influences men's behaviours (Anderson, 2011). The theory suggests that in homohysteric cultures men are forced to behave in certain ways and follow strict behavioural patterns to avoid the accusation of being gay. Similarly, as with HMT (Connell, 1995), in homohysteric cultures, there is one dominant form of masculinity which is culturally exalted within a hierarchy. This means that, at the end of the twentieth century, anyone who feared being perceived as gay aligned their behaviours in anything socially perceived as the opposite in order to cast off homosexual suspicion (Burstyn, 1999). Thus, an example of how homohysteria distances heterosexual men from each other, emotionally, was the inability for men to even admit liking one another.

The level of homohysteria differs in every culture and changes over-time. Anderson (2009a, 2009b) argues that—as the twentieth century progressed—homohysteria grew to such an extent that even a hug between men became symbolic of homosexuality (Derlega et al., 2001). In explicating cultural change in relation to masculinity across societies and time periods, Anderson et al. (2016) propose three stages that are influenced by social, cultural and legislative processes:

1. Homoerasure. This refers to societies in which homosexuality is not recognised as a sexual identity. In such cultures, men can freely engage in behaviours considered feminine without fear of being perceived as gay due to the erasure of homosexuality as an accepted phenomenon.
2. Homohysteria. This describes societies where awareness of homosexuality is high, along with antipathy towards it, and thus a homophobic culture exists. Not only does this impact homosexual populations, but the cultural antipathy towards homosexuality leads to the over emphasise on heteronormative masculinities and femininities. Here, males must distance themselves from homosexuality and prove heterosexuality and thus orthodox forms of masculinity flourish and intra-male intimacy and emotional bonding is avoided.
3. Inclusivity. This refers to societies where the prevailing attitudes towards sexual diversity are positive. Homophobia still exists but is not the dominant cultural attitude. Sexual minorities have greater respect culturally, socially and legally. Even more so, the gendered behaviours of all people, particularly males, are opened up as there is no longer cultural stigma attached to homosexuality or feminine

behaviours. Liberal and inclusive attitudes are normalised, and attitudes associated with homohysteric cultures are stigmatised.

Research on men and their masculinities in the 1970s and 1980s continued to show men in a state of homohysteria until around the turn of the twenty-first century where the culture shifted towards inclusivity. In contemporary Western societies, boys and men are no longer socially pressured into aligning with one orthodox conception of masculinity at the top of a hegemonic hierarchy, as previously theorised. Rather, IMT conceptualises masculinities as existing on a horizontal plane in which multiple masculinities are equally esteemed (Anderson, 2009a, 2009b). There now exists a spectrum in which a plethora of masculinities are equally esteemed and reflect the diversity seen across men's gender performances. This affords boys and men more diversity in routes to gain social capital, and high social capital is no longer the exclusive domain of orthodox masculine boys. We see a shift; adherence to traditional gendered behaviours is no longer the predictor of a masculine hierarchy.

McCormack (2012) demonstrates shift through his ethnographic research in British high schools which reported that charisma, authenticity, emotional supportiveness and social fluidity are now far greater received amongst adolescent boys. Here, we see adolescent boys now have far greater diversity in routes to obtain social capital and esteem amongst their peers, particularly within school settings. There is now significant empirical research documenting the changes in male behaviours in the West (see Anderson & McCormack, 2015; Robinson et al., 2019; Anderson et al., 2012). Importantly, we are seeing this shift in sporting contexts too.

THEORISING MASCULINITIES IN SPORT

Whilst organised competitive sport serves several functions for boys and men, a common thread amongst research on the area is that sport traditionally functioned as a social institution primarily organised around the political project of defining certain forms of masculinity as culturally acceptable and esteemed, while eschewing others (Anderson, 2005a; Crosset, 1990; Connell, 1987; Cunningham, 2008; Kimmel, 1994a, 1994b; Majors, 1990; Kimmel & Messner, 1992).

Much of IMT was developed to explain masculinities in sporting contexts. Anderson (2009a, 2009b) has described sport as a bastion of masculinity which serves as a litmus test for masculinity in broader society. This is because of the hegemonic position of sport in society and because organised and competitive sports often have strong subcultures which influence and drive behaviours, a subject of interest to sport sociologists since the 1980s (Donnelly, 1985; Donnelly & Young, 1988). Furthermore, Anderson and White (2018) have described competitive sport as a near 'total institution', drawing on Goffman's (1959) work to explicate the powerful influence sport has over many people's everyday lives.

The development of much of the Western world's most treasured competitive sports occurred during the Industrial Era (Coakley et al., 2011a, 2011b), in which competitive sport was developed to instil a certain archetype of masculinity to match the demands of the culture at the time. Furthermore, with sport being an exclusively male domain during this time (Dunning, 1986), it provided an environment in which boys could be socialised by older and more physically superior males (Anderson et al., 2012). There was an environment created in which boys had contact and could learn from each other and, crucially, from older more masculine boys who held the most legitimate power (Spring, 1974).

Key to sport shaping gender relations was gender segregation within sport (Hargreaves, 1990). For masculinity to maintain its position as the dominant model in the culture, men needed to be deemed naturally superior to women (Connell, 1995). Here, sport offered a perfect pedestal for men to display physical authority through competitive aggression and physical violence (Cooky et al., 2015). Sports fields have historically been a vehicle to justify the superiority of men over women and Connell suggests, 'men's greatest sporting prowess has become symbolic proof of superiority and right to rule' (1995, p. 54). The historical development of sport as it relates to masculinity is explored in greater depth in the following chapter.

Traditional team sports developed in a homohysteric culture in which characteristics of orthodox masculinity were valued and reproduced. This was achieved through socialising boys into physical violence, aggression, competitiveness, sexism, obedience to authority, willingness to sacrifice bodily health, default heterosexuality and opposition to homosexuality (Bosson & Vandello, 2011; Kimmel, 1994a, 1994b). However, as discussed above, the macro culture in the Western world is transitioning towards the inclusive stage of Anderson's (2009a, 2009b) model. As sport and society are inseparable, we are seeing changes in sporting contexts too.

The culturally dated gendered structures of competitive sport are increasingly being met with resistance, particularly amongst millennial youth. Research has found athletes are rejecting the hypermasculine frameworks that still exist in sport (Adams, 2010). Anderson (2014) suggests athletes are no longer subject to the hypermasculine risk-taking narratives of previous generations. Additionally, empirical research from across Western sporting contexts has shown athletes to be increasingly emotionally open (Robinson et al., 2019), physically tactile (White & Hobson, 2017) and, importantly, gay men are not stigmatised or excluded in sport as previously seen (Anderson et al., 2016; White et al., 2021). An extension of this is the increasing existence of loving 'bromances' amongst athletes (Anderson, 2014; Robinson et al., 2019; Robinson & Anderson, 2022). Further, Magrath (2016) found similar behaviours in male UK academy football players. His research findings reported that professional football players would engage in same-sex touch as a form of emotional support for one another.

Whilst the macro culture is transitioning towards inclusivity, and many sports are reflecting this shift, competitive sport remains a highly gendered institution where orthodox masculinities can flourish (Stick, 2021). It has been recognised that masculinities can vary between athletes and non-athletes in the same culture (Andreasson, 2015) and, importantly, that not all sports promote the same forms of masculinity to the same degrees (Anderson, 2014). Thus, it is important for scholars interested in sport to not view it as a homogenous phenomenon. As McDonald discusses when considering masculinities in sport, 'Each sport has to be understood on its own terms' (McDonald, 2014, p. 484). For example, there is evidence of the micro (sub)cultures of competitive sports deviating from the macro culture in attitudes towards masculinity (Stick, 2021). Williams' (1977) concept of Dominant, Residual and Emergent culture and Ogburn's (1957) concept of Cultural Lag are useful, here, to explicate masculinities in subcultural settings in contemporary society, namely, sport settings.

Firstly, Williams' (1977) theorising of culture and cultural change is useful in understanding the shifts seen in masculinity as they relate to social-cultural and historical change, as discussed above. Williams suggests that all cultures contain elements of its past, but the visibility of these in contemporary culture is highly variable. To theorise this, Williams (1977) discusses three typologies: dominant, residual and emergent cultural artefacts. The dominant culture refers to the hegemonic cultural practices of the time at the macro level. Residual culture are features of culture that were formed in the past but remain active in contemporary cultural processes. This differs from archaic culture, which refers to outdated and abandoned cultural practices. Rather, residual culture is the enduring influence of old cultural practices on modern societies, both implicitly and explicitly. Emergent culture describes new forms of cultural practices that are produced and reproduced within a society by social groups and individuals. These practices can oppose the dominant culture, such as counter-culture subgroups, or they can be dominant in themselves and develop into being absorbed as part of the dominant culture.

Second, Ogburn's (1957) concept of Cultural Lag supplements this discussion through offering a framework to further understand the transitional process of cultural change. The concept refers to the differing rates that segments of culture respond and adapt to social change and align with the dominant culture. As the dominant culture changes at the macro level, this concept helps us understand variances amongst other segments of culture where cultural practices may deviate from the hegemonic practices. For example, this book will present the argument that much of competitive road cycling culture, and male cyclist's behaviours, presents a cultural lag in attitudes towards and practices of masculinity in relation to the dominant culture.

Applying this theorising to understand cultural change and masculinity offers some insight to understanding sporting subcultures. Firstly, Williams' (1977) concepts can be mapped on to the paradigm shifts in understandings of masculinity. As discussed above, masculinity scholarship was largely developed during the twentieth century where orthodox masculinity was culturally exalted and considered the dominant cultural practice of masculinity, a cultural hangover from the nineteenth century. However, the new, inclusive, forms of masculinity that began to be documented at the turn of the twenty-first century (Anderson, 2005a, 2005b, 2008a, 2008b, 2009a, 2009b) were representative of emergent forms of culture that challenged and opposed the hegemony of orthodox masculinity. In the past 20 years, inclusive masculinities have been consumed into the dominant culture and now represent the dominant cultural practice amongst white, university-attending males in Western societies and increasingly so in wider demographics and geographic locations.

However, this shift is not absolute, and segments of culture exist where residual cultural processes are visible. Here, orthodox masculinity, which was the hegemonic form in the nineteenth- and twentieth-century society, can be considered a facet of residual culture as it represents old cultural practices that continue to have an influence on modern society. Williams (1977) discusses how cultural and social institutions are central to the production and reproduction of culture and provide environments in which residual or emergent culture can be hosted. One such institution that can act as a host for residual culture is a sporting subculture.

Both these conceptual frameworks will be used throughout this book to make theoretical and empirical arguments that prominent features of orthodox masculinity, and idolisation of it, are present amongst competitive male road cyclists and embedded within the sports subculture. As such, these cyclists can exist within a culture that is inclusive at the macro level, but the subculture of the sport creates an environment representative of homohysteric cultures on the micro level.

Contentions and Different Approaches to Theorising and Understanding Masculinities

I have focused predominantly on Hegemonic Masculinity Theory and Inclusive Masculinity Theory in this chapter as they represent the most prominent paradigms in recent times to study masculinities. However, other approaches exist and there are contentions within the field of masculinity research. A key contention amongst masculinity scholars, and masculinity research more broadly, is the question: Is masculinity theory concerned with the gender of men or the attributes of sex? Different answers to this question amongst scholars problematise the research field of men and masculinities, of which a detailed exploration is not in the scope of this book. Importantly, IMT scholars are mostly concerned with the gender of men, and this analysis provides rationale for IMT forming the theoretical framework for this work.

Dominant frameworks for understanding masculinity have shifted through paradigms, from Sex Role Theory (Bem, 1981) to Connell's (1995) concept of hegemonic masculinity and, more recently, to Anderson's Inclusive Masculinity Theory (Anderson, 2009a, 2009b). Borkowska (2020) has described the modern epoch of sociological research into masculinities as 'Andersonian'. However, other approaches to understanding masculinities must be acknowledged, particularly in light of concerns highlighted over the 'hegemony' of masculinity theories undermining empirical research (Hearn, 2004; Matthews, 2016).

A common misconception of IMT is that the theoretical framework can only be used if homosexuality is a variable of interest in the research. This is not true. However, homosexuality is the primary explanatory factor, amongst many other variables examined by Anderson (2009a, 2009b) for understanding broad societal changes in masculinity. There are other prominent theorists that do not include homosexuality as a variable for understanding masculinities. For example, Atkinson's (2010) work examines conditions of late modernity, arguing that historical 'certainties' have been broken down resulting in men having to construct new ways of being a man within institutional spaces and social relations. Atkinson (2010) claims that in response to this lack of certainty some men seek certainty by entrenching themselves in orthodox masculinity, whilst others 'discover innovative ways to reframe their bodies/selves as socially powerful in newly masculine manners' (Atkinson, 2010, p. 5), what Atkinson terms 'pastiche hegemony'.

Another alternative theorising of masculinity is Aboim's (2016) concept of 'Plural Masculinities', which examines the multiple, sometimes contradictory, ways in which men construct a masculine identity. Aboim's (2016) work examines men's behaviours in their relationships with women and their changing femininities, and the analysis is situated within understanding changes to the family and women and the resulting influence on masculinities.

Other scholars have adopted the term 'hybrid masculinities' in a development of hegemonic masculinity that recognises the changing nature of masculinities (Arxer, 2011). Bridges (2014) claims that the changing behaviours seen amongst young straight men widely documented are somewhat malicious in that they are done so 'without challenging the systems of inequality from which they emerge' (p. 80). Whilst IMT scholars document this phenomenon as significant evidence of broader social change, Bridges (2014) contends it is an embracement of 'gay aesthetics' without positive attitudes towards gay men. This is reflective of a feminist orientated approach to understanding masculinities.

IMT was developed in fraternity and sport settings, with data collected from white middle-class youth. No claim to wider generalisation is made in Anderson's (2009a) original work. However, the theory has since been refined and expanded, with scholars developing a class analysis. For example, Roberts' (2013) work on heterosexual working-class men in the service industry, where softer versions of masculinity were found that are consistent with IMT. McCormack (2014) also examined class, through deploying Bourdieu's conceptualisation of a symbolic economy of class in a working-class high school in England. Whilst there is no current research using the IMT framework to examine the intersect of ethnicity and masculinity, amongst other variables, it has been welcomed by the theory's architect (Anderson & Magrath, 2019). This is not an exhaustive list of different approaches to theorising and understanding masculinities, but instead aims to highlight there is prominent work outside of the dominant frameworks of masculinity scholarship. The rationale for using IMT as the framework for this book is discussed below.

Theoretical Framework of the Book

There are many theoretical frameworks within the study of sport and the specific study of sporting masculinities. IMT is the chosen framework for this book as it accounts for the large societal shifts seen in masculinity and changes across cultures and time periods. Furthermore, it is an inductive and data-driven theory that Anderson and McCormack (2018) have described as an 'open theory', which welcomes critique and refinement. It has also been substantially developed to account for early criticisms (see Anderson & McCormack, 2018 for a detailed overview of this).

The theory is used to explicate this research as it explains the historical social shift of men from a position in which an orthodox archetype of masculinity was valued in the nineteenth century to the current situation in which inclusive forms of masculinity are valued in the twenty-first century. This is of use as the book uses socio-historical analysis of the development of competitive road cycling, examining it within the context of the broader changes in masculinity. In sum, the non-dogmatic, meso-level and data-driven approach to understanding contemporary masculinities, particularly in sport settings, outlines the utility and rationale for using IMT as the theoretical framework for this book.

As discussed, IMT has been described as an 'open theory'. This book uses the theory as the overall framework but extends it by using it to consider masculinities within subcultural contexts. In short, I discuss male athletes that exist within a macro culture which is inclusive whilst simultaneously being in a highly structured micro (sub)culture in which traits or orthodox masculinity and homohysteria are exhibited. As such, these male athletes can have conflicting notions of masculinity and operate in spaces where different forms may be valued. Thus, this book adds to the corpus of literature using IMT by examining competitive male cyclists for the first time and considering how sporting subcultures can conflict with broader society in the relationship to masculinity. Working from this theoretical framework, I examine the interaction of masculinity in competitive cycling culture as it relates to specific phenomena such as risk taking, injury management and doping.

Furthermore, the book works within an interdisciplinary framework based on the social sciences for its approach to sporting studies. This is because sport is a complex social context that requires a complex approach. Wheaton (2007, p. 15) suggests that when researching sporting subcultures, scholars should 'borrow from, and integrate with, theorising in other areas of sport and mainstream sociological work'. Throughout this book, a range of sociological theory and concepts from sport studies are used to explicate the research and broader arguments made throughout. The material used in the book is also wide ranging as I advocate the approach suggested by Robinson (2008) for studying sport in which sports media, websites, blogs, forums and social media are used alongside academic material to provide a rich and in-depth insight to the area of study. As such, alongside the empirical work reported on in the book, a wide range of material is used to supplement the discussion and provide greater insight to the research area.

Chapter Summary

This chapter has provided a brief overview of the scholarship on masculinities and the theorising of sporting masculinities. The purpose of this chapter is to provide the reader a foundation of understanding on the development of masculinity scholarship and how this maps on to the study of masculinities in sport. As discussed, we can see that the study of masculinity is complex and there are different perspectives on how to understand masculinities in society. I have discussed Connell's (1995) concept of Hegemonic Masculinity, which has been the dominant paradigm since the twentieth century, and then introduced Anderson's (2009a, 2009b) Inclusive Masculinity Theory which offers an alternative understanding of contemporary masculinities. In doing so, I have positioned this book within the broader scholarship on masculinities as working within the theoretical framework of IMT. The following chapter continues this discussion but moves to a more specific consideration of masculinities within Victorian Britain and the influence it had on the development of competitive cycling.

REFERENCES

Aboim, S. (2016). *Plural masculinities: The remaking of the self in private life*. Routledge.

Adams, A. (2010). "Josh wears pink cleats": Inclusive masculinity on the soccer field. *Journal of Bomosexuality, 58*(5), 579–596.

Adams, A. (2011). "Josh wears pink cleats": Inclusive masculinity on the soccer field. *Journal of Homosexuality, 58*(5), 579–596.

Anderson, E. (2002). Openly gay athletes: Contesting hegemonic masculinity in a homophobic environment. *Gender & Society, 16*(6), 860–877.

Anderson, E. (2005a). *In the game: Gay athletes and the cult of masculinity*. SUNY Press.

Anderson, E. (2005b). Orthodox and inclusive masculinity: Competing masculinities among heterosexual men in a feminized terrain. *Sociological Perspectives, 48*(3), 337–355.

Anderson, E. (2008a). 'I used to think women were weak': Orthodox masculinity, gender segregation, and sport. *Sociological Forum, 23*(2), 257–280.

Anderson, E. (2008b). Inclusive masculinity in a fraternal setting. *Men and Masculinities, 10*(5), 604–620.

Anderson, E. (2009a). *Inclusive masculinity: The changing nature of masculinities (Routledge research in gender and society)* (1st ed.). Routledge.

Anderson, E. D. (2009b). The maintenance of masculinity among the stakeholders of sport. *Sport Management Review, 12*(1), 3–14.

Anderson, E. (2011). Masculinities and sexualities in sport and physical cultures: Three decades of evolving research. *Journal of Homosexuality, 58*(5), 565–578.

Anderson, E. (2014). *21st century jocks: Sporting men and contemporary heterosexuality*. Palgrave Macmillan.

Anderson, E., & Magrath, R. (2019). *Men and masculinities* (1st ed.). Routledge.

Anderson, E., Magrath, R., & Bullingham, R. (2016). *Out in sport* (1st ed.). Routledge.

Anderson, E., & McCormack, M. (2015). Cuddling and spooning: Heteromasculinity and homosocial tactility among student-athletes. *Men and Masculinities, 18*(2), 214–230. https://doi.org/10.1177/1097184X14523433

Anderson, E., & McCormack, M. (2018). Inclusive masculinity theory : Overview, reflection and refinement. *Journal of Gender Studies, 27*(5), 547–561.

Anderson, E., McCormack, M., & Lee, H. (2012). Male team sport hazing initiations in a culture of decreasing Homohysteria. *Journal of Adolescent Research, 27*, 427–448.

Anderson, E., & McGuire, R. (2010). Inclusive masculinity theory and the gendered politics of men's rugby. *Journal of Gender Studies, 19*(3), 249–261.

Anderson, E., & White, A. (2018). *Sport, theory and social problems*. Routledge Taylor & Francis Group.

Andreasson, J. (2015). Reconceptualising the gender of fitness doping: Performing and negotiating masculinity through drug-use practices. *Social Sciences, 4*(3), 546–562. MDPI AG. Retrieved from https://doi.org/10.3390/socsci4030546

Arxer, S. L. (2011). Hybrid masculine power: Reconceptualizing the relationship between homosociality and hegemonic masculinity. *Humanity and Society, 35*(4), 390–422.

Atkinson, M. (2010). *Deconstructing men & masculinities (themes in Canadian sociology).* Oxford University Press.

Bem, S. L. (1981). Bem sex role inventory. *Journal of Personality and Social Psychology.*

Borkowska, K. (2020). Approaches to studying masculinity: A nonlinear perspective of theoretical paradigms. *Men and Masculinities, 23*(3–4), 409–424.

Bosson, J. K., & Vandello, J. A. (2011). Precarious manhood and its links to action and aggression. *Current Directions in Psychological Science, 20*(2), 82–86.

Brannon, R., & David, D. (1976). The male sex role: Our culture's blueprint of manhood, and what it's done for us lately. In *The forty-nine percent majority: The male sex role* (pp. 1–48). Addison-Wesley.

Bridges, T. (2014). A very "gay" straight? Hybrid masculinities, sexual aesthetics, and the changing relationship between masculinity and homophobia. *Gender & Society, 28*(1), 58–82.

Burstyn, V. (1999). *The rites of men: Manhood, politics and the culture of sport.* University of Toronto Press.

Chvatík, V., Hardwicke, J., & Anderson, E. (2022). Inclusive masculinity and Czechia youth. *International Sociology, 37*(1), 124–142.

Clements, B., & Field, C. D. (2014). Public opinion toward homosexuality and gay rights in Great Britain. *Public Opinion Quarterly, 78*(2), 523–547.

Coakley, J., Hallinan, C., & McDonald, B. (2011a). *Sports in society 2: Sociological issues & controversies.* McGraw-Hill.

Coakley, J., Hallinan, C. J., & McDonald, B. (2011b). *Sports in society: Sociological issues and controversies.* McGraw Hill.

Connell, R. W. (1987). *Gender and power: Society, the person, and sexual politics.* Stanford University Press.

Connell, R. W. (1995). *Masculinities.* University of California Press.

Connell, R. W., & Messerschmidt, J. W. (2005). Hegemonic masculinity: Rethinking the concept. *Gender & Society, 19*(6), 829–859.

Cooky, C., Messner, M. A., & Musto, M. (2015). It's dude time!: A quarter century of excluding women's sports in televised news and highlight shows. *Communication & Sport, 3*(3), 261–287.

Courtenay, W. H. (2000). Constructions of masculinity and their influence on men's well-being: A theory of gender and health. *Social Science & Medicine, 50*(10), 1385–1401.

Crosset, T. (1990). Masculinity, sexuality, and the development of early modern sport. In *Sport, men and the gender order: Critical feminist perspectives* (pp. 45–54). Human Kinetics.

Cunningham, M. (2008). Changing attitudes toward the male breadwinner, female homemaker family model: Influences of women's employment and education over the lifecourse. *Social Forces, 87*(1), 299–323.

Derlega, V. J., Catanzaro, D., & Lewis, R. J. (2001). Perceptions about tactile intimacy in same-sex and opposite-sex pairs based on research participants' sexual orientation. *Psychology of Men & Masculinity, 2*(2), 124.

Donnelly, P. (1985). Sport subcultures. *Exercise and Sport Sciences Reviews, 13*(1), 539–578.

Donnelly, P., & Young, K. (1988). The construction and confirmation of identity in sport subcultures. *Sociology of Sport Journal, 5*(3), 223–240.

Dunning, E. (1986). Sport as a male preserve: Notes on the social sources of masculine identity and its transformations. *Theory, Culture & Society, 3*(1), 79–90.

Floyd, K., & Morman, M. T. (2000). Affection received from fathers as a predictor of men's affection with their own sons: Tests of the modeling and compensation hypotheses. *Communications Monographs, 67*(4), 347–361.

Goffman, E. (1959). *The presentation of self in everyday life*. Anchor Books.

Hargreaves, J. A. (1990). Gender on the sports agenda. *International Review for the Sociology of Sport, 25*(4), 287–307. https://doi.org/10.1177/101269029002500403

Hasan, M. K., Aggleton, P., & Persson, A. (2018). The makings of a man: Social generational masculinities in Bangladesh. *Journal of Gender Studies, 27*(3), 347–361.

Hearn, J. (2004). From hegemonic masculinity to the hegemony of men. *Feminist Theory, 5*(1), 49–72.

Hu, L. (2018). Is masculinity 'deteriorating'in China? Changes of masculinity representation in Chinese film posters from 1951 to 2016. *Journal of Gender Studies, 27*(3), 335–346.

Kimmel, M. (1994a). Masculinity as homophobia: Fear, shame and silence in the construction of gender identity. In H. Brod & M. Kaufman (Eds.), *Theorizing masculinities* (pp. 119–141). Sage.

Kimmel, M. S. (1994b). Fear, shame, and silence in the construction of gender identity. In *Theorizing masculinities* (pp. 119–141). Sage.

Kimmel, M. (1995). *Manhood in American: A cultural history*. Free Press.

Kimmel, M. S., & Messner, M. A. (1992). *Men's lives*. Macmillan Publishing Co, Inc.

Lorber, J. (1994). *Paradoxes of gender*. Yale University Press.

Magrath, R. (2016). *Inclusive masculinities in contemporary football: Men in the beautiful game*. Routledge.

Majors, R. (1990). Cool pose: Black masculinity and sports. In M. A. Messner & D. F. Sabo (Eds.), *Sport, men and the gender order*. Human Kinetics.

Martin, P. Y., & Hummer, R. A. (1989). Fraternities and rape on campus. *Gender & Society, 3*(4), 457–473.

Matthews, C. R. (2016). The appropriation of hegemonic masculinity within selected research on men's health. *NORMA, 11*(1), 3–18.

McCormack, M. (2012). *The declining significance of homophobia.* Oxford University Press.

McCormack, M. (2014). The intersection of youth masculinities, decreasing homophobia and class: An ethnography. *The British Journal of Sociology, 65*(1), 130–149.

McCormack, M., & Anderson, E. (2014a). Homohysteria: Definitions, context and intersectionality. *Sex Roles, 71*(3), 152–158.

McCormack, M., & Anderson, E. (2014b). The influence of declining homophobia on men's gender in the United States: An argument for the study of homohysteria. *Sex Roles, 71*(3–4), 109–120.

McCreary, D. R. (1994). The male role and avoiding femininity. *Sex Roles, 31*(9), 517–531.

McDonald, I. (2014). Portraying Sporting masculinity through film: Reflections on Jorgen Leth's A Sunday in hell. In *Routledge handbook of sport, gender and sexuality* (pp. 480–487). Routledge.

Morris, M., & Anderson, E. (2015). 'Charlie is so cool like': Authenticity, popularity and inclusive masculinity on YouTube. *Sociology, 49*(6), 1200–1217.

Ogburn, W. F. (1957). *Cultural lag as theory.* Sociology & Social Research.

Philip, S. (2018). *A city of men? An ethnographic enquiry into cultures of youth masculinities in urban India.* (Doctoral dissertation, University of Oxford).

Plummer, D. C. (2001). The quest for modern manhood: Masculine stereotypes, peer culture and the social significance of homophobia. *Journal of Adolescence, 24*(1), 15–23.

Roberts, S. (2013). Boys will be boys… won't they? Change and continuities in contemporary young working-class masculinities. *Sociology, 47*(4), 671–686.

Roberts, S. (2018). *Young working-class men in transition.* Routledge.

Robinson, V. (2008). *Everyday masculinities and extreme sport: Male identity and rock climbing.* Berg.

Robinson, S., & Anderson, E. (2022). *Bromance: Male friendship, love and sport.* Springer International Publishing.

Robinson, S., White, A., & Anderson, E. (2019). Privileging the bromance: A critical appraisal of romantic and bromantic relationships. *Men and Masculinities, 22*(5), 850–871.

Sanday, P. R. (1992). *Fraternity gang rape: Sex, brotherhood, and privilege on campus.* NYU Press.

Spring, J. H. (1974). Mass culture and school sports. *History of Education Quarterly, 14*, 483–499.

Stick, M. (2021). Conflicts in sporting masculinity: The beliefs and behaviors of Canadian male athletes. *The Journal of Men's Studies, 29*(3), 315–334.

Theberge, N. (2000). Gender and sport. In *Handbook of sports studies* (pp. 322–333). Sage.

Twenge, J. M., Sherman, R. A., & Wells, B. E. (2016). Changes in American adults' reported same-sex sexual experiences and attitudes, 1973–2014. *Archives of Sexual Behavior, 45*(7), 1713–1730.

Vilanova, A., Soler, S., & Anderson, E. (2020). Examining the experiences of the first openly gay male team sport athlete in Spain. *International Review for the Sociology of Sport, 55*(1), 22–37.

Way, N., Cressen, J., Bodian, S., Preston, J., Nelson, J., & Hughes, D. (2014). "It might be nice to be a girl... Then you wouldn't have to be emotionless": Boys' resistance to norms of masculinity during adolescence. *Psychology of Men & Masculinity, 15*(3), 241.

Wheaton, B. (2007). After sport culture: Rethinking sport and post-subcultural theory. *Journal of Sport and Social Issues, 31*(3), 283–307.

White, A., & Hobson, M. (2017). Teachers' stories: Physical education teachers' constructions and experiences of masculinity within secondary school physical education. *Sport, Education and Society, 22*(8), 905–918.

White, A. J., Magrath, R., & Emilio Morales, L. (2021). Gay male athletes' coming-out stories on Outsports.com. *International Review for the Sociology of Sport, 56*(7), 1017–1034.

Williams, R. (1977). *Marxism and literature* (Vol. 392). Oxford Paperbacks.

CHAPTER 3

The Gentlemen's Club: Cycling and Masculinity in Victorian Britain

INTRODUCTION

During the late nineteenth and early twentieth centuries, the imaginations of citizens in Britain, and across the West, were captivated by a novel and revolutionary invention: the bicycle (Hutchinson, 2018; Manners, 2018). In addition to the technological advances that came with this invention, these two wheeled machines transformed many aspects of social life in Victorian Britain (Rubinstein, 1977). Bicycle use offered new opportunities for transport and health pursuits. It also allowed for close social interaction between people through a connection of shared experience as, phenomenologically, the experience of riding a bicycle would have been extremely novel and exciting (Fleming, 2015).

Commentary on the social history of cycling largely focuses on class relations. Indeed, Norcliffe (Norcliffe, 2001a, 2001b, p. 187), drawing on Ritchie's (1999) work, suggests 'cycling had a bigger influence on social modernity through its class relations than through its gender relations'. Notwithstanding the importance of class, this chapter (and book) is located predominantly in the examination of gender relations. Specifically, it will explicate how the social construction of masculinity in Victorian society influenced the formation of competitive road cycling to gain an understanding of the roots of the contemporary sport.

© The Author(s), under exclusive license to Springer Nature   41
Switzerland AG 2023
J. Hardwicke, *Masculinities and the Culture of Competitive Cycling*,
Palgrave Studies in Masculinity, Sport and Exercise,
https://doi.org/10.1007/978-3-031-26975-2_3

The invention of the bicycle had a role in the construction of gender for both men and women in Victorian society. For men, it was a tool to assert a dominant masculinity in line with the esteemed archetype of what it meant to be a man in the era, and for women, it was a tool for challenging constructs of what it meant to be female. Indeed, Mackintosh and Norcliffe (2007, p. 172) comment on this:

> Many bourgeois men, reacting to the influence of domesticity in their upbringing and emulating the mores and discipline of the cavalry, developed a decidedly masculine cycling ethos, one that mimicked the gentlemanly fraternalism of the era. These men formed bicycle clubs governed by their own interpretations of masculine morality; masculine cycling obliged chivalrous masculine behaviour. Other men, beguiled by the speed of bicycles, scorched through cities in an openly anti-domestic manner. Women, on the other hand, used the bicycle as a form of domestic embourgeoisement.

Aside from this work, most gendered analyses of this area are largely dominated by the role the bicycle had in the liberation of women and first-wave feminism (Strange, 2002). Fleming (2015, p. 13) notes that 'The sense of independence cycling afforded to women, as well as the opportunities for unification in defence of a cause that arose in light of controversies over the pursuit, were important in forming the foundation for later events'. The bicycle significantly increased women's stake in society at the time and aided the fight for equality through various means. For example, women no longer had to rely on men for transportation, and the relatively inexpensive and accessible technology provided women more control over when and where they went (Hallenbeck, 2015).

Whilst this phenomenon has rightfully occupied much of researchers' and historians' interests, there exists little academic attention examining the relationship between men and masculinity and the development of competitive cycling in Victorian Britain. However, examining cycling practices amongst men in this era can teach us a lot about the early development of cycling for sport, which is deeply tied to masculinity. To explore this, I first discuss masculinities in Victorian Britain more broadly before using this foundation to understand the development of competitive sports and how road cycling maps onto this historical process.

Masculinities in the Victorian Era

The latter half of the nineteenth century marks a significant epoch for understanding many social processes in contemporary society. Britain, and other Western societies, went through a rapid process of structural and organisational change in line with technological advancements and innovations in machinery (Cancian, 1987). An agrarian society was to undergo a process of great change: with the advances in machinery, farmland work became far more efficient and less dependent on workers, resulting in widespread redundancies in this industry.

Concurrently, there were rising opportunities in cities such as London, Manchester and Newcastle, where the technological advancements seen in factories meant that there was a requirement for large workforces. Here, there was a mass migration of the agrarian workforce to the new urban environments in pursuit of employment and the allure of the novel urban living. Indeed, Cancian (1987) estimates that over 50% of the population transitioned from rural living to the new urban industry in the nineteenth century. Consequently, Western society underwent a 'transition process from a completely agrarian (feudal) society to a society based on market exchange' (Wittenberg, 2005, p. 21).

This mass urbanisation of Western society influenced cultural processes and transformed many aspects of social life. Indeed, Tosh notes how industrial Britain in the period 1800–1914 was increasingly characterised by distinctions of gender and sexuality (2005, p. 330). One area that contributed to changes in societal understandings of gender was the family structure. Prior to this epoch, families would typically live and work as a unit in a farm environment, all contributing to its function, forming a central focus point of the family structure. In this structure, there were less defined gender roles. Scholars suggest that there was an overlap of duties for men and women; thus, there were less defined gender roles within the family and, as a result, the wider society (Goldstone, 1996). With the urbanisation of society, there was a restructuring of associated gender roles in both work and household spheres. Women became responsible for the domestic sphere, and men became the sole income providers (White & Vagi, 1990). Here, Cancian (1987) observes the introduction of distinct gender roles that formed within this changing cultural context.

This new division of gender responsibilities in the nuclear family unit played a role in the collective moral panic over the absence of a male figure in the household to regulate the development of young boys (Anderson &

White, 2018). This job was now the responsibility of women, with children of both genders receiving their primary socialisation from women for the first time. Rotundo (1993, p. 31) comments that within the domestic environment, 'Motherhood was advancing, fatherhood was in retreat…women were teaching boys how to be men'.

This presented a problem to late nineteenth- and early twentieth-century society, where there was a cultural fear of effeminate men associated with the new urban living (Ditz, 2004). A further factor contributing to this was the increasing visibility of homosexuality in the novel urban environments (Anderson & White, 2018). For the first time, with the increased population density, there were high concentrations of homosexuals in cities, whereas previously, in agrarian life, homosexuals would be dispersed, producing a feeling of isolation and relative deprivation in sexuality. However, in the new urban environments, gay identities and communities had collective power and flourished, with a homosexual population being established in cities such as London and Manchester (Spencer, 1995).

In this time, the increasing visibility of homosexuality because of increased population density was not the collective understanding of the phenomenon. Rather, homosexuality was perceived to be a result of feminine gender socialisation, which was delivered by mothers, since fathers were absent working in the factories and taking the role of the breadwinners. Freud et al.'s (1905) work 'Three Essays on the Theory of Sexuality' sought to explain homosexuality and the apparent rise seen in these new societies, which provides some insight into the thinking at the time. Crucially, Freud's theories were grounded in the understanding that sexuality and gender were not innate, both being socially constructed. He suggested that childhood experiences were central to the understanding of how men became heterosexual or homosexual, which the latter he referred to as inversion. For Freud, homosexuality was the result of a disruption to the gendering process caused by the absence of a father figure and over-domineering mothers. He writes 'the presence of both parents plays an important part. The absence of a strong father in childhood not infrequently favours the occurrence of inversion' (1905, p. 146).

As such, in this social zeitgeist, the meaning of what it was to be a man in the late nineteenth and early twentieth centuries was predicated on being the opposite of a woman (Anderson & White, 2018). As homosexuals were associated with behaviours coded as feminine, being heterosexual was conceived as not being perceived as homosexual (Anderson & White,

2018). Kimmel (1994a, 1994b) suggests that the heterosexual identity expanded based on an aversion to any behaviours coded as feminine, and a stricter archetype of masculinity was constructed.

With the collective social concern over the new societal structure and urban living producing young feminine and homosexual boys, solutions to this problem were sought after to undo the perceived damage of gender inversion that mothers were causing. Alongside this, there was increasing demand for boys to be brought up to be disciplined, docile and stoic to risk their bodies in dangerous factory environments (Anderson, 2009a, 2009b). This was also reinforced by increasing global tensions at the time, with World War One on the horizon and the strong emphasis on the need for a 'strong' nation and accompanying army. As such, Anglo-American society perceived itself to have a serious problem with masculinity, and a number of institutions were shaped to deal with this. One such institution was competitive, organised and violent sport, which was developed to instil an orthodox archetype of masculinity that was culturally desired in this period (Anderson & White, 2018).

COMPETITIVE SPORT AS A POLITICAL PROJECT

In this collective societal concern, sport was restructured as a political project with a function and answer to the perceived crisis of masculinity and feminising of young boys. Sport and its administrators were now responsible for addressing this issue by producing heterosexual, masculine boys (Anderson & White, 2018). As a by-product, sport also served to maintain men's hierarchical position over women in society and reinforced the view that male bodies were superior to women's (Connell, 1995).

In this time, sport had three key functions that would benefit the novel urbanised society. The first of these was the development of attributes in men that would benefit the new factory-based industry (Cancian, 1987). The bourgeoisie (ruling classes, e.g. the factory owners) needed certain qualities from their workers for the successful continuation of their production; they required brave men to not be put off by the dangerous factory environments; they needed to be disciplined, docile and accept orders; and they needed to be fast and efficient in performing physical tasks (Eitzen, 2001). For these factories to maximise profit, workers needed to accept risk and work through pain, injury and fatigue (Anderson, 2009a, 2009b). As Bailey puts it, sport offered an excellent instrument to preserve 'the fitness of the nation's physical stock' (2014, p. 126).

46   J. HARDWICKE

Sharing characteristics with the first, the second function was to produce a strong and obedient workforce using military discourse. The military required men that were brave, stoic and disciplined. It also needed men who would face almost certain death or would need to take another man's life at the sound of an order (Anderson & White, 2018). Sport offered an excellent arena for this, with its 'mock battle' (Dunning and Sheard, 1973, p. 7) approach to competition. The same cultural processes were mirrored in American society and Coakley (2016a, p. 1) comments on this:

> Youth sports were believed to create in young men the energy, nationalism, and competitive spirit that would sustain personal health, fuel industrial expansion, and create American military power. Programs in selected team sports were used to Americanize immigrant children, convert unruly boys in crowded tenements into efficient and compliant workers, foster good health although outdoor activities, prepare boys to be fit and willing soldiers, and masculinize middle-class boys who were perceived to lack the assertive and competitive character to become political and economic leaders because they had been socialised in female-dominated households. Fuelled by anecdotal evidence, the personal testimonies of athletes, stories circulated through popular culture, and the pronouncements of physical educators and coaches, the belief that sport participation produced positive development among youth became a taken-for-granted cultural truth in most Western societies.

The third function is situated within the increased social concern surrounding the feminisation of young men (Anderson, 2005a, 2005b). With the primary socialisation of young men becoming the responsibility of women and the rising public awareness of homosexuality, many at the time perceived this to be an issue in the gendering of children (White & Vagi, 1990). Previously discussed, Freud et al.'s (1905) work aligned this issue with the absence of a father figure. Due to this absence on account of the long working hours that came with industrial life, the working classes needed another source of male influence (Anderson, 2009a, 2009b).

The masculinising potential of sport to address this issue was recognised and utilised. Sport offered a mechanism to develop the archetype of men that was required for the social environment to be of benefit, both socially and economically. Anderson notes, 'It was in this atmosphere that sport became associated with the political project to reverse the feminising and homosexualising trends of boys growing up without father figures'

(2014, p. 30). With sport being a 'male preserve' (Dunning & Sheard, 1973), it provided an environment in which boys could be socialised by older and more physically superior males (Anderson et al., 2012). Boys could now have contact and learn from each other and, crucially, from older boys who held the most legitimate power (Spring, 1974).

Key to this gendered socialisation was gender segregation within sport (Hargreaves, 1990). Mothers were perceived to be the cause of inversion (Freud et al., 1905), combined with women being deemed physiologically inferior to men. For masculinity to maintain its position as the dominant model in the culture, men needed to be perceived as naturally superior to women (Connell, 1995). Here, sport offered a perfect pedestal for men to display physical authority through competitive aggression and physical violence (Cooky et al., 2015). Connell suggests, 'men's greatest sporting prowess has become symbolic proof of superiority and right to rule' (1995, p. 54). Thus, competitive organised sports became institutionalised during this period, with gender having a significant influence on its development and organisational structuring within society.

CYCLING PRACTICES AND MASCULINITY IN VICTORIAN BRITAIN

Much of the literature on the development of traditional organised sports as they relate to masculinity is situated in team sports such as rugby (Nauright & Chandler, 1996) and football (Taylor, 2013; Magrath, 2017), as these sports, particularly contact sports, are prominent vehicles in the development of highly gendered and socially esteemed notions of masculine characters (Anderson & White, 2018). The development of competitive cycling has received little academic attention for its relationship to masculinity and the 'making of men' in this era (Chandler & Nauright, 2013). It is not the purpose of this chapter, or book, to provide a detailed account of the history of competitive cycling (see Ritchie, 2018 for this); rather, this section highlights how the development of competitive cycling was influenced by the culture of the time, particularly regarding gender. This is important, as Anderson and White (2018) notes that sports reflect the culture from which they emerge. With the historical context detailed above, we can examine how competitive cycling was developed during the eighteenth and nineteenth centuries and how the culture of the time influenced this development.

Bicycle use in the mid-1800s was dominated by males and mostly privileged upper-class males (Mackintosh & Norcliffe, 2007). It largely consisted of bourgeoisie males riding notoriously dangerous early models of bicycles known as 'velocipedes' for recreational purposes, and this would be considered an 'extreme' sport for the time (Hutchinson, 2018). Then, tricycles and 'high-wheelers' (Penny Farthings) were the dominant models that saw the gradual growth in cycling popularity from 1870 onwards. However, it was the late 1880s and 1890s that saw a dramatic rise in the number of cyclists on the roads (Rubinstein, 1977, p. 50). This was due to the invention of the Rover Safety bicycle in the 1880s, which largely represents what we would recognise as a bicycle today. The safety bicycle had a chain-driven rear wheel, pneumatic tires and equally sized wheels. With the increasing technology of the time allowing mass production and more accessible pricing, the safety bicycle soon became the dominant bicycle model (Oosterhuis, 2016, p. 233). The invention of the Rover Safety bicycle also shifted the cultural perception of cycling in the 1890s as, for the first time, bikes were adopted and used by both men and women (Mackintosh, 2005), as opposed to solely being a risky leisure pursuit for bourgeoisie males.

The increased strain for men to assert and confirm their masculinity in opposition to the rising urban effeminacy was previously outlined and is widely cited in the literature (see Chauncey, 1994; Kimmel, 1996; Ditz, 2004). Here, the cultural shift of cycling from an exclusively male leisure pursuit to an accessible mode of transport, adopted by both men and women, threatened men's position on the use of bicycles in fear of the increasing feminised coding of bicycles (Mackintosh & Norcliffe, 2007). As Kimmel (1994a, 1994b) states, the heterosexual male identity expanded based on an aversion to any behaviours coded as feminine at this time. As such, the bicycle required masculinising for men to continue using them.

The first stage of this was the conspicuous use of high-wheeled bicycle models (Penny Farthings) by men, as opposed to the 'Safety bicycle' model increasingly being used by women and children as a mode of transport and leisure pursuit (Norcliffe, 2006). Early cycling clubs and cycling culture were beginning to be established by men riding penny farthings throughout the 1870s (Manners, 2018). With the introduction of the Rover Safety bicycle in the 1880s, the persistence of men to use the penny farthing models is important to note. Indeed, the attitude at the time was that 'Manly men would always prefer the ordinary [Penny Farthing]' (Bartleet, 1931, p. 67).

3 THE GENTLEMEN'S CLUB: CYCLING AND MASCULINITY IN VICTORIAN...   49

Although this may seem trivial, it teaches us a lot about masculinity at the time. The penny farthing was extremely dangerous, and crashes were frequent. Indeed, the most common injury was riders being thrown over the handlebars from a height and landing headfirst—termed 'headers', these injuries were often fatal (Norcliffe, 2001a, 2001b). Norcliffe (2006) notes that the choice of men to use this bike model over the Rover Safety bicycle and, accepting the inherent risks that came with it, was an overt expression of 'cavalier masculinity', allowing men to detach themselves from the increasingly feminised connotations of the safety bicycle.

The second process of masculinising the bicycle was the institutionalisation of cycle racing and club culture, bringing in a competitive aspect to further separate cycling from the transport and leisure domain that was becoming increasingly popular with women and children. It is here we see the birth of the sport recognised today. It is important to note that at this time, it was almost exclusively in the domain of the bourgeoisie, and early competitive cycling culture was surrounded by elitist and social hierarchical attributes (Mackintosh & Norcliffe, 2007).

However, a subgroup was formed that did not have the social capital to join this elite but instead used public displays of masculinity as a tool to gain access. Termed 'scorchers', they consisted of fearless young male riders who took 'substantial risks to demonstrate their prowess' (Mackintosh & Norcliffe, 2007, p. 161); it is suggested that this subgroup was perhaps the early orchestrators of the 'badass' masculinity seen in sport, particularly in cycling (Mackintosh & Norcliffe, 2007). In this early conception of cycling as a competitive pursuit, Chauncey (1994, p. 114) writes:

> Crashes were quite frequent, and their consequent wounds were badges of an aggressive masculinity that exemplified the era's resulting 'cult of muscularity', which identified firm muscles and 'manly' fitness as necessary attributes of bourgeois masculinity.

Crashes were a regular feature of early cycling, as well as a focus on fitness and competition, which helped construct a hypermasculine culture around cycling. Mackintosh and Norcliffe (2007, p. 160) comment:

> Club racers were expected to maintain a high level of fitness: letting the club down in competition with another club was not viewed favourably. For MBC members, two places of special significance and bodily improvement were the Blue Bonnets (horse) racing track, where cyclists were allowed to

train and race occasionally, and the practice track at the grounds of the Montreal Lacrosse Club, where during summer, racers trained two mornings a week before going to work. Here, the masculinist side of early cycling was most in evidence: male athletes coaxed their unstable machines to speeds as high as 25 miles an hour. Crashes were quite frequent as racers caught each other's pedals and handlebars or their rear wheels slid out on the bends.

Many cycling practices were shaped in line with the culture at the time and to protect the culturally esteemed archetype of masculinity of the era. It was perceived to 'teach us strength of limb, soundness of mind, fleetness of foot, accuracy of the eye, readiness in emergency, persistence in accomplishing an end' (The Bristol Bicycle and Tricycle Club Monthly Gazette, 1897; Manners, 2015). Cyclists were described as men who were well put together, 'firm, strong, healthy and manly' (*Cycling*, 1892, p. 254; Manners, 2015).

Whilst racing had formed part of cycling culture during the 1870s on Penny Farthings prior to the invention of the Rover Safety cycle, it was during the 1880s with the increase of leisure and utility cycling amongst women and children that the sport of road cycling was truly institutionalised and popularised amongst men. Indeed, sports were given particular credence for the way in which they tested and pushed men, aiding the development of the archetype of man that was culturally esteemed at the time. One late Victorian commentator in 1897 stated that:

> Sport promotes not merely bodily health and vigor but all the higher forms of manliness, alertness in observation, promptitude in judgment and action, the determination never to lose and always deserve to win, and the disciplined temper to accept defeat without degradation and victory without vaunting. (McDevitt, 2004, p. 138)

The emphasis now placed on competition and the associated risks that came with the increased speeds helped protect the bicycle use as a masculine pursuit. One article on cyclists in the *Fortnightly Review* (a nineteenth-century popular culture magazine) commented that you can often see them [cyclists], 'swarm out of the large towns on the first and last days of the week- hot, dust stained and pressing forwards as if their lives depended on it' (Mecredy, 1891, pp. 76–77; Manners, 2015). With the processes outlined above, the origins of a competitive sport predicated on principles of orthodox masculinity were born.

The English Cycling Club and the Reproduction of Masculinity

Alongside the introduction of competitive cycling, an important aspect to examine is the construction and reproduction of masculinity in the exclusively male cycling clubs of England in the era (Norcliffe, 2006; Manners, 2015, 2018). Sports clubs were (and are today) social locations of high social cohesion and identity development, yet there exists limited literature examining their importance. Richard Holt's, 1990 study, Sport and the British, recognised that sports clubs were sites that have often been 'neglected' by historians. This argument was reinforced by Jeffrey Hill in 2003 when he argued that the functions and effects of sports clubs 'have not been subject to a great deal of scrutiny by historians' (2002, p.144). Nearly a decade later, he retained this opinion, as he stated that sports clubs remain a 'neglected field', which represent 'one of the gaps in our knowledge of the history of sport' (2010, p. 44).

Furthermore, in a 2013 special edition of *The International Journal of the History of Sport*, which focussed on 'The Sports Club in History', again acknowledged that these institutions represent an under conceptualised area of historical research. Vamplew (2013, pp. 1569–1570) suggests that:

> There has been relatively little British academic research exploring sports clubs in aggregate as sociocultural, political, or economic forces. There have been many histories of individual clubs in many sports...but the authors, often themselves members of the club, tend to focus on events at the club rather than having a broader contextual view.

As such, using the lens of masculinity, I examine English cycling clubs in Victorian Britain within the broader social context of the time. In doing so, I will suggest that cycling clubs served as a social location where men negotiated and positioned their masculinities, as well as the esteemed notion of masculinity of the era being reproduced.

In the Victorian period, it is estimated that there were over 2000 cycling clubs in England, with over 300 in London alone (Rubinstein, 1977). To formulate an analysis of masculinities, here, historical material provides in-depth insight to cycling clubs of the time, particularly 'gazettes'. Gazettes were small-scale publications, approximately 6–12 pages long, produced by cycling clubs and were aimed primarily at their own membership (Manners, 2018). They were used to inform members about upcoming club events and dedicated much of their space to articles written by members detailing excursions and activities that had occurred over the course of the previous month. Through a sociohistorical analysis of material from Gazettes, as well as other available literature, four primary areas cycling clubs served to instil an orthodox archetype of masculinity were clear. These are (1) the use of military discourse and discipline; (2) the idolisation of physical attributes; (3) the exclusion of women and (4) the use of public spaces. Much of these overlap with the broader development of competitive organised sports during this period.

First, military discourse and discipline. As noted earlier, the utility of sports to develop disciplined boys in Victorian Britain has been previously discussed (Coakley, 2016a, 2016b; Anderson & White, 2018). This was required as the era needed men who would face almost certain death or would need to take another man's life at the sound of an order (Anderson & White, 2018). Furthermore, discipline and obedience to authority were desired characteristics for the new industrial work force. Sport offered a vehicle to achieve both of these, with its 'mock battle' structures, military discourses and ranking structure that required obedience to authority (coaches, captains, older males) (Dunning and Sheard, 1973, p. 7).

Cycling practices and club structure in England reflected these characteristics and masculinising processes. The membership of these cycling clubs was highly regulated and organised, guided by military rhetoric. Indeed, Mackintosh and Norcliffe (2007, p. 158) comment:

> The responsibilities of cycling club members were organised hierarchically, and quite formally, in contrast to the much greater informality that was to suffuse mixed recreational cycling in the 1890s. The captain was to 'take command', as would any cavalry officer, assisted by his road officer—the lieutenants, the bugler and the standard bearer.

Reflecting the requirement and expectation of men in this era, English cycling clubs provided a site in which men constructed masculinity through ideals of discipline, hierarchy and obedience to authority. This was very visible to members and outsiders, with 'Officers' of cycling clubs having set uniforms, badges and whistles signifying their rank within the club (Mackintosh & Norcliffe, 2007, p. 158).

Second, the value of physical attributes and athleticism to gain masculine capital and peer kudos was evident amongst cycling clubs, symbolic of the 'cult of muscularity' in the era (Kimmel, 1994a, 1994b; McDevitt,

2004). This has been a central feature in the relationship of masculinity and sport since the industrial era and is still largely true today. Coakley et al. (2011a, 2011b) suggest that a strong, muscular and athletic body can provide men with social status among peers, as it symbolises self-control and discipline, while the ability to endure pain is a sign of physical strength and stoicism.

This is evident in early cycling practices with the masculine capital gained from accepting the risks of crashing and injury (Chauncey, 1994) and to deal with injury in an appropriately 'manly' manner. Commenting on this, Mackintosh and Norcliffe note 'Like mediaeval knights at a jousting tournament, club members who suffered injuries during rides were expected to endure them without complaint' (Mackintosh & Norcliffe, 2007, p. 158). Chauncy (Chauncey, 1994) discusses how early cycling culture embraced the era's 'cult of muscularity', with muscular physiques and fitness being necessary attributes for the esteemed archetype of masculinity. Historical material suggests that physical attributes were important for individuals within cycling clubs to gain social capital and status among their peers. This can be seen through one cycling member description of his captain in an 1891 Gazette:

> One of the best-known Birmingham cyclists. His jovial face and everlasting humour have won him friends wherever he has gone. He has an iron constitution, and his burly physique impresses one with this fact. He has been Captain of the Nechells C.C. for four years, and his strong right arm has come in useful with his 'boys' on several occasions [A reference to altercations between cyclists and highwaymen which was a common occurrence at the time]. He is the model of a captain, and the Nechellites would indeed be sorry to lose their jolly Frenchman. (Cycling, 1891)

Physical attributes were regularly cited as a requirement to gain respect and status among cycling club members. This can be seen in one of the monthly character pieces in the gazette of the Bristol Bicycle and Tricycle Club, which detailed their committee member, C.J. Ford. Ford was described as having won the respect and admiration of his fellow clubmen not only through his 'honest, straightforward qualities and genial temperament' but also his 'great strength and wonderful stamina' (Bristol Bicycle and Tricycle Club Gazette, 1897, p. 103; Manners, 2018). Furthermore, an extract from an 1893 Gazette comments similar:

54   J. HARDWICKE

> A very extraordinary and awe-inspiring combination, no less than the union of a pair of lungs of abnormal capacity with an exceptional flexibility of the ankle muscles...In a very short period of time you will find this member the oracle of the club and (unless he under Providence, rises superior to it) becoming chief director of its destinies. (*Cycling*, 1893, p. 449)

Commensurate with the culturally desired archetype of men in this era, early cycling culture also contributed to reproducing the notion that muscularity and athleticism were required attributes in men. In early cycling practices, this was demonstrated through overt displays of physical fitness and to endure any subsequent injuries from crashing without complaint, something of a core value in the contemporary sport, which will be discussed in greater detail in the following chapters.

Third, the exclusion of women amongst early cycling culture worked to reinforce the Victorian archetype of masculinity predicated on an aversion to femininity. Early cycling clubs were exclusively male sites (Norcliffe, 2006). Indeed, cycling practices were highly gendered, and a large part of women's emancipation was rejecting this narrative around how they should ride bikes, what they should wear doing so and how fast they could ride them (Mackintosh & Norcliffe, 2007). Unfortunately, many women cyclists in the 1890s were victims of catcalling, jeers and attempts of getting knocked off when riding in public spaces (Rubinstein, 1977).

This attitude was slow to shift (there are still problems with sexism in the sport today, which is covered in Chap. 9), with the male-only cycling clubs contributing to the notion that women should be strictly regulated in their use of bicycles. To provide some insight to the cycling clubs of the late nineteenth century, we can briefly glance over the website for the Pickwick Bicycle Club (http://www.pickwickbc.org.uk/). Established in 1870 in Hackney, London, the Pickwick Bicycle Club is one of the world's oldest running bicycle clubs. Unfortunately, the club continues to cling on to traditions of the era that do not match up with the world we live in today. All the above discussion can be seen on the website, with a strict rule book members must adhere too, a cycling uniform and 'officers' of the club. It also stubbornly remains a (white) male-only club (Reid, 2018). Whilst the club is culturally dated (almost amusingly so), it provides some contemporary insight into the culture of the clubs in the nineteenth century, of which the Pickwick Bicycle Club is trying to preserve.

One major area that contributed to this attitude and regulated women's participation in sports and the use of bicycles in the Victorian era was commentary on health. Cycling was framed as dangerous for female health, despite a lack of historical epidemiological work on bicycle-related injuries, as this was such a novel invention. Kiersnowska (2019, p. 92) notes that 'various figures of authority cautioned against its detrimental effects on women's moral constitution, health and reproductive capacity'. Further medical concerns included risk of chronic diseases, risk of injury due to over exertion and uneven terrain, hardening of abdominal muscles causing problems during labour, spinal shock, body deformity and, at the most extreme, sudden death (Vertinsky, 1990, p. 79; McCrone, 2014, pp. 179–80). However, during the late 1890s, more progressive voices of the medical world gained a platform, and these concerns were largely negated, with cycling being recommended as an alternative to walking and a healthy exercise for women (see Kiersnowska, 2019 for a more detailed commentary on this).

The issue of women using bicycles became more significant concerning competitive cycling, which was largely forbidden for much of this period through restricted access to cycling clubs and racing events. Whilst medical concerns were also used here, a large amount of the argument against female participation was based on moral principles of the era. Competitive sports promoted values of hypercompetitiveness, rivalry and determination (Anderson & White, 2018), which all contributed to the construction of Victorian masculinity. These values existed in opposition to the desired archetype of femininity for women in the era. As such, female participation in competitive cycling was seen to conflict with the acceptable female behaviour of the era and to impinge on a strictly male domain (Kiersnowska, 2019). Here, we see how early cycling culture aided the construction of Victorian masculinity through the exclusion of women.

Finally, social geographers have observed the gendering of the streets that occurred through men's use of bicycles in Victorian society. Mackintosh and Norcliffe (2007, p. 160) note:

> Men's bicycle clubs of the 1880s, despite their relatively small number of members, succeeded in their efforts to display the masculinity of a decidedly modern technology. In a demonstrably geographic and public way, these men gendered the street with their physical presence and reinforced the masculine athlete/gentleman stereotype.

Unlike other common sports and leisure pursuits, cycling was (and is today) a very overt activity that took place in the public sphere. This is important to examine as it contributed to the construction of a dominant masculinity, as well as a masculine-influenced culture around cycling. This

56 J. HARDWICKE

was achieved in a number of ways. First, young males would go 'scorching', which involved riding at high speeds in public spaces demonstrating their physical fitness, fearless constitution and acceptance of risk (Hutchinson, 2018; Norcliffe, 2006), which are all tenets of orthodox masculinity (Anderson, 2005a, 2005b). Second, cycling clubs would have regular group rides, termed 'club runs', which contributed to the gendering of the streets in Victorian Britain. Club runs would involve members riding abreast along streets in their uniform presenting an overt expression of masculinity through a physical presence on the streets (Manners, 2018). Finally, related to this, it was a regular practice for the clubs to have a designed member that carried a bugle. This member would use the bugle when approaching small villages or towns while on a club run to announce the club's arrival (Hutchinson, 2018). This contributed to the physical presence of the riders and instilled a dominance of the public roads, reflecting men's hegemonic position in society at the time (Connell, 1995).

CHAPTER SUMMARY

In summary, this chapter has endeavoured to provide a comprehensive account of the relationship between cycling and the social construction of masculinity in Victorian Britain. Through a discussion of wider social changes resulting from the industrial era and how these impacted the function of sport, an overview of the development of cycling practices has been explicated. We can see how masculine values and wider social forces of the Victorian era shaped early competitive cycling, which can inform contemporary research into the sport. Previous literature has overlooked this relationship, but I argue it offers valuable insight into how the sport of competitive cycling evolved as well as the intersection of sport and masculinity (as it pertains to cycling) in this era. With the 'roots' of competitive cycling discussed as it relates to masculinity, the following chapter will consider what contemporary sports look like.

REFERENCES

Anderson, E. (2005a). *In the game: Gay athletes and the cult of masculinity.* SUNY Press.

Anderson, E. (2005b). Orthodox and inclusive masculinity: Competing masculinities among heterosexual men in a feminized terrain. *Sociological Perspectives, 48*(3), 337–355.

Anderson, E. (2009a). *Inclusive masculinity: The changing nature of masculinities (Routledge research in gender and society)* (1st ed.). Routledge.

Anderson, E. D. (2009b). The maintenance of masculinity among the stakeholders of sport. *Sport Management Review, 12*(1), 3–14.

Anderson, E. (2014). *21st century jocks: Sporting men and contemporary heterosexuality.* Palgrave Macmillan.

Anderson, E., & White, A. (2018). *Sport, theory and social problems.* Routledge Taylor & Francis Group.

Anderson, E., McCormack, M., & Lee, H. (2012). Male team sport hazing initiations in a culture of decreasing Homohysteria. *Journal of Adolescent Research, 27,* 427–448.

Bartleet, H. W. (1931). *Bartleet's bicycle book.* Edward J. Burrow & Co.

Cancian, F. M. (1987). *Love in America: Gender and self-development.* Cambridge University Press.

Chandler, T. J., & Nauright, J. (2013). *Making the rugby world: Race, gender, commerce.* Routledge.

Chauncey, G. (1994). *Gay New York: Gender, urban culture, and the making of the gay male world, 1890–1940* (Illustrated ed.). Basic Books.

Coakley, J. (2016a). Positive youth development through sport: Myths, beliefs, and realities. In *Positive youth development through sport* (pp. 21–33). Routledge.

Coakley, J. (2016b). Youth sports in the United States. In K. Green & A. Smith (Eds.), *Routledge handbook of youth sport.* Routledge.

Coakley, J., Hallinan, C., & McDonald, B. (2011a). *Sports in society 2: Sociological issues & controversies.* McGraw-Hill.

Coakley, J., Hallinan, C. J., & McDonald, B. (2011b). *Sports in society: Sociological issues and controversies.* McGraw Hill.

Connell, R. W. (1995). *Masculinities.* University of California Press.

Cooky, C., Messner, M. A., & Musto, M. (2015). It's dude time!: A quarter century of excluding women's sports in televised news and highlight shows. *Communication & Sport, 3*(3), 261–287.

Cycling, (1891–1900).

Ditz, T. L. (2004). The new Men's history and the peculiar absence of gendered Power: Some remedies from early American gender history. *Gender History, 16*(1), 1–35. https://doi.org/10.1111/j.0953-5233.2004.324_1.x

Dunning, E. G., & Sheard, K. G. (1973). The rugby football club as a type of "male preserve": Some sociological notes. *International Review of Sport Sociology, 8*(3), 5–24.

Eitzen, S. (2001). *Sport in contemporary society: An anthology.* MacMillian.

Fleming, J. E. (2015). The bicycle boom and women's rights. *The Gettysburg Historical Journal, 14*(1), 3.

Freud, S., Strachey, J., Marcus, S., & Chodorow, N. J. (1905). *Three essays on the theory of sexuality* (Revised ed.). Basic Books.

Goldstone, J. A. (1996). Gender, work, and culture: Why the industrial revolution came early to England but late to China. *Sociological Perspectives, 39*(1), 1–21. https://doi.org/10.2307/1389340

Hallenbeck, S. (2015). *Claiming the bicycle: Women, rhetoric, and technology in nineteenth-century America.* SIU Press.

Hargreaves, J. A. (1990). Gender on the sports agenda. *International Review for the Sociology of Sport, 25*(4), 287–307. https://doi.org/10.1177/1012690290 02500403

Holt, R. (1990). *Sport and the British: A modern history.* Oxford University Press.

Hutchinson, M. (2018). *Re: Cyclists: 200 years on two wheels.* Bloomsbury Publishing.

Kiersnowska, B. (2019). Female cycling and the discourse of moral panic in late Victorian Britain. *Atlantis, 41*(2), 85–104.

Kimmel, M. (1994a). Masculinity as homophobia: Fear, shame and silence in the construction of gender identity. In H. Brod & M. Kaufman (Eds.), *Theorizing masculinities* (pp. 119–141). Sage.

Kimmel, M. S. (1994b). Fear, shame, and silence in the construction of gender identity. In *Theorizing masculinities* (pp. 119–141). Sage.

Kimmel, M. (1996). *Manhood in America* (4th ed.). Oxford University Press.

Mackintosh, P. G. (2005). Scrutiny in the Modern City: The domestic public and the Toronto local Council of Women at the turn of the twentieth century. *Gender, Place & Culture, 12*(1), 29–48. https://doi.org/10.1080/096636 90500082852

Mackintosh, P. G., & Norcliffe, G. (2007). Gender and social geography of Cycling in the late nineteenth-century. In *Cycling and society* (p. 153). Ashgate.

Magrath, R. (2017). *Inclusive masculinities in contemporary football: Men in the beautiful game.* Taylor & Francis.

Manners, W. (2015). *Uncle, grandpa and the boys: Re-imagining relationships and masculinities within 1890s English Cycling clubs.* (Doctoral dissertation, University of York).

Manners, W. (2018). *Revolution: How the bicycle reinvented modern Britain.* Prelude Books.

McCrone, K. (2014). Individual sports: Lawn tennis, golf and Cycling. In *Sport and the physical emancipation of English women (RLE sports studies)* (pp. 184–221). Routledge.

McDevitt, P. (2004). *May the best man win: Sport, masculinity and nationalism in Great Britain and the empire, 1880–1935.* Palgrave Macmillan.

Mecredy, R. J. (1891). Cycling. *Fortnightly review, 50,* 75–88.

Nauright, J., & Chandler, T. J. L. (Eds.). (1996). *Making men: Rugby and masculine identity* (Vol. 10). Psychology Press.

Norcliffe, G. (2001a). *Ride to modernity: The bicycle in Canada, 1869–1900* (Illustrated ed.). University of Toronto Press, Scholarly Publishing Division.

Norcliffe, G. B. (2001b). *The ride to modernity: The bicycle in Canada, 1869–1900*. University of Toronto Press.

Norcliffe, G. (2006). Associations, modernity and the insider-citizens of a Victorian highwheel bicycle club. *Journal of Historical Sociology, 19*(2), 121–150. https://doi.org/10.1111/j.1467-6443.2006.00275.x

Oosterhuis, H. (2016). Cycling, modernity and national culture. *Social History, 41*(3), 233–248.

Reid, C. (2018, December 6). *Time-warp lunching at the World's oldest, poshest and Most eccentric bicycle Club*. Forbes. https://www.forbes.com/sites/carltonreid/2018/12/06/time-warp-lunching-at-the-worlds-oldest-poshest-and-most-eccentric-bicycle-club/

Ritchie, A. (1999). The origins of bicycle racing in England: Technology, entertainment, sponsorship and advertising in the early history of the sport. *Journal of Sport History, 26*(3), 489–520.

Ritchie, A. (2018). *Early bicycles and the quest for speed: A history, 1868–1903*. McFarland.

Rotundo, A. E. (1993). *American manhood: Transformations in masculinity from the revolution to the modern era* (Reprint ed.). Basic Books.

Rubinstein, D. (1977). Cycling in the 1890s. *Victorian Studies, 21*(1), 47–71.

Spencer, C. (1995). *Homosexuality a history* (0th ed.). Fourth Estate Ltd.

Spring, J. H. (1974). Mass culture and school sports. *History of Education Quarterly, 14*, 483–499.

Strange, L. S. (2002). The bicycle, women s rights, and Elizabeth cady Stanton. *Women's Studies, 31*(5), 609–626.

Taylor, M. (2013). *The association game: A history of British football*. Routledge.

The Bristol Bicycle and Tricycle Club Monthly Gazette. (1897, January–December).

Vamplew, W. (2013). Theories and typologies: A historical exploration of the sports club in Britain. *The International Journal of the History of Sport, 30*(14), 1569–1585.

Vertinsky, P. A. (1990). *The eternally wounded woman: Women, doctors, and exercise in the late nineteenth century*. Manchester University Press.

White, P. G., & Vagi, A. B. (1990). "Rugby in the 19th-century British boarding-school system: A feminist psychoanalytic perspective." pp. 67–78 in Sport, Men, and the Gender Order, ed. Michael Messner and Don Sabo. Champaign, IL: Human Kinetics. Whitehead, N. J., & Hendry, L. B. (1976). Teaching Physical Education.

Wittenberg, M. (2005). *Industrialisation and surplus labour: A general equilibrium model of sleep, work and leisure*. School of Economics, University of Cape Town.

CHAPTER 4

'Don't be soft': Cycling and Masculinity in the Twenty-First Century

INTRODUCTION

It's quite a famous phrase in cycling, you're almost 'soft' if you don't do it [Get back on the bike after a crash]. And I guess you wanna live up to that expectation of being macho and getting on with it and being the person that got over the hurdle if you like. (27-year-old, first category, male cyclist)

In the previous chapter, I provided an overview of the early roots of competitive cycling and the role the masculinity of the Victorian Era played in the development of the sport. The question to be addressed in this chapter is how has cycling changed from the early inception of the sport? Competitive road cycling emerged in the Industrial era with strict codes of conduct that were heavily influenced by societal understandings of gender at the time. This chapter considers how this culture has changed, or not, and what the contemporary sport looks like.

THE MACHO CULTURE OF COMPETITIVE ROAD CYCLING

Academic attention to masculinity in competitive cycling is limited (Hardwicke, 2022a, 2022b, 2022c). However, there exists much popular media, non-academic books and journalism that suggests the sport remains predicated on a strong macho culture. The idealisation of the 'hard man' image within cycling culture is somewhat of a norm, something I was

© The Author(s), under exclusive license to Springer Nature Switzerland AG 2023
J. Hardwicke, *Masculinities and the Culture of Competitive Cycling*, Palgrave Studies in Masculinity, Sport and Exercise, https://doi.org/10.1007/978-3-031-26975-2_4

61

immersed in during my time as a competitive cyclist. The antonym of this masculine ideal is the phrase 'Don't be soft', a commonly used term amongst amateur competitive cyclists (Hardwicke, 2022a, 2022b, 2022c). The connotations of this are the use of gendered discourse to challenge an athlete's masculinity and encourage certain behaviours that align with the esteemed archetype of masculinity in the sport. This has been reported amongst football (soccer) coaches, where gendered discourse that drew on war, gender and sexuality was used by coaches to try enhance athletic performance or make athletes aware the coach was not happy (Adams et al., 2010). Similar language is frequently used amongst competitive cyclists, and military discourse is often present in journalistic writings on the sport in which cyclists are painted as warriors that 'battle' on the roads (Sidwells, 2019).

It could be said that this imagery of 'toughness' is somewhat fetishized within the cycling world, and this will feature throughout the book as I examine various aspects of road cycling. An interesting example, that almost all competitive cyclists will be familiar with, is the 'Velominati' who self-describe as the 'Keepers of the Cog' (Velominati, 2022). This Internet-based informal organisation offers a tongue-in-cheek (with serious undertones) take on the cycling world. Importantly, they 'maintain the sacred text wherein lie the simple truths of cycling etiquette known as 'The Rules' (Velominati, 2022). The discourse of toughness, and other orthodox masculine traits, is embedded in much of their outputs, as well as the cult-like undertones of the need to obey these 'rules' in order to be a 'proper' cyclist. This is explored further in the following chapter, where a subcultural consideration of the sport will be considered.

Of the 95 rules presented, number 5 is of particular relevance here. That being, 'Harden the fuck up' commonly known as HTFU. The sentiment of this is ever present amongst competitive road cyclists and spills into behaviours around injury, the management of risk and approaches to training (Hardwicke, 2022a, 2022b, 2022c). As discussed in Chap. 3, this is not a new thing in cycling. With the sport being heavily influenced by orthodox notions of masculinity, this feature of the sport harks back to its origins. Whilst we live in a vastly different society now, these features of the sport are still clung unto and fetishized. Examples are numerous across popular media and journalism. To highlight one in line with the discussion, published by Velominati, the book 'The Hardmen: Legends and

Lessons from the Cycling Gods' highlights the argument I am making. The blurb reads:

> In cycling, suffering brings glory: a rider's value can be judged by their results, but also by their panache and heroism. Prepared to be awed and inspired by Chris Froome riding on at the Tour de France with a broken wrist or Geraint Thomas finishing it with a broken pelvis. (Velominati, 2017)

This is an appealing image; it draws on emotions and images of sacrifice for eternal sporting glory which has interested sociologists of sport for a long time. Indeed, it relates to something Hughes and Coakley (1991) conceptualised as 'the sport ethic'. This being the cultural expectation within sport for athletes to sacrifice their bodies and health for sporting success, something that would be deviant in broader society but is normative in sport (Hughes & Coakley, 1991).

Competitive road cycling is replete with examples of the adoration for such an ethic. I have previously written on this, arguing that the management of injuries in cycling often involve bodily sacrifice to the entrenched "hardman" culture of the sport and the macho environment (Hurst & Hardwicke, 2020; Hardwicke, 2022a, 2022b, 2022c). In Chap. 5, I discuss in more detail the intersects of masculinity and injury in cycling and why this imagery and attitude is problematic. An over-riding thesis of this book is that, as a sport, there needs to be a move towards a culture in which health is prioritised over fluffy, traditionalist, emotional attachments to a certain image of the sport.

In sum, the sport of competitive road cycling has been described as having a macho culture surrounding it which can influence injury management, risk management, attitudes towards gender and sexuality, health and performance. As such, road cycling masculinity can be understood to prioritise, and value, competition, risk, winning and physicality (Barrie et al., 2019). The remainder of this chapter will explicate this in more detail by first considering what the sport looked like during the twentieth century. The contemporary sport in the twenty-first century will then be discussed, drawing on my own research to consider what the sport looks like today and if indeed a 'macho' culture still exists.

ROAD CYCLING IN THE TWENTIETH CENTURY

As discussed in the previous chapter, modern sport was developed on the late nineteenth- and early twentieth-century notion that it was an institution that could aid the prevention of young boys exhibiting characteristics associated with femininity (Anderson, 2009a, 2009b). The construction of sport as a masculine enterprise influenced how sport was played, organised and understood in society. Anderson (2009a, 2009b, p. 8) comments that it 'created a social space in which boys were taught to value and perform a violent, stoic and risky form of masculinity'. This is a thesis put forward by sport sociologists for over 30 years (Messner & Sabo, 1990). The influence of this on competitive road cycling has, to my knowledge, not been previously examined.

The early cycling culture during the late nineteenth century has been discussed in the previous chapter. As the sport grew in popularity, and became increasingly institutionalised and commercialised, the baton was picked up during the twentieth century as competitive road cycling culture established itself. Much of the idealised macho culture of competitive road cycling comes from this era, where the sport was steeped in notions of pain and suffering. Rider welfare was pretty much non-existent, and races were designed around pushing bodies to absolute limits. For example, the early Tour de France races from 1910 through to the 1930s required riders to cover 5000+ kilometres in just 15 stages (Bike Race Info, 2022). Only about a third of the peloton would finish each year, with the 1919 tour only having ten finishers. To put that in perspective, the 2022 Tour de France was 3343.8 km covered over 21 stages with rest days. And one must consider the advances in technology and sport science available to riders in the contemporary sport. It is perhaps not a surprise cycling developed a doping culture early on with such physical demands placed on the body, of course competitors would be looking for any help available. This era of the sport, and doping more specifically, is covered in greater detail in Chap. 7.

Within cycling discourse, what is commonly referred to as the 'Old school' approach in cycling was developed throughout the twentieth century. Much of this is underpinned by orthodox notions of masculinity where stoicism, violence, risk taking and bodily sacrifice were highly valued. For example, Wagner (2022) comments on the image of Eddy Merckx, perhaps the most famous ever road cyclist who was competing in the twentieth century, getting back on the bike with a broken jaw which has been widely celebrated as a visual testament to the toughness of cycling and celebrates a macho ideal of stoicism in the face of injury. Further, McDonald (2014, p. 485) comments on racing in this time that 'The nature of cycling demands a particular kind of masculinity based on courage, determination, a hard body and a strong competitive spirit'.

In summary, the sport of road cycling was popularised during the twentieth century and many facets of the early culture in the sport were predicated on orthodox notions of masculinity which directed behaviours of the athletes. Notions of pain and suffering were central to the development of the sport, and this imagery was given life by journalist's presentation of the sport during this period.

Male Cyclists and Their Masculinity in the Twenty-First Century

Whilst the macro culture of Western society has shifted towards more inclusive forms of masculinity being valued, cycling culture remains a context in which orthodox forms are still prevalent (Hardwicke, 2022a, 2022b, 2022c). The sport continues to propagate orthodox notions of masculinity where stoicism, violence, risk taking and bodily sacrifice are highly valued and promoted. A lot of this is driven by the nature of the sport, which involves frequent crashes and high injury rates (see Silberman, 2013; De Bernardo et al., 2012; Barrios et al., 2015; Decock et al., 2016). Research reports that bodily health is often sacrificed in favour of sporting performance in competitive cycling (Hurst et al., 2019; Hardwicke & Hurst, 2020; O'Reilly et al., 2020; Hardwicke et al., 2022). Dahlquist et al. (2015) reported a high acceptance rate of injury and willingness to compete when injured amongst amateur road cyclists. This is covered in more detail in Chap. 5.

There is a large amount of prima facie evidence of the macho culture of competitive road cycling which was discussed earlier in this chapter. In terms of academic literature, there has been just one study on competitive road cyclists and masculinity conducted by Powell et al. (2005) based on US males. The researchers administered a self-report survey using the Bem Sex Role Inventory to a sample of 32 collegiate male cyclists, aged 20–26, from a cycling-related conference in the US. From the statistical analysis the authors concluded that the sample showed statistically significant stronger identity with masculinity than seen in the general population. This is a limited study both in sample size, selection and the instrument used but is one of the only available studies on this area in the literature. Furthermore, the study's application to the contemporary study of masculinities is quite limited, as it was conducted around the time researchers began seeing a shift in team sport athletes from orthodox to inclusive forms of masculinity (Anderson, 2009a, 2009b).

Since the Powell et al. (2005) study, mainstream youth culture has shifted in response to declining homophobia. For example, researchers find that behaviours once coded as feminine or gay, such as young heterosexual men kissing in the UK, are now widely accepted, or increasingly accepted, social behaviours amongst heterosexual males in the UK (Anderson et al., 2012, 2019; Wignall et al., 2020). These changes are apparent in the athletic domain, as well. Empirical research from across Western sporting contexts has shown athletes to be increasingly emotionally open (Anderson & McCormack, 2015; Robinson et al., 2019), physically tactile (White & Hobson, 2018) and, importantly, gay men are not as stigmatised or excluded in sport as previously seen (Anderson et al., 2016). For example, recent research from White et al. (2021) highlights the positive experiences of gay male athletes coming out and the changing landscape of inclusivity of the LGBT+ community in sport.

However, much of the literature is predicated on organised team sports, such as Rugby and Football. Anderson (2009a, 2009b) has described these sports as primary domains for studying shifts in masculinity because they have been theorised to be social locations of men steeped in orthodox understandings of gender. Thus, little is known about masculinities within competitive road cycling with the Powell et al. (2005) study now being nearly 20 years old at the time of writing. As such, I conducted research into this to try to understand if anything has changed and to examine competitive road cyclist's notion of their gender.

To do so, I had 105 UK competitive male road cyclists complete a self-reported survey (see Hardwicke, 2022a, 2022b, 2022c for study). I took participant's self-reported identity with masculinity and femininity as the measure for the study. An 8-point Likert scale was administered which ranged from 'Exclusively masculine' to 'Exclusively feminine', with an eighth option of 'Prefer not to say' provided. Full options were as follows: Exclusively masculine, Mostly masculine, More masculine than feminine, Equally masculine and feminine, More feminine than masculine, Mostly feminine, Exclusively feminine and Prefer not to say. This instrument was modelled on that used by YouGov (2016) in a survey on the UK general population to allow a comparison to be made. Figure 4.1. displays the participant responses to the scale in my study.

Results from the study indicated the sample more closely identified with an explicit notion of masculinity than seen in the general male population, and this finding was consistent across age groups. The comparative was made with survey data from 1692 British residents conducted by YouGov (2016). Using the same instrument as my study, YouGov (2016) data showed males identifying as 'Exclusively masculine' were at lower rates than found amongst the cyclists I surveyed, across all age groups. Rates from that data (YouGov) were 18–24 (2%), 25–49 (21%), 50–64 (32%) and 65+ (56%). A similar trend is present in both data sets of increased explicit identity with masculinity as groups increase with age, but far higher rates amongst younger age groups were found in the road cyclists.

Furthermore, in the younger cohorts of the national data, the most selected option across the 18–24 (47%) and 25–49 (28%) age groups was 'More masculine than feminine' (YouGov, 2016). Although the same trend was seen with younger cyclists selecting this option at higher rates than older groups, the net responses here were far lower in the current

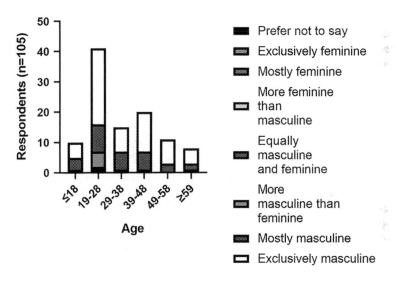

Fig. 4.1 Responses of male competitive cyclists to self-reported gendered identity

study. This highlights the large cohort differences of these competitive cycling males and the general population, reinforcing the findings reported by Powell et al. (2005). The statistical analysis of the data found that neither age nor ability were predictors of holding the explicit notion of masculinity, but the overall sample trend was towards this explicit notion, regardless of these factors.

These findings contradicted what previous research would predict. For example, the older age cohorts would be expected to exhibit closer identity to masculinity than the younger, being reflective of generational cultural changes. Exemplifying this in the general population, Anderson and Fidler (2018) conducted in-depth interviews with 27 heterosexual British men aged between 65 and 91. Findings demonstrated a generational gap in attitudes, with participants expressing negative views towards the softer masculinities that are increasingly visible today. Here, Anderson and Fidler (2018) conclude that these attitudes reflect the cultural homophobia and homohysteria the participants experienced growing up in the early decades of the twentieth century. The data from the cyclists contrarily indicates age was not a factor on notions of masculinity held by participants.

Similarly, holding higher athletic capital and excelling in sport has been cited as characteristics of orthodox masculinities (Wellard, 2010). Yet amongst the cyclists, the higher ability of the participant (the more they have achieved in the sport) was not a predictor of holding the explicit notion of masculinity. Of course, all participants were involved in competitive road cycling, in some capacity, so may exhibit this close identity to masculinity because of the competitive environment, explaining the elevated rates against the general population.

The structures of competitive sport have been noted as a vehicle to encourage excessive competitiveness and establish masculinity amongst males (Adams et al., 2010). This structure can influence individual behaviours and beliefs towards gender. For example, Ogilvie and McCormack (2020) suggested that the formal structure of sport led elite male and female athletes to focus on gender differences which they attributed to biology, but when mixed-gender training was introduced, this belief was dissipated. Further, Magrath's (2017) research on homosexually themed chanting amongst football fans found that men use language in sport they would not in other contexts and that may diverge from their own personal beliefs. This research supports the notion that the structures of competitive sport may still reproduce orthodox notions of gender and associated behaviours. This may explain the results of the above study, where cycling exists as a sport that still perpetuates many aspects of orthodox masculinity within its culture.

Ogburn's (1957) concept of Cultural Lag offers a framework to theorise these findings, with the understanding that competitive cycling may hold a strong subculture that influences individual behaviours and beliefs. The concept refers to the differing rates that segments of culture adapt to social change (see Chap. 2). Inclusive Masculinity Theory (IMT) recognises the changing nature of masculinities towards a softer archetype as a product of wider social changes (see Anderson, 2009a, 2009b; McCormack, 2012; Anderson & McCormack, 2015). This is particularly salient with the sample from the current study being more heavily weighted towards younger age groups, which the literature would suggest are less restrictive in their gender performances (see Carrillo & Hoffman, 2017; McCormack, 2012; McCormack & Anderson, 2014a, 2014b). As such, the culture of competitive cycling may present a lag behind changes in the macro culture—an argument explored throughout this book.

This research, as well as the overall thesis of this book, has several implications for men in competitive road cycling. First, a body of literature examines the role of strong identification with orthodox masculinity in predicting risky or health-avoidant behaviours. Orthodox masculinity has been shown to be a predictor for risky behaviours and higher propensity for injury (Adams et al., 2010). Orthodox masculinity is also associated with men refraining from seeking medical help for fear of this detracting from masculine status or from seeking help for mental health issues (see Fleming et al., 2014; Levant & Wimer, 2014; Morioka, 2014; Reed, 2013). Increased willingness to take risks and under-reporting of medical issues are particularly relevant in the current concussion crisis in sport (Harmon et al., 2013; Baron et al., 2013).

For example, in a study of male college athletes, Schlosser (2016) found that those who identified closer with orthodox scriptures of masculinity were associated with more harmful attitudes towards concussion, such as that they were not a serious issue. This was also supported by Baron et al. (2013) who note the role of orthodox masculinity and the reporting of injury being coded as a sign of weakness (Baron et al., 2013). This influence of masculinity has been researched in American football players (Anderson et al., 2012) and seen to impact both male and female athletes (Sanderson et al., 2016). These attitudes are, therefore, a concern for safer cycling, as survey studies on competitive cyclists and concussion reporting suggest that cyclists were willing, in considerable numbers, to mask injuries to continue in competition (Hurst et al., 2019; O'Reilly et al., 2020; Hardwicke & Hurst, 2020; Hardwicke et al., 2022). This is explored in more detail in Chap. 5.

The next area of concern is that orthodox masculinity can negatively impact attitudes towards diversity and inclusion, particularly sexual minorities. There is a large body of academic work in sporting domains that demonstrate straight athletes accept and support openly gay teammates, particularly amongst youth athletes (see Magrath, 2017; Magrath, 2018; Roberts et al., 2017; White et al., 2021); however, academic attention lacks in this cultural aspect of cycling. Prima facie evidence suggests that homophobia might still be a salient issue in cycling (Reimer, 2021). Competitive road cycling is regularly described as having a conservative culture (Cycling News, 2017) and insights from professional riders have noted that being gay is coded as a weakness in competitive cycling (Guardian, 2018). Competitive road cycling, particularly the professional level, is also noticeably absent from positive gay institutional discourses, as well as there being no openly gay athletes at the time of this study. This is discussed further in Chap. 7.

A final problematic area is how this hypermasculine and competitive culture manifests in public spaces. Competitive cycling is unique in that its participants spend large amounts of time training on public roads, and a body of literature exists on masculinities in cycling within the transport field (see Zheng et al., 2020; Ravensbergen et al., 2019; Balkmar, 2018). However, there are no studies on cyclists using these public spaces for sporting pursuits. The concern here is that competitiveness, coupled with aggression, have been cited as aspects of orthodox masculinities (Clyde & Franklin, 2012) and that Wijlhuizen et al. (2016) noted competitive attitudes amongst cyclists as a variable for increased risk of crashing when on public roads. My research suggests that competitive cyclists more closely identify with orthodox scriptures of masculinity. An area that would be interesting for future research is if this identification with orthodox masculinity has any association with accidents on public roads with those using them for transport purposes alone.

CHAPTER SUMMARY

In summary, current research suggests male cyclists hold a closer identity with a stricter archetype of masculinity than we would expect to see amongst males in the general population. Combined with an understanding of the history of the sport and its close relation to masculinity, this is perhaps unsurprising. This chapter has brought the discussion on from the historical roots of the sport to consider what the contemporary sport looks like. In doing so, I have made the argument that competitive road cycling presents a cultural lag behind the broader culture in its understandings and relationship to masculinity. The following chapter continues this discussion with a more detailed analysis of the (sub)culture of competitive cycling and why this is important to examine.

REFERENCES

Adams, A., Anderson, E., & McCormack, M. (2010). Establishing and challenging masculinity: The influence of gendered discourses in organized sport. *Journal of language and social psychology, 29*(3), 278–300.

Anderson, E. (2009a). *Inclusive masculinity: The changing nature of masculinities (Routledge research in gender and society)* (1st ed.). Routledge.

Anderson, E. D. (2009b). The maintenance of masculinity among the stakeholders of sport. *Sport Management Review, 12*(1), 3–14.

Anderson, E., & Fidler, C. O. (2018). Elderly British men: Homohysteria and orthodox masculinities. *Journal of Gender Studies, 27*(3), 248–259. https://doi.org/10.1080/09589236.2017.1391690

Anderson, E., Adams, A., & Rivers, I. (2012). "I kiss them because I love them": The emergence of heterosexual men kissing in British institutes of education. *Archives of Sexual Behavior, 41*(2), 421–430.

Anderson, E., Magrath, R., & Bullingham, R. (2016). *Out in sport* (1st ed.). Routledge.

Anderson, E., & McCormack, M. (2015). Cuddling and spooning: Heteromasculinity and homosocial tactility among student-athletes. *Men and Masculinities, 18*(2), 214–230. https://doi.org/10.1177/1097184X14523433

Anderson, E., Ripley, M., & McCormack, M. (2019). A mixed-method study of same-sex kissing among college-attending heterosexual men in the US. *Sexuality & Culture, 23*(1), 26–44.

Balkmar, D. (2018). Violent mobilities: Men, masculinities and road conflicts in Sweden. *Mobilities, 13*(5), 717–732. https://doi.org/10.1080/17450101.2018.1500096

Baron, D., Reardon, C., & Baron, S. H. (2013). *Clinical sports psychiatry: An international perspective.* John Wiley & Sons, Ltd.

Barrie, L., Waitt, G., & Brennan-Horley, C. (2019). Cycling assemblages, self-tracking digital technologies and negotiating gendered subjectivities of road cyclists on-the-move. *Leisure Sciences, 41*(1–2), 108–126.

Barrios, C., Bernardo, N. D., Vera, P., Laíz, C., & Hadala, M. (2015). Changes in sports injuries incidence over time in world-class Road cyclists. *International Journal of Sports Medicine, 36*(3), 241–248. Available at: https://www.thieme-connect.de/products/ejournals/abstract/10.1055/s-0034-1389983

BikeRaceInfo. (2022). *Bicycle race results.* https://bikeraceinfo.com/annual/race2022.html

Carrillo, H., & Hoffman, A. (2017). 'Straight with a pinch of bi': The construction of heterosexuality as an elastic category among adult US men. *Sexualities, 21*(1–2), 90–108.

Clyde, L., & Franklin, W. (2012). *The changing definition of masculinity (perspectives in sexuality) (softcover reprint of the original 1st ed. 1984th ed.).* Springer.

Cycling News. (2017, December 12). Philippa York: Cycling's conservative culture suppresses LGBT issues. Cyclingnews.Com. https://www.cyclingnews.com/news/philippa-york-cyclings-conservative-culture-suppresses-lgbt-issues/

Dahlquist, M., Leisz, M. C., & Finkelstein, M. (2015). The club-level road cyclist: Injury, pain, and performance. *Clinical Journal of Sport Medicine: Official journal of the Canadian Academy of Sport Medicine, 25*(2), 88–94. https://doi.org/10.1097/JSM.0000000000000111

De Bernardo, N., Barrios, C., Vera, P., Laiz, C., & Hadala, M. (2012). Incidence and risk for traumatic an overuse injury in top-level road cyclists. *Journal of Sports Science, 30*(10), 1047–1053. https://doi.org/10.1080/0264041 4.2012.687112

Decock, M., De Wilde, L., Van den Bossche, L., Steyaert, A., & Van Tongel, A. (2016). Incidence and aetiology of acute injuries during competitive road cycling. *British Journal of Sports Medicine, 50,* 669–672. Available at: https://bjsm.bmj.com/content/50/11/669

Fleming, P. J., Lee, J. G., & Dworkin, S. L. (2014). "Real men don't": Constructions of masculinity and inadvertent harm in public health interventions. *American Journal of Public Health, 104*(6), 1029–1035. https://doi.org/10.2105/AJPH.2013.301820

Guardian. (2018, May 1). *Philippa York says macho culture prevents cyclists coming out.* The Guardian. https://www.theguardian.com/sport/2018/apr/30/philippa-york-macho-culture-cyclists-coming-out.

Hardwicke, J. (2022a). *An investigation into attitudes towards, and experiences of, sexual minorities in cycling.* University of Northampton. https://doi.org/10.24339/5011a1d2-7adb-4584-9373-de911f4d91cb

Hardwicke, J. (2022b). An investigation into masculinity among competitive road cyclists. *Journal of Emerging Sport Studies, 7.*

Hardwicke, J. (2022c). *Inside the peloton: An exploration into the culture of competitive road cycling with reference to masculinity, risk and injury, with a principle focus on concussion* (Doctoral dissertation, University of Winchester).

Hardwicke, J., Baxter, B. A., Gamble, T., & Hurst, H. T. (2022). An investigation into helmet use, perceptions of sports-related concussion, and seeking medical care for head injury amongst competitive cyclists. *International Journal of Environmental research and public health, 19*(5), 2861.

Hardwicke, J., & Hurst, H. T. (2020). Concussion knowledge and attitudes amongst competitive cyclists. *Journal of Science and Cycling, 9,* 53–66.

Harmon, K., Drezner, J., Gammons, M., et al. (2013). American medical society for sports medicine position statement. *Clinical Journal of Sport Medicine, 23*(1), 1–18. https://doi.org/10.1097/jsm.0b013e31827f5f93

Hughes, R., & Coakley, J. (1991). Positive deviance among athletes: The implications of overconformity to the sport ethic. *Sociology of Sport Journal, 8*(4), 307–325.

Hurst, H., & Hardwicke, J. (2020, September 22). *Cycling: Head injuries ignored because of entrenched macho culture.* The Conversation. https://theconversation.com/cycling-head-injuries-ignored-because-of-entrenched-macho-culture-146374

Hurst, H., Novak, A., Cheung, S., & Atkins, S. (2019). Knowledge of and attitudes towards concussion in cycling: A preliminary study. *Journal of Science and Cycling, 8*(1), 11–17. Available at: http://www.jsc-journal.com/ojs/index.php?journal=JSC&page=article&op=view&path%5B%5D=10.28985%2F1906.jsc.03&path%5B%5D=534

Levant, R. F., & Wimer, D. J. (2014). Masculinity constructs as protective buffers and risk factors for Men's health. *American Journal of Men's Health, 8*(2), 110–120. https://doi.org/10.1177/1557988313494408

Magrath, R. (2017). 'To try and gain an advantage for my team': Homophobic and homosexually themed chanting among English football fans. *Sociology, 52*(4), 709–726. https://doi.org/10.1177/0038038517702600

Magrath, R. (2018). 'To try and gain an advantage for my team': Homophobic and homosexually themed chanting among English football fans. *Sociology, 52*(4), 709–726.

McCormack, M. (2012). *The declining significance of homophobia.* Oxford University Press.

McCormack, M., & Anderson, E. (2014a). Homohysteria: Definitions, context and intersectionality. *Sex Roles, 71*(3), 152–158.

McCormack, M., & Anderson, E. (2014b). The influence of declining homophobia on men's gender in the United States: An argument for the study of homohysteria. *Sex Roles, 71*(3–4), 109–120.

McDonald, I. (2014). Portraying Sporting masculinity through film: Reflections on Jorgen Leth's A Sunday in hell. In *Routledge handbook of sport, gender and sexuality* (pp. 480–487). Routledge.

Messner, M. A., & Sabo, D. F. (1990). *Sport, men, and the gender order: Critical feminist perspectives* (Vol. 10). Human Kinetics.

Morioka, R. (2014). Gender difference in the health risk perception of radiation from Fukushima in Japan: The role of hegemonic masculinity. *Social Science & Medicine*, *1982*(107), 105–112. https://doi.org/10.1016/j.socscimed.2014.02.014

O'Reilly, M., Mahon, S., Reid, D., Hume, P., Hardaker, N., & Theadom, A. (2020). Knowledge, attitudes, and behavior toward concussion in adult cyclists. *Brain Injury*, *34*(9), 1175–1182. https://doi.org/10.1080/02699052.2020.1793386

Ogburn, W. F. (1957). *Cultural lag as theory*. Sociology & Social Research.

Ogilvie, M. F., & McCormack, M. (2020). Gender-collaborative training in elite university sport: Challenging gender essentialism through integrated training in gender-segregated sports. *International Review for the Sociology of Sport*, *56*(8), 1172–1188.

Powell, D., Stiles, B., Haff, G., & Kilgore, L. (2005). The notion of masculinity in male collegiate road cyclists. *Creative Sociology*, *33*(2), 153. https://ojs.library.okstate.edu/osu/index.php/FICS/article/view/1558

Ravensbergen, L., Buliung, R., & Laliberté, N. (2019). Toward feminist geographies of cycling. *Geography Compass*, *1*. https://doi.org/10.1111/gec3.12461

Reed, K. (2013). Beyond hegemonic masculinity: The role of family genetic history in Men's accounts of health. *Sociology*, *47*(5), 906–920. https://doi.org/10.1177/0038038513494505

Reimer, A. (2021, August 25). *Cyclist clay Davies comes out, calls out his sport for homophobia*. Outsports. https://www.outsports.com/homophobia/2021/8/25/22641481/clay-davies-british-cycling-gay-homophobia

Roberts, S., Anderson, E., & Magrath, R. (2017). Continuity, change and complexity in the performance of masculinity among elite young footballers in England. *The British Journal of Sociology*, *68*(2), 336–357. https://doi.org/10.1111/1468-4446.12237

Robinson, S., White, A., & Anderson, E. (2019). Privileging the bromance: A critical appraisal of romantic and bromantic relationships. *Men and Masculinities*, *22*(5), 850–871.

Sanderson, J., Weathers, M., Snedaker, K., & Gramlich, K. (2016). "I Was Able to Still Do My Job on the Field and Keep Playing": An Investigation of Female and Male Athletes' Experiences With (Not) Reporting Concussions. *Communication & Sport*, *5*(3), 267–287. https://doi.org/10.1177/2167479515623455

Schlosser, A. J. (2016). *Concussion knowledge and attitudes: The impact of hegemonic masculinity*. The University of North Dakota.

Sidwells, C. (2019). *The call of the Road: The history of cycle Road racing*. William Collins.

Silberman, M. (2013). Bicycling injuries. *Current Sports Medicine Reports*, *12*(5), 337–345. https://doi.org/10.1249/JSR.0b013e3182a4bab7

Velominati. (2017). *The hardmen – Legends and lessons from the Cycling gods*. Pegasus.

Velominati – Keepers of the Cog. (2022, June 25). https://www.velominati.com/

Wagner, K. (2022, July 13). The sport of cycling fixates on pain too much. Bicycling. https://www.bicycling.com/tour-de-france/a40578977/sport-of-cycling-fixates-pain/

Wellard, I. (2010). Men, sport, body performance and the maintenance of 'exclusive masculinity'. *Leisure Studies, 21*(3–4), 235–247. https://doi.org/10.1080/0261436022000030641

White, A., & Hobson, M. (2018). Teachers' stories: Physical education teachers' constructions and experiences of masculinity within secondary school physical education. *Sport, Education and Society, 22*(8), 905–918.

White, A. J., Magrath, R., & Emilio Morales, L. (2021). Gay male athletes' coming-out stories on Outsports.com. *International Review for the Sociology of Sport, 56*(7), 1017–1034.

Wignall, L., Scoats, R., Anderson, E., & Morales, L. (2020). A qualitative study of heterosexual men's attitudes toward and practices of receiving anal stimulation. *Culture, Health & Sexuality, 22*(6), 675–689.

Wijlhuizen, G., van Gent, P., & Stipdonk, H. (2016). Sport Cycling crashes among males on public roads, the influence of bunch riding, experience and competitiveness. *Safety, 2*(2), 11. https://doi.org/10.3390/safety2020011

YouGov. (2016, May 13). *Only 2% of young men feel completely masculine (compared to 56% of over 65s)*. https://yougov.co.uk/topics/politics/articles-reports/2016/05/13/low-young-masculinity-britain

Zheng, Y., Ma, Y., & Cheng, J. (2020). Cycling anger in China: The relationship with gender roles, cycling-related experience, risky and aggressive riding. *Transportation Research Part F: Traffic Psychology and Behaviour, 68*, 52–66. https://doi.org/10.1016/j.trf.2019.12.002

CHAPTER 5

Joining the Peloton: The Cult(ure) of Competitive Road Cycling

INTRODUCTION

As discussed already throughout this book, competitive road cycling has long been a sport that cherishes tradition and romanticises imagery that is steeped in notions of orthodox masculinity (Brittain, 2022). The purpose of this chapter is to discuss the culture of competitive cycling more broadly by building on the previous chapters that have outlined the masculine tenets in which much of the sports culture has been developed around. To achieve this, the sociology of sporting subcultures will firstly be discussed and then applied to the sport of road cycling. Then the everyday experiences of the competitive road cyclist within a sport with a strong, often cult-like, subculture associated with it will be considered. The chapter concludes with an argument put forward that competitive road cycling is a sport that operates within a 'culture of risk', and this theoretical framing provides the starting point of analysis for Chaps. 6 and 7.

UNDERSTANDING SUBCULTURES

To understand subcultures, we must first understand what is meant by culture, which is not an easy task. 'Culture' has been previously argued to be one of the most complex words to understand, study and conceptualise in the English language (Williams, 1983). Notwithstanding this

© The Author(s), under exclusive license to Springer Nature   77
Switzerland AG 2023
J. Hardwicke, *Masculinities and the Culture of Competitive Cycling*,
Palgrave Studies in Masculinity, Sport and Exercise,
https://doi.org/10.1007/978-3-031-26975-2_5

complexity, for the purposes of this chapter I will take the textbook understanding of culture in that it is the values, beliefs, systems of language, communication, practices and behaviours in which people share in common and, when brought together, allow a group to be defined as a collective. Whereas a subculture is a group in which such characteristics deviate from the dominant culture they are situated. Yinger (1960) describes subcultural groups in the ways they 'differ in such things as language, values, religion, diet, and style of life from the larger social world of which they are a part' (p. 626). Young and Atkinson (2008, p. 9) expand on this by suggesting that subcultures are 'small social structure[s] within the larger dominant culture, composed of individuals sharing similar values, behaviours, attitudes, symbols, and rituals, which set them apart from the larger culture, dominating their style of life and stabilising over time'.

To give an applied example of this in practice, let us consider a common practice in the sport of road cycling in the UK (and internationally). Within the *subculture* of road cycling, it is a social norm for male cyclists to have shaved legs. Indeed, a competitive cyclist with hairy legs would be socially stigmatised in this group. But in the broader *culture* of the UK, it is largely a deviant behaviour for males to shave their leg hairs. The act of shaving leg hairs conflicts with dominant gendered norms associated with men. Therefore, we can see how an act can be the norm within one space (e.g. a subculture) but deviates from the norm in another (e.g. the broader culture).

This was one of the first moments which brought sociology to life for me as a keen 16-year-old cyclist. Armed with a very basic understanding of culture and social norms gained from studying sociology for an A-Level, I found myself in an interesting conundrum. Do I shave my legs in order to fit in with the cycling subculture I was involved in and thus deviate from the norm within the larger social world I occupied (in other words, risk being mocked by my peers)? My dad coming home to me sitting with my legs covered in tissues with a bloody trail from the bathroom to my room confirms I opted for shaving.

Subcultures, and how they can influence human behaviours, have been of interest to sociologists for some time. Before considering sporting subcultures, I briefly discuss the development of theorising on subcultures which can largely be thought of in three waves with differing foci: subcultures as deviance, subcultures as resistance and subcultures as distinction. The development of understandings of subcultures broadly aligns with three eras of research, but this is not clear cut and there are overlaps between subcultural theorising.

Much of the early subcultural work was spearheaded by the Chicago School, which developed urban sociology and qualitative approaches to understand the significant social and cultural change Chicago experienced due to population increase throughout the early to mid-twentieth century. Here, the social organisation of the city was restructured leading to the development of inner-city subcultures.

Much of this early research focused on deviance being a key aspect of these subcultures, largely because of the relation between subcultural membership and crime (Park, 1915; Thrasher, 1927; Venkatesh, 2008). However, with the seminal work of Becker (1963, 1967), deviancy as the unit of analysis moved away from a focus on crime per se, and moral failings of individuals, and towards an understanding that deviance was just difference from the norm. In short, no behaviour is inherently deviant but becomes so if society deems it to be (Becker, 1967). As such, theorising was focused on subcultures, particularly amongst youth, as social locations in which groups reacted to being negatively labelled as deviant by dominant societal norms.

The next paradigm shift in subcultural studies was a move away from a focus on a subculture's relationship to the broader culture and towards a focus on the individual experiences within the subculture. This saw a shift from deviance towards resistance. This work was largely directed by the Birmingham Centre for Contemporary Cultural Studies (CCCS) and focused on resistance to dominant societal norms and structures. Here, subcultures were understood as sites in which members held symbolic power through resisting hegemonic cultural norms and societal power and status structures. This power was understood as symbolic as it did not enact social change, but the act of resistance was cathartic to the members (Hall & Jefferson, 2006).

This approach has been criticised for taking a reductionist approach to understanding working-class culture (Muggleton, 2000; Murdock & McCron, 1976). Further, the CCCS subcultural analysis was mostly on white British, working-class males (Waters, 1981), thus making the application to wider subcultures that face different constraints, or no constraints, not easy. This is particularly the case for sporting subcultures which can include a range of different people not unified by resistance to dominant societal norms due to lack of social status or capital.

80   J. HARDWICKE

As a result of this, a more nuanced understanding of subcultures was needed, and the third shift was to view subcultures as forms of distinction. Subcultures are still understood as sites in which resistance and deviance are exhibited, but contemporary frameworks broadly conceptualise them as expressions of a collective identity that deviate from dominant cultural norms. Subcultures are still distinct from broader society but are united around shared values, behaviours and practices as opposed to being united around shared experiences of oppression or being labelled as deviant (Hodkinson, 2005). As will be discussed in more detail below, recent theorising has also further considered the workings of subcultures on the micro-level and the importance of the individual in this setting in terms of differing levels of membership, involvement and capital within a subculture.

As with most concepts in the social sciences, and particularly sociology, subculture is still a contested term with much history behind the changing understandings of the word. Alternative concepts have been posited to try refine theorising such as idioculture (Fine, 1979), scene (Irwin, 1977), neo-tribe (Maffesoli, 1996) and post-subculture (Muggleton, 2000). Whilst this work is useful, I adopt the original terminology of subculture as I believe this to still be the best operational word for the discussion of this book, as well as it being better recognised and understood in popular culture.

Whilst I offered some definitions of subcultures at the beginning of this section, there is no universally accepted definition of the concept. Building on these, I will outline some core tenets of my understanding of a subculture relevant to the field of study this book is located:

- The subculture is formed around a shared interest and/or activity and this is the reason it exists.
- There are explicit (formal) and implicit (informal) shared rules in which members must learn and adopt.
- There are shared norms, behaviours and language which deviate from mainstream culture.
- Members invest significant resources into membership to the subculture, as well as material and bodily sacrifice.
- Emphasis is placed on membership having to be earnt and this leads to feelings of distinctiveness from mainstream culture.
- A hierarchy exists within the subculture in which not all members are equal, and some members hold greater status, power and capital than others within the group.

Understanding Subcultures in Sport

Whilst being a key area of interest for mainstream sociology, subcultures have also been of interest to sociologists of sport for some time. Indeed, much of the early research within the subdiscipline of sport sociology focused on understanding sport subcultures and the everyday experiences in these. It was largely concerned with gaining an understanding of the 'back regions' (Goffman, 1959) of sport (Crosset & Beal, 1997) and, following suit with the early classical work, was largely focused on deviancy and resistance to dominant culture (Abramson & Modzelski, 2010). Perhaps one of the earliest studies of sporting subcultures was Weinberg and Arond's (1952) study of boxers, where fighting was reported to be an important pathway to social status amongst lower socioeconomic groups, particularly youth. This was followed by a range of seminal studies across sport such as horse racing (Scott, 1968), surfing (Pearson, 1977) and pool (Polsky, 1969). Then, later in the twentieth century, saw the continuation of this tradition with studies of subcultures in rugby (Young, 1988), bodybuilding (Klein, 1986), mountain climbing (Donnelly & Young, 1988), windsurfing and running (Nash, 1977). There now exists much contemporary literature in the sociology of sport that uses the notion of subcultures to understand behaviours, practices and attitudes found across sports (Anderson & White, 2018).

In understanding this development of the sociology of sporting subcultures, Donnelly (2007) highlights the importance of Ingham's (1975) work in which a combination of the work of Marx, Weber and Goffman was deployed in his analysis of subcultures in occupational spaces in the sporting world. Here marked a shift towards a sharper understanding of culture as something that was socially constructed, produced, reproduced and, in the case of subcultures, could be resisted. This is important when considered in a sporting context as sport holds such an esteemed position within Western culture and thus over individuals lives. Indeed, Anderson and White (2018) have described competitive sport as a near 'total institution', drawing on Goffman's (1963) work to explicate the powerful influence sport has over many people's everyday lives. Therefore, the (sub) culture of competitive cycling is explored in this chapter, and throughout the book, as it is an important site in which behaviours, attitudes and practices are learnt by participants of the sport.

A key consideration here is constructing a theoretical understanding of *why* people join and identify with sporting subcultures. Much of the early sociological and ethnographical work on subcultures focused on groups in society that did not have access to orthodox means of gaining social status and thus subcultures offered a route to gain social capital through reputation, shared values and respect. However, the theories built on this early work had a shortcoming in explaining why members of society that held high social capital and had access to orthodox social status would still participate in subcultures that involve material and bodily sacrifice (this is the case in many sports) with no clear benefits to them in the larger social world.

It is here that the work of Abramson and Modzelski (2010) is particularly useful for the context of this book. They build on theories of sporting subcultures in an examination of middle-class participation in cage-fighting subcultures. These being individuals with significant social capital and access to orthodox means of social status. Abramson and Modzelski (2010) conclude from their empirical work that fighters were drawn to the cage-fighting subculture because 'they feel it gives them visceral access to widespread American ideals, such as being rewarded for hard work, "being true to oneself," and forming voluntary communities' (p. 174). They argue that beliefs, practices and attitudes within the cage-fighting subculture share constituent elements of middle-class morality and habitus. Despite the seemingly extreme and non-conforming image of the subculture to the outsider, the underlying belief systems of the subculture were 'scarcely different than the social psychology of the ideal typical middle-class life' (Atkinson, 2008, p. 309). Abramson and Modzelski (2010, p. 174) comment:

> Fighters feel the local status systems created in the gym and supported by their pugilistic peers, better reflect who they "really are" and who they "want to be," than their positions in society proper. Participation becomes an organizing principle of life, one that assumes great importance through the powerful draw associated with a perceived match between ideals and practice.

This sense of micro-level community is constructed through both extraordinary and mundane rituals (Durkheim, 1933; Goffman, 1963), which makes involvement in [Insert any activity in which a subculture is formed around] seem uniquely real and meaningful to the participant (Geertz, 1966, 2000). Whilst theoretical inconsistencies remain around the draw and function of subcultures in sport (Young & Atkinson, 2008; Wheaton, 2007), I am interested in explicating road cycling subculture through a similar theoretical lens outlined by Abramson and Modzelski (2010) of understanding the wide-ranging appeal of subcultures to individuals across different social strata. This is a particularly useful approach for understanding road cycling culture as it exists as a sport largely dominated by white, middle-class males (Falcous, 2017), who typically hold high levels of social capital and access to social status within Western cultures.

Membership and Identity in a Subculture

I have discussed what a subculture is, their history in the sociology of sport and some thoughts on the 'pull' factors towards becoming a member of one. But what is the process of joining one? Here, I will draw on relevant theory to outline this process before applying it specifically to competitive road cycling. The discussion here is largely directed by the seminal work of Donnelly and Young (1988) 'The Construction and Confirmation of Identity in Sport Subcultures'.

In anthropology and sociology, the term assimilation refers to the process in which an individual, or group, acquires the culture of the dominant culture in which they have entered by adopting aspects of its attitudes, values and practices. This is more of a macro process (on a large scale), but the same process occurs on the micro-level (small scale) when an individual seeks to join a sporting subculture. A key analytical distinction to make when considering sporting subcultures is that they are a social location in which a choice is made to participate (notwithstanding considerations for processes of socialisation influencing that choice, particularly with boys in sport), as opposed to an individual belonging to a subculture due to characteristics assigned at birth (Fine & Kleinman, 1979). Therefore, to be clear, the focus and research context of this book is on a subculture (road cycling) in which people have made the conscious decision to join.

Donnelly and Young (1988, p. 225) suggest there are a variety of means in which individuals assimilate into a subculture, with the most significant being modelling. Modelling refers to new members of subcultures deliberately adopting mannerisms and attitudes, styles of dress, speech and behaviours (like me shaving my legs for the first time) that they perceive to be required of them and are observed in established members of the subculture (Donnelly, 1985). As such, as an individual spends time within the group and doing whatever activity it is, they start shaping their behaviours and reflecting that of the group to increase chances of membership

84   J. HARDWICKE

and acceptance amongst the members. In turn, an individual's identity begins to be shaped around these practices as they become more immersed in the culture. This can be a staged process. For example, a new road cyclist may go through steps in forming an identity aligned with the cycling subculture such as first wearing lycra, purchasing certain cycling technologies, entering their first race and choosing to shave their legs (often the final frontier before gaining acceptance as a 'proper' road cyclist).

However, simply engaging in these acts and adopting the behaviours of the group does not always secure acceptance and membership. Donnelly and Young (1988, p. 225) comment:

> Acceptance in subcultures is directly related to demonstrations of appropriate job and/or skill requirements, appropriate roles and identities under specific circumstances, successful socialization procedures, and general value homophyly between the actor and the larger group. Acceptance may also necessitate the actor's flexibility toward activities he or she usually considers negatively but which are condoned in the larger context of the subculture.

In some cases, role conflicts can arise and members of subcultures that do not meet the requirements of the group or sufficiently follow the processes above can face ostracism and possible banishment from the group (Donnelly & Young, 1988). The extent of this varies across subcultures, with some having very strict internal policing and others being more fluid in their acceptance of members. As will be considered below, and discussed in previous chapters, road cycling has developed a culture of strict policing of membership. We can see how this formed, and this discussion of subcultures applies to the early days of the sport discussed in Chap. 2 where membership to cycling clubs were strictly regulated and members had a number of, formal and informal, rules that must be followed.

In the twenty-first century, there has been a rise in subcultures based around a sporting and/or leisure activity, but limited accompanying research and theory to understand it. However, the literature on 'Serious leisure' is useful here. Serious leisure refers to 'the systematic pursuit of an amateur, hobbyist or volunteer activity sufficiently substantial and interesting in nature for the participant to find a career there acquiring and expressing a combination of its special skills, knowledge, and experience' (Stebbins, 1992). Importantly, the key distinction here to other recreational pursuits in leisure is the level of commitment and meaning of the activity to the participant. Such an activity requires a total commitment from the participant, which significantly shapes their life and social identity. Green and Jones (2005) highlight that serious leisure participants belong to a clearly identifiable group with its own norms, values, behaviours and even language. Competitive road cycling can be considered a 'serious leisure' pursuit, and a deeper discussion of this is offered below, but first a consideration of power hierarchies within subcultures is offered.

POWER HIERARCHIES WITHIN A SUBCULTURE

Within subcultures (and culture more broadly), power is rarely evenly distributed and certain members will hold greater status within the group. A key concept here which I have used at various times already is 'cultural capital'. This is another slippery term with much debate and controversies around its use and conceptualisation, but that debate is not in the scope of this book. To operationalise the term for the purposes of the analysis here, cultural capital can be understood as the socio-cultural assets of a person that can promote social mobility in a stratified society.

The concept was developed during the 1970s by French sociologist, Pierre Bourdieu. He developed the concept to attempt to explain how power in society operated and was transmitted amongst different social classes. Whilst Karl Marx famously posited that economic capital (material assets such as money) was the sole determinant of an individual's position in a social order, Bourdieu was interested in material *and* non-material assets that contributed to a person's social standing. Both Marx and Bourdieu suggested that the more capital a person has, the higher their social standing and more powerful they are.

Bourdieu (1986) defined cultural capital as 'familiarity with the legitimate culture within a society', what is sometimes referred to as 'high culture'. For example, why theatre may be valued over soap operas on TV, with theatre representing 'high culture'. Bourdieu (1986) identified three sources of cultural capital: objective (cultural goods, books, works of art), embodied (language, mannerisms, preferences) and institutionalised (qualifications, education credentials). This theorising has since been developed to better reflect contemporary society with other forms of capital such as technological proficiency and emotional intelligence being included (Noble & Davies, 2009; Holden, 2015).

Whilst much of this operates on the macro-level, this same process has been considered on a micro, subcultural, level to explain hierarchies within subcultures. Thornton's (1995) work on dance club cultures is germane here, where she sought to fill a theoretical gap of cultural distinctions and hierarchies within subcultures. In her work she highlights the importance of internal power hierarchies within and between subcultures. Using Bourdieu's (1986) concept of cultural capital, she coined the term 'subcultural capital' to denote distinctions and power differences between members of a subculture. Using dance club culture as the site of analysis, Thornton (1995) discussed how there were distinctions within this world largely directed by claims of authenticity. For example, the authentic versus the phony or the hip versus the mainstream. Thus, whilst a subculture may distance itself from the broader culture, there also exists tensions within a subculture where certain members may hold greater subcultural capital and develop distinctions between 'us' and 'them'.

If we consider this process in road cycling, the book 'The Rules: The Way of the Cycling Disciple' from Velominati (2014) offers a good, applied example. The book uses the advertising slogan of 'We are CYCLISTS, the rest of the world merely rides bikes' which is reinforced with undertones throughout publications by Velominati that although an individual may be a cyclist, they are not a *proper* cyclist unless the rules outlined are followed. Thus, a distinction is created within a subculture. Furthermore, road cycling culture often operates on hierarchical principles in which members with greater subcultural capital will hold the most status amongst the group. This is explored in more detail below. The importance of this discussion, and why I have dedicated this chapter to a discussion of subculture, is how these processes can influence and encourage certain behaviours within the sport, such as dealing with injury as will be explored in the following chapter.

THE CULT(URE) OF COMPETITIVE ROAD CYCLING

A common thread across decades of socio-cultural research on road cycling is that it is a somewhat 'closed' sport with a strong subculture that can be hard to access for 'outsiders' (Williams, 1989; Albert, 1999; Rees et al., 2014; Hardwicke, 2022). Indeed, the sport was largely built on this exclusive premise, as discussed in Chap. 2. The social world of road cycling is full of implicit behaviours, mannerisms, values and attitudes that an individual must learn and adopt in order to achieve membership in the sports subculture. On this, Drinkell (2021, p. 5) comments on how 'there are literally thousands of unwritten rules – from the length of your socks to the "luft" of your cap to the nuances of behaviour when cycling in a group'. Further, Rees et al. (2014, p. 466) comment on the road cycling setting:

> This social setting functions as a secret world, the organisation of which is governed by unwritten rules and unspoken knowledge, a social world with an intricate system of values invisible and unknown to outsiders.

As such, the subculture of road cycling offers an interesting site for social analysis. Here, I will provide a brief overview of some of the core structures of this complex social world, as well as discuss social order amongst competitive road cyclists. And given the importance that is placed on learning and abiding by these rules, I provide an over-arching argument that road cycling members can be considered as cult members. A cult can be understood as a social group defined by unusual religious, spiritual or philosophical beliefs and rituals but with greater devotion to what we may expect in subcultures. Whilst I make this argument tongue in cheek, it is done so to highlight the importance the sport holds over many of its participants' lives which can come with negative consequences, as will be discussed over the following chapters.

Firstly, it must be made clear that the sport of road cycle racing is an extremely physiologically demanding endurance-based sport (Clarsen et al., 2010). As such, participants must dedicate a lot of time and effort to complete a race (often 70+ miles in length with average speeds of 25mph+), let alone be competitive in one. It is not uncommon for amateur competitive cyclists to spend upward of 20 hours training a week. (This often does not go down well with partners, from personal experience.) This level of commitment to a physical activity makes it a fascinating site for sociological analysis. From ethnographic research on a Canadian amateur road cycling club, Williams (1989, p. 320) notes the general behaviour of a club member:

> He [Third person reference to a general club member] had to expend a lot of time and effort in training. Just to keep up with the peloton in a race of 70 miles required daily training for up to three hours a day. It was extremely demanding exercise, so demanding in fact that he had to eat and drink frequently while in the saddle and once off the bike it was very common for him to have difficulty walking. As a result of this, the cyclist had very little 'spare' time during a normal day, after going to work or studying, nor the

88   J. HARDWICKE

energy to devote to non-cycling activities and this represented a serious and
heavy commitment to the activity.

As such, the first step for a cyclist's introduction to the culture of the
sport is the sacrifice it demands from its participants. This physical demand
required can lead to the sport becoming all-consuming to a participant's
life. The popularity of this sport amongst white male professional workers
offers an interesting discussion point for the meanings attached to this
activity and what the draw towards such a total commitment is. To my
knowledge, this has not been explored in detail and is out of the scope of
this book, however both Falcous (2017) and Glackin and Beale (2018)
offer some interesting discussion on understanding serious, non-
competitive, amateur road cyclists' attraction to the activity.

Once this commitment has been made which, of course, is often a gradual process as a participant becomes increasingly embedded in the sport,
the next important area to consider within the subculture of cycling are
the formal and informal rules that must be learnt. These have been of
interest to the social sciences since the early inception of most disciplines
within the field. Often referred to as implicit and explicit norms, they refer
to the ways in which we learn behaviours and ways to act in social contexts. Formal rules/explicit norms refer to norms that are codified in formal structures, such as cyclists in competition are not permitted to take
erythropoietin (EPO), whereas informal rules/implicit norms refer to the
'un-written' rules that have been agreed upon amongst a social group,
such as a cyclist shaving their legs. It is the latter that is of interest here,
and I will not cover the formal rules of the sport of road cycling, rather the
informal rules will be considered. Indeed, Albert (1991, p. 343) suggests
that socialisation into a sporting subculture is 'not attained by internaliz-
ing the formal rules but must be accompanied by incorporation into the
informal rule-like practices of the game'.

As discussed above, the sport of road cycling offers a complex social
world in which many informal rules exist. Neophytes (new members of a
subculture) must learn these and integrate them into their behaviours to
successfully become a member of the subculture. Firstly, the nuances of
competition in road cycling are important to note. There has been previous discussion on the nuances of the sport of road cycling which involves
ideologies of both individualism and collectivism, and cyclists must learn
when each is appropriate (Williams, 1989; Albert, 1991; Rees et al.,
2014). On this, Albert (1991, p. 344) comments:

Contrary to expectations, within the sport of bicycle racing the two themes of conflict and association coexist (Williams, 1989). On the one hand, the theme of individualism reflects the unambiguous aspects of conflict, emphasizing individual or team effort that occurs within the framework of basic rules and results in a win or loss. On the other hand, a theme of collectivism has emerged, reflecting some of the situational particularities of the sport that require an association between opponents, called "drafting." In practice the bicycle race presents a somewhat anomalous situation in which apparent opponents shift between antagonistic competition and associative efforts. The competitive/associative phasing that pervades this sport is, in part, a feature of the social space of the bicycle race whereby riders compete in close proximity to one another and wherein competitive advantage is to be gained through the use of an opponent's slipstream, a practice known as drafting. It may also be to one's further advantage to cooperate with another, each in turn making an effort while the other rests in the slipstream. By combining, competitors limit the tendency of one rider to race particularly on the efforts of others.

Therefore, the sport of cycling deviates from dominant understandings of competition in sport as 'such structures as pelotons and pacelines create both the opportunity for and the requirement of cooperative efforts between opponents, standing in stark contrast to more conventional conceptions of sport in which only unambiguous conflict between competitors is seen as legitimate' (Albert, 1991, p. 345). Because of this, socialisation into the subculture of road cycling involves the internalisation of an ideology where competition is flexible and competitors move between opposition and cooperation, alongside the expected knowledge any neophyte must learn such as formal rules, equipment use and training routines (Albert, 1984).

A phenomenon here that can prevent a new member from gaining acceptance or membership within a road cycling subculture is if these informal rules are violated by not adhering to collectivism when required. This can occur when a rider does not contribute to a group effort, whether that be in a race setting or training, and this leads to social ostracising and is a stigmatised behaviour. This can happen if a rider does not take a 'turn' on the front to contribute to the collective effort by allowing others to draft in the slipstream, and this can lead to being labelled as a 'Wheel sucker' (Albert, 1991; Rees et al., 2014). An extension of this is that all riders must keep this internal social order and coherence to gain a benefit, and if one rider 'loses the wheel' of the rider in front, the cohesion of the group breaks down and a 'split' is caused, providing the riders in front an advantage and disadvantaging the riders behind (Rees et al., 2014). This is often a cause of conflict in races and in my time racing I regularly saw those that 'lost the wheel' receive verbal abuse for doing so (I won't pretend I have not also been on the receiving end of this abuse at times, also). As such, this forms another key feature which a new cyclist must learn and Rees et al. (2014, p. 467) comment:

> [T]he ability to hold the wheel is central to the activity and is the standard by which all participants are judged and is a further reflection of the intrinsic nature of surveillance in learning skills that are essential to cycling competition.

This contributes to a cyclists' standing within the subculture, which relates to the above discussion of hierarchies within a subculture. Drawing on Bourdieu's (1986, p. 71) discussions of power and dominance in social situations coming from possession of cultural and social capital, Rees et al. (2014) suggest that racing cycling culture is replete with internal competition over status, and power and dominance takes a number of forms. Within road cycling subculture, members which hold the most power are often referred to as 'Hitters' (Rees et al., 2014; Hardwicke, 2022). This status is largely gained through displays of physical fitness and previous successes in competition and can be seen to map onto core tenets of orthodox masculinity. Rees et al. (2014, p. 473) comment:

> Being one of the fittest riders has significant value amongst racing cyclists and confers physical capital related to an individual's strength and athleticism. This overt and highly prized individualised component of the racing cyclist is studied, understood and admired by all within this subculture. Thus, 'physical capital', as it is expressed in the Bourdieusian sense, also confers status through social capital related to reputation and image.

This has also been reported in other research. Kolsrud (2014) conducted participant observation and interviews with amateur competitive road cyclists, finding that cyclists within the group and local area clearly differentiated between 'recreational' and 'competitive' riders. Here, those that engaged with the sport competitively set themselves apart from recreational riders with undertones of there being greater value in engaging in the sport competitively. Kolsrud (2014, p. 1) comments on the experiences of competitive cyclists as opposed to recreational:

> Competitive cyclists put themselves at risk in group training rides and races, they put others around them at risk, and they also put their reputations as riders at risk. Hence, competitive cyclists' behaviours, actions, and identities were constantly undergoing evaluation through their performance on the bikes.

Here, we see a hierarchy within cycling more broadly, in which competitive cyclists assign themselves to the top of over other cycling practices. Furthermore, Barrie et al. (2019) discuss the influence of Strava on (re) producing the hierarchal and competitive nature of road cycling subcultures. Strava, a self-tracking mobile application for recording cycling activities, is described by Barrie et al. (2019, p. 109) in the following way:

> Strava not only tracks the cycling body (heart rate, distance, times, routes, speed, cadence, power, elevation and calories burnt) but also shares this data within a social network of athletes underpinned by the myth of sports as an egalitarian activity. Hence, competition becomes possible.

Here, the research reported how the road cycling masculinity predicated on competition, risk, winning, speed and physicality is (re)produced through Strava. Barrie et al. (2019, p. 116) discuss how the platform encourages public competition amongst cyclists whereby 'On the bike, friends become rivals and a social hierarchy is produced through cycling masculinities, enhanced by the affective qualities of self-tracking data and surveillance'. This research further reinforces the notion that the subculture of road cycling is strongly based on a hierarchy largely based on masculine tenets.

This, of course, leads to concerns around the inclusivity of such groups and those that do not meet these demands of the sporting subculture may be marginalised. It is also important to consider this through the lens of masculinity. I discussed in Chap. 2 how the sport was built upon orthodox masculine norms and developed within a cultural climate where masculinity significantly shaped the structuring of sport. What can be considered forms of social and physical capital within competitive road cycling have significant overlaps with notions of masculine capital (Anderson, 2005). Anderson and White comment that 'The more a male adheres to these [masculine norms] in cultures that value orthodox masculinity, the more he raises his masculine capital – his worth among other boys and men' (2018, p. 111). Thus, male competitive road cyclists often exist within a hierarchy where a constant negotiation of position happens and traits of orthodox masculinity, such as physical fitness and risk taking, are highly valued and offer members a route to gaining social status and capital within the group.

In assimilating into the road cycling culture and learning the formal and informal rules of the game outlined above, individuals within a road cycling subculture will often form a social identity based on the sport. In short, they become a 'Road cyclist'. This is sociologically interesting and important to consider when studying the lives of the sport participants. As highlighted above, the sport requires significant material and bodily commitment, and this may be a significant factor in the formation of the strong subculture associated with the sport. The aspects of road cycling discussed align with the conceptualisations of 'Serious leisure' activities (Green & Jones, 2005), and road cyclists develop an identity based on their engagement with the activity.

Dellanebbia's (2020) research reported that being a 'competitive road cyclist' formed a large part of the participants' primary identity in the study. This led to accounts from participants suggesting an enduring passion for the activity and the notion that road cycling becomes their 'whole life' and 'all consuming' (Dellanebbia, 2020). Whilst this is not unique to road cycling and individuals participating in a sport, particularly adolescents, will often shape their primary identities on this (Anderson & White, 2018), it is particularly common in road cycling and, interestingly, is present across all ages of participants.

Whilst the above discussion is of interest and important to consider, my focus in this book is how these informal cultural rules in the sport can encourage negative behaviours and how the identity of being a 'road cyclists' can lead to an attitude where performance is prioritised over health. And as discussed throughout, analysing this through the lens of masculinity provides some useful insight to the existence and reproduction of such features within the subculture of road cycling. The influence on health is discussed in greater depth in the following chapter, but first I provide a consideration for another key component of road cycling culture: risk.

Road Cycling as a 'Culture of Risk'

Risk is a core part of road cycling. In this section I will present the argument that road cycling operates within a culture of risk in which taking and accepting physical risks are both normalised and accepted within the sport. This then provides the theoretical grounding for the following two chapters focused on injury and doping, where health is compromised for performance.

There is a large body of sociological literature that examines the intersects of pain, injury and risk in sport. Indeed, this has been of interest to sport sociologists for over 30 years (Young, 2019). Pain and injury are discussed in the following chapter, the focus is on risk in this section. Nixon's (1992) seminal work is germane here, where the argument is made that sporting contexts operate within 'cultures of risk' which encourage athletes to accept risk, and risk taking, in sport as the norm. Further, pain and injury are to be brushed off and an athlete's ability to tolerate both is valorised. Nixon (1992) theorised that these attitudes towards injury, pain and risk flourish in sporting cultures because of 'sports nets' which are the influential social networks around athletes such as teammates, coaches, fans and the media. Through this interaction with sporting culture, athletes learn what Hughes and Coakley (1991) term 'the sports ethic'. This leads to athletes being culturally expected to sacrifice their bodies and health for sporting success, something that would be deviant in broader society but is normative in sport (Hughes & Coakley, 1991; Anderson & White, 2018). This ethic also normalises the presence of risk and encourages risky behaviours in sporting contexts. As such, many athletes will continue to compete despite pain and/or injury (Nixon, 1992).

Much previous sociological studies on injury and risk have focused on elite athletes and those in highly organised settings where an athletic identity is the individual's primary identity. Early sociological work was also largely focused on hierarchal environments like high-school and college-level athletes (Curry & Strauss, 1994; Messner, 1992; Nixon, 1994, 1996) and within a professional context (Messner, 1990; Messner & Sabo, 1994; Young & White, 1995). But how relevant is this theorising for understanding risk and injury experiences in more individualised sports and amongst amateur athletes? There have been studies into risk within specific sporting subcultures that are more focused on sport-as-leisure and athletes that have less extrinsic rewards and pressures of the professional athlete or institutionalised college athlete.

Lyng's (1990, 2005) research is important here. Focusing on voluntary risk taking, Lyng argues that individuals engage in high-risk environments, such as skydiving, to temporarily escape from social boundaries and constraints of everyday life. This is known as the notion of 'edgework', where individuals flirt with the edge of mental and physical boundaries resulting in a feeling of control over their lives, whilst simultaneously pushing limits. The concept has been applied to studies on BMX riding (Scott & Austin, 2016), skateboarding (O'Conner, 2016) and skydiving (Laurendeau, 2006). Further, subcultural research on risk in non-mainstream, individualised sport provides some insight. For example, experiences of risk in skateboarding cultures have been explored, finding that risk formed a central feature to the subculture (see Atencio et al., 2009; Haines et al., 2010; Kern et al., 2014). Matthews' (2020) research into boxing suggests risky body cultures are ingrained into boxing subcultures resulting in physical risks to the body being a normal, and expected, phenomenon.

There is limited research that explores the nexus of risk and subculture within competitive road cycling. Albert's (1999) study of risk in road cycling culture outlines the first (and only) comprehensive work in this area. Drawing on interview data, participant observation, media analysis and internet blog posts, Albert presents the argument that competitive road cyclists negotiate risk and injury by embodying both as inherent features of the sport. Road cyclists were not seen to 'court risk for it's own sake' (1999, p. 169), but as risk was deemed so inherent to the sport it is normalised amongst cycling subcultures. As a sport that takes place at high speeds, often on only semi-closed public roads, with minimal protective clothing, the risks of crashing and injury are ever present within road cycling. Indeed, it can be seen as a central feature of the sport. However, it is important to distinguish that competitive road cyclists do not seem to enter the sport because of the risk, rather that this is just part and parcel of competing in the sport and must be dealt with accordingly (Hardwicke, 2022).

As such, the sport of road cycling can be seen to operate within a 'culture of risk'. Importantly, members of the subculture must appropriately deal with this risk to gain membership. Similar to the discussion above on the intricacies and unwritten rules of the sport, cyclists must also negotiate risk. Indeed, Albert suggested that accepting these risks served to 'exhibit and to assert membership in the cycling subculture' (1999, p. 157).

Understanding this provides us a foundation to examining common practices amongst cyclists in which health is often sacrificed for performance, which is addressed in the following chapters.

THE ACCEPTANCE AND NORMALISATION OF RISK IN ROAD CYCLING

Through my research using interviews with a range of competitive cyclists, two main themes represent how cyclists appeared to deal with risk within their sport: acceptance and normalisation (Hardwicke & Hurst, Forthcoming). Before explicating these, it is important to highlight that competitive road cyclists are acutely aware of the high risks of physical injury. As will be discussed in the following chapter, competitive road cyclists commonly report experiences of crashing and injury which is supported by epidemiological research into the sport. There is no denial of this in the sport and the presence of such risks forms a large part of the culture and romantic 'allure' of the professional sport that many journalists draw on when writing about the sport.

Firstly, acceptance of risk is common amongst competitive road cyclists. My research suggests the acceptance of risk by competitive road cyclists is largely processed by the perceived benefits that cyclists report gaining from participation in the sport. For example, one 19-year-old first category rider said to me 'The feeling of doing well and getting a good result definitely outweighs any risk I face'. Other riders made similar comments during interviews which resonate with this notion of risk acceptance:

> The fitness element, the friends, it feels you're achieving something, it gives you some consistency in life this all outweighs the risk of injury.
> The rewards definitely outweigh the risks, definitely.
> Yeah 100% the risks are worth it, it's amazing, I love it. The enjoyment takes over any worrying about risks.

Much of the rewards cited by competitive road cyclists were mostly intrinsic and included improved mental wellbeing, personal fitness and enjoyment. This intrinsic drive perhaps explains why this attitude appears to be consistent across cyclists, regardless of level of competition. (My research includes beginners right up to professional athletes.) One participant, a 39-year-old second category rider, recalled a story from a previous

96 J. HARDWICKE

injury that provides an insight to this mentality and interaction with risk. They commented:

> I had a crash...last year? Yeah, last year, I snapped the chain during team pursuit, stopped and just used my leg as a break at 50 kph. I mean, I didn't hit anything. I didn't hit my head or anything. Just like cheese grater down my leg. My whole leg was bandaged up for a while and I remember a work colleague asked if I was mental doing this sport. And I just thought, this is purely transactional for me. I get so much out of cycling that this is a price worth paying.

In understanding this risk-taking behaviour, I draw on Lyng's (1990, 2005) concept of 'Edgework'. This is a particularly useful framework for understanding attitudes present amongst participants in my research, particularly those at the 'lower levels' of the sport representing serious amateurs that competed alongside work and family responsibilities. Lyng makes the argument that individuals engage in high-risk environments to temporarily escape from social boundaries and constraints of everyday life. Whilst no participants reported being motivated to participate in road cycling because of the risks involved, which was also reported by Albert (1999), there was evidence of the deviation from mundane 'day-to-day' life being a motivating factor for participation. For example, a 37-year-old working professional said 'Racing at the weekend and training in the week provides me a release from the 9-5 and being stuck at a computer. I just love the thrill of competition and adrenaline rush from racing at 40kph plus with a bunch of guys at 8am on a Sunday morning'.

As mentioned earlier in this chapter, a large 'pull' factor towards subcultures is how a community builds around a shared experience which involves both extraordinary and mundane rituals (Durkheim, 1933; Goffman, 1963). In turn, involvement in road cycling seems uniquely real and meaningful to the participant (Geertz, 2000). Amongst competitive road cyclists, the shared acceptance of risk and engagement in an activity with a high risk of physical injury forms part of the identity of the competitive road cyclist and helps bond the subculture together.

Another angle of analysis draws on notions of class. As mentioned previously, competitive road cycling is largely made up of white, middle-class males (Falcous, 2017), and this is reflected in the participants in my research. Wilson (2006) has suggested that middle-class service and managerial work is a variable in increasing likelihood for involvement in sporting subcultures, such as road cycling. Lyng's (1990, 2005) concept of 'Edgework' provides some insight into understanding the risk practices amongst competitive cyclists, where engagement with the high-risk sport of road cycling offers an outlet to push mental and physical boundaries that contrasted from mundane 'everyday' experiences. Atkinson (2008) reported similar findings amongst triathletes, where pushing physical limits and enduring pain and suffering were an attraction to the sport and an 'escape' from normal life.

Similar to the acceptance of risk, within the culture of competitive road cycling risks are normalised contributing to the 'culture of risk' (Nixon, 1992) within the sport I outlined above. For example, one 26-year-old elite category rider commented 'There's a sense of normalisation to the risk. Because I've been cycling for so long, I don't really notice the risks'. Similarly, a 29-year-old elite said similar 'When I'm training on my own, I know there's risks, but I don't really think about it. For me it's normal. When you are racing you don't think about the risks'. It is common amongst competitive road cyclists that awareness of risk is high, but they are accepted and thus normalised into the everyday experience of the racing cyclist. Highlighting this, one 32-year-old said 'With the risk, you've just gotta try push it out your mind haven't you'. Similarly, a 20-year-old elite racer that was a 'sprinter', this means they are frequently involved in high-speed sprint finishes which are considered one of the most dangerous aspects of road cycling, commented on this suppression and acceptance of risk:

> I mean, I don't really think about it too often, really, I just sort of try not to dwell on it and, you know, like, well, I'm not really a risk taker as such, but eventually like when you come into a sprint finish you've just got to do it and you know you don't really think about the risks there, you just sort of act so quickly you don't really get time to process anything. Yeah, just that sort of that racing brain takes over really.

In summary, risk forms a central feature of competitive road cycling culture and to the experience of the individual in the sport. Road cyclists must negotiate this in order to participate in the sport and the acceptance of the inherent risks serves as a key behaviour to gain acceptance within the subculture.

98   J. HARDWICKE

CHAPTER SUMMARY

This chapter serves a range of purposes. Firstly, a discussion of subcultures more broadly has been provided to locate this work within the literature. I have explicated my understanding of subcultures and the features which are used to examine road cycling subculture throughout this book. This is important as subcultural theorising is important to understand the intricacies and processes associated with sporting subcultures. As will be discussed in the following chapters, this can also lead to behaviours which can be harmful to health and an adherence to the subculture comes before the individual's needs. To lay the foundations of the nature of road cycle racing, I discussed some key elements of the sport and the range of informal rules in which new members must learn. It has been argued that competitive road cycling is a serious leisure pursuit which participation in forms a large part of a participant's social identity. Furthermore, the subculture of the sport is hierarchically arranged and status within the subculture is largely gained through exhibiting masculine behaviours of risk taking, competition and physicality. In concluding the chapter, I present my thesis that road cycling operates within a 'culture of risk' and this understanding provides the theoretical framing for the following chapters where I discuss a range of areas where this impacts the everyday experience of the racing cyclist.

REFERENCES

Abramson, C. M., & Modzelewski, D. (2010). Caged morality: Moral worlds, subculture, and stratification among middle-class cage-fighters. *Qualitative Sociology, 34*(1), 143–175.

Albert, E. (1984). Equipment as a feature of social control in the sport of bicycle racing. *Sport and the Sociological Imagination*, 318–338.

Albert, E. (1991). Riding a line: Competition and cooperation in the sport of bicycle racing. *Sociology of Sport Journal, 8*(4), 341–361.

Albert, E. (1999). Dealing with danger: The normalization of risk in cycling. *International Review for the Sociology of Sport, 34*(2), 157–171.

Anderson, E., & White, A. (2018). *Sport, theory and social problems.* Routledge Taylor & Francis Group.

Atencio, M., Beal, B., & Wilson, C. (2009). The distinction of risk: Urban skateboarding, street habitus and the construction of hierarchical gender relations. *Qualitative Research in Sport and Exercise, 1*(1), 3–20. https://doi.org/10.1080/19398440802567907

Atkinson, M. (2008). Triathlon, suffering and exciting significance. *Leisure Studies, 27*(2), 165–180. https://doi.org/10.1080/02614360801902216

Barrie, L., Waitt, G., & Brennan-Horley, C. (2019). Cycling assemblages, self-tracking digital technologies and negotiating gendered subjectivities of road cyclists on-the-move. *Leisure Sciences, 41*(1–2), 108–126.

Becker, H. (1963). *Outsiders: Studies in the sociology of deviance.* The Free Press.

Becker, H. (1967). History, culture, and subjective experience. *Journal of Health and Social Behavior, 8,* 163–176.

Bourdieu, P. (1986). The Forms of Capital. In: Education, Globalisation and Social Change, eds H. Lauder, P. Brown, J.-A. Dillabough and A.H. Halsey. Oxford: Oxford University Press.

Bourdieu, P. (1986). *Distinction (Routledge classics)* (1st ed.). Routledge.

Brittain, J. J. (2022). Atrophying masculinity within professional Road Cycling. In *The Routledge handbook of gender politics in sport and physical activity.* Routledge.

Clarsen, B., Krosshaug, T., & Bahr, R. (2010). Overuse injuries in professional Road cyclists. *The American Journal of Sports Medicine, 38*(12), 2494–2501. https://doi.org/10.1177/0363546510376816

Crosset, T., & Beal, B. (1997). The use of "subculture" and "subworld" in ethnographic works on sport: A discussion of definitional distinctions. *Sociology of Sport Journal, 14*(1), 73–85.

Curry, T., & Strauss, R. H. (1994). A little pain never hurt anyone: A photo-essay on the normalization of sports injury. *Sociology of Sport Journal, 11,* 195–208.

Dellanebbia, A. M. (2020). *The experiences of women competitive road cyclists: A qualitative study* (Doctoral dissertation, Texas Woman's University).

Donnelly, P. (1985). Sport subcultures. *Exercise and Sport Sciences Reviews, 13*(1), 539–578.

Donnelly, P. (2007). *Sport culture and subcultures.* The Blackwell Encyclopedia of Sociology.

Donnelly, P., & Young, K. (1988). The construction and confirmation of identity in sport subcultures. *Sociology of Sport Journal, 5*(3), 223–240.

Drinkell, P. (2021). *The Road Cyclist's companion* (Revised PB edition) (Revised). Cicada Books.

Durkheim, E. (1933). *The division of labor in society.* Free Press.

Falcous, M. (2017). Why we ride: Road cyclists, meaning, and lifestyles. *Journal of Sport and Social Issues, 41*(3), 239–255.

Fine, G. A. (1979). Small groups and culture creation: The idioculture of little league baseball teams. *American Sociological Review,* 733–745.

Fine, G. A., & Kleinman, S. (1979). Rethinking subculture: An interactionist analysis. *American Journal of Sociology, 85*(1), 1–20.

Geertz, C. (1966). Religion as a cultural system. In M. Banton (Ed.), *Anthropological approaches to the study of religion* (pp. 1–46). Tavistock.

Geertz, C. (2000). Deep play: Notes on the Balinese cockfight. In *Culture and politics* (pp. 175–201). Palgrave Macmillan.

Glackin, O. F., & Beale, J. T. (2018). 'The world is best experienced at 18 mph'. The psychological wellbeing effects of cycling in the countryside: An interpretative phenomenological analysis. *Qualitative Research in Sport, Exercise and Health, 10*(1), 32–46.

Goffman, E. (1959). *The presentation of self in everyday life.* Anchor Books.

Goffman, E. (1963). Embarrassment and Social Organization. In N. J. Smelser & W. T. Smelser (Eds.), *Personality and social systems* (pp. 541–548). John Wiley & Sons.

Green, B. C., & Jones, I. (2005). Serious leisure, social identity and sport tourism. *Sport in Society, 8*(2), 164–181.

Haines, C., Smith, T. M., & Baxter, M. F. (2010). Participation in the risk-taking occupation of skateboarding. *Journal of Occupational Science, 17*(4), 239–245. https://doi.org/10.1080/14427591.2010.9686701

Hall, S., & Jefferson, T. (Eds.). (2006). *Resistance through rituals: Youth subcultures in post-war Britain.* Routledge.

Hardwicke, J. (2022). Inside the peloton: An exploration into the culture of competitive road cycling with reference to masculinity, risk and injury, with a principle focus on concussion (Doctoral dissertation, University of Winchester).

Hodkinson, P. (2005). 'Insider research' in the study of youth cultures. *Journal of Youth Studies, 8*(2), 131–149.

Holden, J. (2015). The ecology of culture. Available at: http://www.culturalmanagement.ac.rs/uploads/research_file_1/66134e4b60bbb5800408f992fa4d0fe4e2ff6a31.pdf

Hughes, R., & Coakley, J. (1991). Positive deviance among athletes: The implications of overconformity to the sport ethic. *Sociology of Sport Journal, 8*(4), 307–325.

Ingham, A. (1975). Occupational subcultures in the work world of sport. In *Sport and social order* (pp. 333–389). Addison-Wesley.

Irwin, J. (1977). *Scenes.* Sage Publications.

Kern, L., Geneau, A., Laforest, S., Dumas, A., Tremblay, B., Goulet, C., Lepage, S., & Barnett, T. A. (2014). Risk perception and risk-taking among skateboarders. *Safety Science, 62*, 370–375. https://doi.org/10.1016/j.ssci.2013.08.009

Klein, D. J. (1986). *Effects of systematic exercise and body building/weight lifting on self-esteem of female subjects* (Doctoral dissertation, Kean University).

Kolsrud, F. (2014). Exhaustion of leisure: Identity and cycling. NANO: New American Notes Online, (4). Retrieved from https://www.proquest.com/scholarly-journals/exhaustion-leisure-identity-cycling/docview/2326843084/se-2

Laurendeau, J. (2006). He didn't go in doing a skydive: Sustaining the illusion of control in an edgework activity. *Sociological Perspectives, 49*(4), 583–605.

Lyng, S. (1990). Edgework: A social psychological analysis of voluntary risk taking. *American Journal of Sociology, 95*(4), 851–886. https://doi.org/10.1086/229379

Lyng, S. (2005). *Edgework: The sociology of risk-taking* (1st ed.). Routledge.

Maffesoli, M. (1996). *The time of the tribes: The decline of individualism in mass society* (Trans. D. Smith), Sage.

Matthews, C. R. (2020). 'The fog soon clears': Bodily negotiations, embodied understandings, competent body action and 'brain injuries' in boxing. *International Review for the Sociology of Sport, 56*(5), 719–738. https://doi.org/10.1177/1012690220907026

Messner, M. A. (1990). When bodies are weapons: Masculinity and violence in sport. *International Review for the Sociology of Sport, 25*(3), 203–220. https://doi.org/10.1177/101269029002500303

Messner, M. A. (1992). Like family: Power, intimacy, and sexuality in male athletes' friendships. In P. M. Nardi (Ed.), *Men's friendships* (pp. 215–237). Sage Publications. https://doi.org/10.4135/9781483325736.n12

Messner, M. A., & Sabo, D. F. (1994). *Sex, violence & power in sports: Rethinking masculinity.* Crossing Press.

Muggleton, D. (2000). *Inside subculture.* Berg Publishers.

Murdock, G., & McCron, R. (1976). Youth and class: The career of a confusion. In *Working class youth culture* (pp. 10–26). Routledge and Kegan Paul.

Nash, J. E. (1977). Lying about running: The functions of talk in a scene. *Qualitative Sociology, 3*(2), 83–99.

Nixon, H. L. (1992). A social network analysis of influences on athletes to play with pain and injuries. *Journal of Sport and Social Issues, 16*(2), 127–135. https://doi.org/10.1177/019372359201600208

Nixon, H. L. (1994). Social pressure, social support, and help seeking for pain and injuries in college sports networks. *Journal of Sport and Social Issues, 18*(4), 340–355. https://doi.org/10.1177/019372394018004004

Nixon, H. L. (1996). Explaining pain and injury attitudes and experiences in sport in terms of gender, race, and sports status factors. *Journal of Sport and Social Issues, 20*(1), 33–44. https://doi.org/10.1177/019372396020001004

Noble, J., & Davies, P. (2009). Cultural capital as an explanation of variation in participation in higher education. *British Journal of Sociology of Education, 30*(5), 591–605.

O'Conner, P. (2016). Skateboarding, helmets, and control: Observations from skateboard media and a Hong Kong skatepark. *Journal of Sport & Social Issues, 40*(6), 477–498.

Park, R. E. (1915). The conflict and fusion of cultures with special reference to the negro. *The Journal of Negro History, 4*(2), 111–133.

Pearson, K. (1977). *Surfing subcultures: A comparative analysis of surf life saving and surfboard riding in Australia and New Zealand.* University of New England.

Polsky, N. (1969). *Hustlers, beats, and others*. Routledge.

Rees, A., Gibbons, T., & Dixon, K. (2014). The surveillance of racing cyclists in training: A bourdieusian perspective. *Surveillance & Society, 11*(4), 466–480.

Scott, M. (1968). *The racing game*. Aldine.

Scott, S. D., & Austin, M. (2016). Edgework, fun, and identification in a recreational subculture: Street BMX riders. *Qualitative Sociology Research, 12*(4), 84–99.

Stebbins, R. A. (1992). *Amateurs, professionals, and serious leisure*. McGill-Queen's University Press. http://www.jstor.org/stable/j.ctt81ccj

Thornton, S. (1995). *Club cultures: Music, media, and subcultural capital*. Wesleyan University Press.

Thrasher, F. M. (1927). *The gang: A study of 1313 gangs in Chicago*. The University of Chicago Press.

Velominati, T. (2014). *The rules: The Way of the Cycling disciple (illustrated)*. W. W. Norton & Company.

Venkatesh, S. A. (2008). *Gang leader for a day: A rogue sociologist takes to the streets*. Penguin.

Waters, C. (1981). Badges of half-formed, inarticulate radicalism: A critique of recent trends in the study of working class youth culture. *International Labor and Working-Class History, 19*, 23–38.

Weinberg, S. K., & Arond, H. (1952). The occupational culture of the boxer. *American Journal of Sociology, 57*(5), 460–469.

Wheaton, B. (2007). After sport culture: Rethinking sport and post-subcultural theory. *Journal of Sport and Social Issues, 31*(3), 283–307.

Williams, R. (1983). *Culture and society, 1780–1950*. Columbia University Press.

Williams, T. (1989). Sport, hegemony and subcultural reproduction: The process of accommodation in bicycle road racing. *International Review for the Sociology of Sport, 24*(4), 315–333.

Wilson, B. (2006). *Fight, flight, or chill: Subcultures, youth, and rave into the 21st century*. McGill-Queen's University Press.

Yinger, J. M. (1960). Contraculture and subculture. *American Sociological Review, 25*(5), 625–635.

Young, K. (1988). Performance, control, and public image of behavior in a deviant subculture: The case of rugby. *Deviant Behavior, 9*(3), 275–293.

Young, K. (2019). *Sport, violence and society* (2nd ed.). Routledge.

Young, K., & White, P. (1995). Sport, physical danger, and injury: The experiences of elite women athletes. *Journal of Sport and Social Issues, 19*(1), 45–61.

Young, K. A., & Atkinson, M. (Eds.). (2008). *Tribal play: Subcultural journeys through sport*. Emerald Group Publishing.

CHAPTER 6

Getting Back on the Bike: Debating Injury and Masculinity

INTRODUCTION

Cyclists live with pain. If you can't handle it, you will win nothing.
– Eddy Merckx, Belgian professional cyclist.

As will be highlighted in this chapter, competitive road cycling is a sport with high rates of injury, involves significant physical risks and exhaustive pain. The purpose of this chapter is to discuss injuries in competitive cycling and use understandings of masculinity to elucidate an understanding of the injury management practices of competitive road cyclists. As well as using masculinity as an explanatory factor for the research findings of my own work in the area, I build on the discussions in the previous chapter about how the subculture of the sport leads to certain behaviours and practices regarding attitudes towards pain, injury and suffering. To do this, I will first provide some theoretical background before discussing some of my research on competitive road cyclists in the areas of interest.

UNDERSTANDING PAIN AND INJURY IN SPORT

Closely related to notions of risk in sport discussed in the previous chapter is that of experiences of pain and injury, and sociological examinations of both in sport are numerous. First, whilst seemingly alike, pain and injury

© The Author(s), under exclusive license to Springer Nature   103
Switzerland AG 2023
J. Hardwicke, *Masculinities and the Culture of Competitive Cycling*,
Palgrave Studies in Masculinity, Sport and Exercise,
https://doi.org/10.1007/978-3-031-26975-2_6

are distinctly different, both physically and conceptually (Howe, 2003). Pain (physical, emotional and exhaustive) can be considered a more subjective experience to an athlete, whereas injury refers to a more objective indication of the physical breakdown of a bodily structure (Howe, 2003). It is argued that the acceptance of both is widespread in sport (Anderson & White, 2018). Indeed, Hughes and Coakley comment that 'accepting risks and playing through pain' (1991, p. 309) forms a central tenet of the sport ethic. Athletes are required to endure all constructs of pain and compete with significant risks (Curry & Strauss, 1994; Young & White, 1995). Roderick comments, 'athletes learn to disregard the risk of physical harm to normalise pain and injury as part of their sporting experience' (2006, pp. 18–19). Howe's (2004) ethnographic work highlights how athletes learn to embody exhaustive pain as a positive experience. Further, Atkinson's (2008) ethnographic study of triathlon examines how the athletes bonded over a 'pain community', where physical and mental suffering was valued and sought after. There is limited understanding of the experiences of risk, pain and injury in road cycling and my research reported on in this chapter hopes to start addressing this gap in knowledge.

The Intersection of Masculinity, Injury and Sport

Subscription to orthodox masculine norms and conformity to norms of bodily sacrifice for sporting glory exist across sports. Indeed, Anderson (2009) suggests orthodox notions of masculinity are institutionally codified within sport. Important, here, is the ongoing centrality of injury, and how it should be dealt with, as well as violence in sport. There exists a dissonance between what research is increasingly showing about masculinities and athletes, and the way contemporary sport is still structured and the values it propagates.

In wider society, violence among men is declining and young men are now less interested in the previously dominant violent scriptures of masculinity (Anderson, 2014). Pinker (2012) showed that, across several measures, violent behaviour of men in society is in decline. Men today are less willing or interested in engaging in violent acts. Yet, these now outdated, harmful and redundant discourses around masculinity and warrior narratives are still endemic to much competitive sport in the Western world. Indeed, commenting on this, Anderson notes that unless competitive sport recognises and responds to this dissonance, it faces cultural extinction (Anderson & White, 2018).

6 GETTING BACK ON THE BIKE: DEBATING INJURY AND MASCULINITY   105

If we consider collision and combat sports, core principles of violence, pain and injury are often packaged as 'character building' traits that instil essential values to individuals that engage with such sports (Gatz et al., 2002). This is not dissimilar to sport's function in the Industrial Era to instil orthodox masculine values discussed in Chap. 2. On this phenomenon, Coakley (2002, pp. 15–16) comments:

> I often am amazed by the pervasiveness of beliefs and assumptions about the character-producing and behaviour-shaping potential of sport participation. Dreams of using sports to promote or redirect the development of young people, especially those who have been defined as problems and threats to society.

Much research exists that dispels this thesis of the ability of sport to develop character (Miracle & Rees, 1994; Krause & Priest, 1993; Doty, 2006; Matthews et al., 2022), and the proposed potential of sport to do this is often disproportionality aimed at developing young boys (Anderson & White, 2018). Sports which require (mostly) boys to collide into each other were built on principles of normalising pain and injury which stem from the masculinising enterprise of sport at the turn of the twentieth century (Anderson, 2009).

I discussed above that the acceptance of pain is a widespread, accepted and promoted social norm in sporting culture (Curry, 1993; Young et al. 1994; Waddington, 2000). Athletes are expected to sacrifice their bodies for athletic success, and this is often gendered (Sabo et al., 2004). Even amongst adolescent athletes it is learnt that 'males should ... [be] tolerant of pain' (Pringle & Markula, 2005, p. 482). Furthermore, Sabo suggests athletes must adhere to the pain principle within sport, defining it as a 'patriarchal cultural belief that pain is inevitable and that the endurance of pain enhances one's character and moral worth' (2004, p. 64). Acceptance of pain therefore becomes a predictor for 'self-worth, social acceptance, and status gains' (2004, p. 64) and is prolific in sporting environments.

Looking at exhaustive pain, utilising ethnographic methods, Howe (2004) found some athletes to conceive pain as positive, a notion supported by work from Nixon (1993) that reported athletes 'learn to enjoy pain'. Further, it is not only essential for athletes to accept pain but in many sports athletes are required to inflict pain. This references the military discourses seen around competitive sports, where athletes utilise their

106   J. HARDWICKE

bodies as weapons to inflict and cause pain to opposition players (Messner, 1990).

Research has suggested that athletes engage with injurious activities and downplay injuries as it enhances their masculine and athletic identities (Schlosser, 2016; Parry et al., 2021), which is then praised by the media and spectators (Baron et al., 2013; Sanderson et al., 2016). I have discussed this elsewhere and the influence of masculinity on road cyclists under reporting of concussions, as well as the role of media reporting on injury by glorifying harmful injury management behaviours (see Hurst & Hardwicke, 2020).

It is here we see the intersection of masculinity, injury and pain in sport. Sport, and many of its propagators, continue to socialise young people (mainly boys) to privilege sport over their health (Anderson & White, 2018). This had a function in the context of war and industry in the twentieth century but is no longer a requirement for twenty-first-century society, yet the sentiment remains at the core of many sporting cultures.

Injuries in Competitive Road Cycling

Crashing is part of cycling as crying is part of love.
– Johan Museeuw, Belgian professional cyclist.

It is somewhat of a truism that if you compete in competitive road cycling you will experience crashing, and likely injury, as I outlined in the previous chapter. Albert (1999) comments crashes are 'part of the daily routine' in professional road cycling. When talking with one 26-year-old elite male cyclist, they suggested to me that 'I've crashed more times than I can count, I often say to people that if you road race you are fairly likely to have a big crash at least once a year'. Although I prefer what one 29-year-old elite cyclists commented which rather succinctly sums up the point: 'It's a bloody dangerous sport'. Given that average race speeds at the professional level are 40.5 kph (ProCycling Stats, 2022), with amateur racing being similar, the risks of injury if a crash occurs are evident.

Perhaps unsurprisingly then, injuries in competitive road cycling are common (Barrios et al., 2015). Epidemiological research in competitive cycling classifies injuries into three categories: bicycle contact, overuse and traumatic injuries (Silberman, 2013). Bicycle contact injuries involve any injuries sustained from the contact points on a bicycle, such as Plantar Neuropathy from the foot to pedal connection, 'saddle sores' in the perineal region from saddle contact or Ulnar neuropathy/carpal tunnel syndrome which affects the hand from handlebar contact (Silberman, 2013). Overuse injuries are sustained through the repetitive biomechanics of riding a bike, most often seen through lateral knee pain in the form of iliotibial band syndrome (Farrell et al., 2003). These two injury constructs are not of concern to the scope of this book. Traumatic injuries are the focus of this work, which represent injuries sustained from anything in the external environment that causes a crash, such as the road surface (potholes), contact with road traffic (cars, pedestrians or other cyclists) or human error. In the literature, these injuries are most often seen through fractures and result in the most time off to recover (Silberman, 2013).

Despite the frequency of injury, across all constructs, in competitive road cycling (see De Bernardo et al., 2012; Barrios et al., 2015; Rooney et al., 2020), there is limited epidemiological literature in road cycling focusing on traumatic injury (Silberman, 2013). The focus is predominantly on recreational injuries (Davidson, 2005) or overuse injuries in sport science fields which approach the topic from a performance-oriented angle.

There are also no consistent methodological approaches in the literature, making the cross-comparison of studies in road cycling difficult (Silberman, 2013). Indeed, professional road cycling does not have a robust injury surveillance system in place, making insight to injury rates and trends extremely difficult (Heron et al., 2020). A recent international consensus statement on injury reporting in professional road cycling was published to address this (see Heron et al., 2020). Here, medical experts clarified injury definitions and concluded 'Injury rates should be reported as per 1,000 hours of cycling training, both in and outdoors, and per 1,000 hours of competition as well as per 1,000 hours of non-cycling training' (Heron et al., 2020, p. 1). Although holding some utility for the field moving forward, the statement holds little utility without the support of the UCI (the world governing body for cycling) to implement an injury surveillance system and also does not account for the, largely unknown, injury rates outside of the professional level of the sport.

Drawing on research that is available, we see high rates of traumatic injury in competitive road cycling. Decock et al. (2016) reported in a sample of amateur competitive cyclists, in Flanders between 2002 and 2012, that one in six athletes had a crash resulting in traumatic injury during races. The most common cause of crashing was collisions with other riders.

108   J. HARDWICKE

De Bernardo et al. (2012) conducted a four-year study of 51 professional cyclists. Here, 43 of the cyclists experienced 103 injuries over the period and only 8 were injury free. Overall injury rates were 0.50 per racer/year and 0.007 per 1000 km of training and competition. Given that studies place the approximate figure of kilometres covered per year by professional cyclists in training and competition to be around 25,000–35,000 km (Sanchis-Gomar et al., 2011), this injury rate equates to at least one in two professional athletes being exposed to injury, every season. Leading the authors to the conclusion that competitive cyclists are exposed to a high injury risk and that more research is needed to greater understand incidence rates of injury in the sport (De Bernardo et al., 2012).

Looking at the Tour de France, one of cycling's most iconic races that spans over 21 stages, Haeberle et al. (2018) found, between 2010 and 2017, an average of 17 cyclists had to withdraw annually after suffering a traumatic injury. This was just for one event in a season and does not account for the many that continue to race with serious injury, which is common practice in road cycling. For example, Geraint Thomas in the 2013 tour continued the race with a broken pelvis, so would not have been included in this data (BBC, 2013). Greve and Modabber (2012) note that by stage 9 of the 2011 Tour de France, there were 14 fractures, 16 rider retirements and 1 athlete in intensive care.

The paucity of research into traumatic injury in competitive road cycling, and diversity in methodology, makes cross-comparison of studies, longitudinal insights and identifying a valid picture of injury aetiology somewhat challenging. Much of the work, such as Haeberle et al. (2018), do not capture the true rates of injury as they rely on public data retrospectively compiled to produce the injury rates. Working with the data that is available, however, it is warranted to follow the assumption that road cycling is a high velocity and dangerous sport that carries high rates of traumatic injury.

Sport-Related Concussion in Competitive Cycling

In the 2020 edition of the Tour de France, French rider Romain Bardet crashed heavily on stage 13 was visibly concussed as he struggled to stand straight and gain his balance, which can be seen on the race TV coverage, but continued to complete the remaining 86 km of the stage (Cycling Weekly, 2020). This effort was described as heroic, displaying 'admirable courage' and that he fought 'like a lion' by his team manager (Road,

2020). He was later diagnosed with a brain haemorrhage (a bleed on the brain) the evening of the race and subsequently withdrew from the tour for an indefinite period of rest (Cycling Weekly, 2020). This led to media coverage, and outrage, on cycling 'lagging miles behind other sports' in concussion protocols (Coverdale, 2020). This is a topic I have written extensively on (Hardwicke & Hurst, 2020; Hardwicke, 2022; Hardwicke et al., 2022, 2022; Hardwicke & Hurst, Forthcoming).

Traumatic brain injuries, commonly referred to as sport-related concussion (SRC), represent one of contemporary sports greatest challenges due to the increasing concerns over the linkages to participation in some sports and long-term brain health (Anderson & White, 2018; Malcom, 2019). In the US alone, the Centre for Disease Control estimates that between 1.6 and 3.8 million sport-related concussions occur annually (Langlois et al., 2006), comparable data is not currently available for the UK. This is only a rough estimate with actual numbers likely far higher due to widespread under-reporting of SRC. Indeed, it is estimated that over half of all sport-related concussions go unreported (Harmon et al., 2013). Furthermore, this number does not account for the many sub-concussive impacts that occur across sport (Rawlings et al., 2020). As such, a true picture of the volume of brain trauma sustained by athletes across different sports is hard to determine.

This is of importance as research highlights that both concussive and sub-concussive injuries can have long-term effects on physical and mental health (see Esterov & Greenwald, 2017; Farrell et al., 2019; Wilson et al., 2017; Moore et al., 2017; Hind et al., 2022). Researchers have found a range of neurodegenerative diseases, in elevated rates, amongst contact-sport athletes: including Chronic Traumatic Encephalopathy (CTE) (Kiernan et al., 2015), Dementia (Kulkarni et al., 2019), Alzheimer's (Taghdiri et al., 2019), Parkinson's (Jafari et al., 2013) and Multiple Sclerosis (Montgomery et al., 2017). Important to the context of this book, the risks to brain health from crashes sustained in cycle sports are still largely unknown and under-researched. Silberman (2013, p. 340) comments on this:

> The risk of diffuse cerebral swelling after head injury, a rare occurrence seen more often in boxers and children, is unknown in cycling. The pathophysiology and risk of chronic traumatic encephalopathy, a neurodegenerative tauopathy, diagnosed in post-mortem cases in other contact collision sports

such as hockey and football, also are unknown as they relate to closed head injuries in cycling.

The growing concern over the linkages of multiple types of brain trauma-inducing events that occur in sport (such as heading, tackling, punching, crashing a bicycle), alongside the cultural esteem that competitive sport holds in Western culture (Anderson & White, 2018), makes this a significant, contemporary, cultural concern. Indeed, some scholars suggest there is now a concussion 'crisis' within sport (Malcom, 2019).

Much of the literature to date in this field is situated within medical domains (Malcom, 2017) and focused on mainstream, contact and team sports (Dean & Bundon, 2020). There is little research into SRC in non-mainstream, non-contact and individual sports, such as road cycling. As such, limited attention has been paid to competitive cycling and its numerous sub-disciplines within the SRC field and there remains little research on SRC in road cycling (Elliott et al., 2019). Yet, it is estimated that SRC makes up to 5–15% of injuries in road cycling (Rooney et al., 2020). Importantly, competitive road cycling still represents a large percentage of athletic endeavours globally. For example, British Cycling had 150,000 active members in 2019 representing a three-fold increase since 2012, and the largest recorded membership base since its establishment (British Cycling, 2019). It is therefore crucial that cycling sports be included in research focused on SRC.

I have been researching concussion in competitive cycling since 2018 (for this body of work see Hardwicke & Hurst, 2020; Hurst & Hardwicke, 2020; Hurst et al., 2020; Hardwicke, 2022; Hardwicke et al., 2022, 2022; Hardwicke & Hurst, Forthcoming). This research has used a range of both qualitative and quantitative methods, and some of the overall findings from this work that provide useful context for the book, as well as understanding injury more broadly in competitive road cycling, will be outlined here.

Firstly, in Hardwicke and Hurst (2020) I reported on a self-report survey study assessing the concussion knowledge and attitudes of 118 UK competitive cyclists. Key findings here were that knowledge of concussion as an injury was comparable to other sports and symptom recognition was sound amongst the participants surveyed. However, a considerable number of the participants reported they would mask signs of a suspected concussion or not report the injury in order to remain in a competition. The issue highlighted in this research is that of translation of knowledge to behavioural intent. Despite reporting sound knowledge of the severity of sport-related concussion, in a competition scenario the cyclists reported they would favour performance over health. Furthermore, statistical analysis of the data found that those racing at higher levels (elite and first category) held more dangerous attitudes towards the injury which I theorise to be down to greater investment within the sport which is required to have reached these levels.

In a similar vein, more recently I conducted research on 405 international competitive cyclists assessing helmet use, perceptions of sport-related concussion and seeking medical care for head injury (Hardwicke et al., 2022). Again, using a self-reported survey design, findings suggested a similar theme to the study outlined above. First, the majority of participants reported holding a belief that a bicycle helmet protects from concussion (which it does not). This can be problematic in the effective management of suspected concussions if the athletes believe they are protected from something they are not. More relevant to the current discussion, it was also found that large numbers of the participants reported they would not seek medical care for situations in which this would be advised, such as having a cracked helmet because of a crash. In the context of the discussions already throughout this book, I theorise this to be down to the attitude towards injury more broadly within competitive road cycling culture.

To provide greater contextual understandings to these findings I conducted a number of in-depth semi-structured interviews with competitive road cyclists (Hardwicke, 2022; Hardwicke & Hurst, Forthcoming). Whilst findings from these interviews are used throughout the book, key findings relevant to this discussion include greater detail to the attitude towards injury and sport-related concussion where it was commonly reported across the cyclists that withdrawal from a race is always a last resort, and one must 'get back on the bike' unless this is physically not possible. This is discussed in more detail below. In reference to sport-related concussion, cyclists reported a limited understanding of the injury and those that had personal experience with it were significantly more knowledgeable on the topic and held more positive attitudes towards its potential severity. How these findings can be understood through the lens of masculinity is discussed at the end of the chapter.

Dealing with Pain, Injury and Suffering in Road Cycling

There was nothing physically apparent stopping me riding the bike. If I could breath, and I can see, then I could ride a bike and that's it, I'll continue. There was never any thought like that's it, I'm going to drop out the race or anything. What followed was like an absolute nightmare. Like I couldn't sleep, I was sticking to the bedsheets, I was excessively tired. I don't even know how I managed to drag my carcass around the stages that week it was just terrible. (Elite category UK male cyclist, 29 years old)

The above quote provides a vivid insight to a common attitude towards dealing with pain and injury amongst competitive cyclists around the UK and internationally. The act of continuing competing following a crash and/or injury in road cycling is a shared norm amongst members of competitive cycling (sub)culture. Not only is this a norm, but an expectation which must be met to assimilate into the subculture. For example, one 26-year-old competitive male cyclist suggested to me 'I think you could call it an expectation, if you have a crash, you carry on. There is no real kind of thought process behind it'.

Atkinson's (2008) work on pain and suffering narratives in Triathlon can be used to provide some interesting insight here. The athletes Atkinson studied viewed the sport as inherently involving 'suffering' and exhaustive pain due to the physiological demands, which was viewed positively and 'relished' (Atkinson, 2008). Similar narratives are present amongst competitive road cyclists with the sport regularly being described as a 'tough' and 'gruelling' sport. Indeed, when I competed in the sport, myself and peers would actively pride ourselves on the idea we were 'tough' because we were racing cyclists. The ability to push to physiological limits and endure physical and mental suffering is highly valued amongst competitive road cyclists and there is often a feeling of this setting them apart from 'normal' people. An application of this is that this cultural lore amongst competitive cyclists of enduring exhaustive pain and suffering appears to cross over into cyclists holding a similar attitude towards physical pain and suffering from injury. In short, the physiological demand of the sport and requirement to endure suffering likely contributes to the attitudes towards dealing with physical injury.

My research has involved a mixed level of competition, from recreational amateurs to professional riders, and I have been closely involved

6 GETTING BACK ON THE BIKE: DEBATING INJURY AND MASCULINITY 113

with riders of all levels throughout my time as a competitive road cyclist. What is of interest is that this attitude towards injury is present across the sport, regardless of level of competition. As one 29-year-old male professional cyclist said to me 'I think in cycling, if you crash and you can get back on the bike and back in contention then you just do it. Even down to the grassroots level that's the attitude'. Previous research in rugby from Liston et al. (2006, 2018) has also found this attitude towards injury management is not just found in elite sport but forms a significant feature in amateur sport also. The following comment from another elite rider summarises this attitude:

> When you're injured, it's always like okay how quickly can I get back on the bike and training. It's not how well can I recover and do what my body needs me to do for long term injury prevention or you know long term wellbeing, it's always how quickly can I get back to doing the thing I love.

This attitude is a core feature of road cycling subculture, and one I certainly subscribed to as detailed in the introductory chapter. I have been interested in understanding how this attitude is produced and reproduced within competitive cycling, and data from the semi-structured interviews conducted provides some indication. Firstly, the idea of 'Pressure' was a commonly reported theme amongst participants that competed at the higher levels of the sport. This pressure to compete when injured and withdrawal from a race being a last resort was reported to come from coaches, team managers, teammates (reports of not wanting to let teammates down were common) and personal expectations held by the athletes. Similar findings were recently reported by Daly et al. (2021) amongst retired ex-professional Rugby players. The following comment from an elite professional male provides some insight to this:

> Yeah, I mean, they're quite hard on it all really. Especially when you get to a fairly decent level they almost see you as like an object. Like we give you money, we give you this kit and we expect you to be on the start line. The minute you're not they are like well get back there as quick as possible. I've never really seen any kind of support, like getting those people saying how can I help or checking in on you on a daily basis, you're almost just left to your own devices. We don't have a team doctor, there's race doctors, but yeah it's up to yourself to decide to race or not.

114   J. HARDWICKE

Other than pressure, the glorification of such behaviours having a significant influence was also reported amongst the participants. This came through the media and peers. The media reporting of injury in cycling was regularly commented on amongst participants, with the argument that riding through injury is 'glorified' by sports journalists and reporting. For example, 'Yeah, like if you compare that to different sports, it probably is praised. Like you see a rider crashed down and their bib shorts get ripped, jerseys ripped, and they carry on riding and the commentators and everyone's like "ahh what a hero"' (26-year-old competitive male cyclist).

There has been previous socio-cultural research exploring the media's influence on athletes' responses to pain and injury (see McGannon et al., 2013; White et al., 2020). The research highlights how the media is a powerful institution in constructing narratives around injuries in sport and can influence athlete behaviours. I have previously discussed the impact of sport journalist reporting on injury in professional cycling, suggesting the media plays a role in contributing to harmful injury management practices in road cycling (Hurst & Hardwicke, 2020). The media is a significant site in which the norm within competitive cycling subcultures to compete whilst injured and to 'get back on the bike' is (re)produced.

As well as the media, peers and teammates were also reported to play a role. As with most competitive sports, road cycling operates with close social networks with high social cohesion where members are regularly negotiating identity and membership within the subculture, as outlined in the previous chapter. My research found that wanting to live up to 'expectations', not let teammates down and to 'earn the respect' of peers are all influential features of the attitudes towards dealing with injury amongst cyclists. For example, one elite female cyclist commented:

> When we did the Ras [International level multi-stage road race] a few years ago, my teammate crashed I think it was literally a kilometre from the finish and she got a lot of road rash and it was sort of like, there was no question, she was going to get back on and we all expected her to get back on. And I think if she hadn't got back on, we would have thought, sort of, like what are you doing? Like come on, that's what you do unless you are seriously injured and cannot ride you are expected to get back on.

Competing whilst injured or returning to competition quickly after injury also acts as a means to 'prove' oneself as a 'proper' cyclist. One of my participants suggested signs of injury were a 'metaphorical badge of pride that cyclists wear'. Anyone familiar with competitive road cycling culture will be aware of the rite of passage that breaking your collarbone is. My findings seem to align with Alberts' (1999) work on the topic where he made the argument that cyclists must accept injury and risk in order to gain and assert membership in the cycling subculture.

Masculinity, Cycling Subculture and Getting Back on the Bike

With the discussion thus far in this chapter, we can understand competitive road cycling as a dangerous sport in which crashing is frequent and the attitude of 'getting back on the bike' is a core principle within the subculture. Here, I provide an account for how examining the management of injury in cycling through the lens of masculinity provides a useful framework to understand this phenomenon.

The sport was built on strict notions of an orthodox/traditional archetype of masculinity which is still influential in the contemporary sport. This archetype of masculinity values risk taking and dealing with injury in a way that does not signify any weakness. As discussed in Chap. 3, these are principles that have been at the core of competitive cycling since its inception in the nineteenth century. As such, I theorise that the idolisation of orthodox masculinity in competitive cycling culture is a significant reason for why we see injuries often trivialised and cyclists so willing to prioritise performance over health.

In Chap. 4, I detailed my study on male competitive cyclists and their masculinity so will not repeat this here, but the main finding was that competitive male cyclists hold a stricter notion of masculinity compared to the general population (Hardwicke, 2022). As discussed in the previous chapter, Rees et al. (2014) suggest competitive cyclists are under constant surveillance and must continuously prove and assert themselves within the cycling subculture. With my argument that the sport operates within a hypermasculine environment, I theorise there is also an influence of masculinity on cyclists' behaviours and commitment to the subculture.

Traditional theorising of masculinity suggests masculinities are arranged within a hierarchy (Anderson, 2011). Within this conceptualisation of masculinity, particularly in sport (Connell & Messerschmidt, 2005), men who display a commitment to traditional masculine values (e.g. strength, aggression, speed, risk taking) ascend to the top of the masculinity hierarchy. Athletes that do not adhere to the traditional masculine expectations would be prevented from rising up the hierarchy. Whilst in the broader culture of Western societies masculinities are now better understood to be arranged along a horizontal plane in which multiple masculinities are equally esteemed (Anderson, 2009), the existence of a masculine hierarchy can still operate on the micro-level, such as in sporting subcultures.

As discussed in the previous chapter, competitive road cycling subculture often has internal hierarchies where members gain subcultural capital through exhibiting characteristics synonymous with orthodox masculinity such as strength, not showing weakness, physical fitness, success in competition, ability to endure suffering and brushing off injuries. As such, I theorise that as cyclists negotiate their position within the sporting subculture, masculinity plays a significant role in influencing attitudes towards injury. Cyclists adhere to the culture of the sport, which is deeply tied to orthodox masculinity, whilst simultaneously proving themselves amongst peers to achieve acceptance and gain subcultural capital. Furthermore, the influence of orthodox masculinity can affect behaviours of both male and female athletes (Sanderson et al., 2016), as displayed with the quote from the female athlete interviewed above. This is discussed further in Chap. 9.

Chapter Summary

This chapter has explored notions of pain, injury and suffering within competitive road cycling. The sport is one that is replete with all three of these features. Drawing on my research into the sport, I have highlighted common attitudes towards dealing with injury amongst competitive road cyclists: that of 'getting back on the bike' at all costs. In understanding this phenomenon, masculinity provides a useful framework of analysis for why these behaviours and attitudes exist within the sport. In understanding the development of the sport and the foundations of its culture being based around tenets of orthodox masculinity, we can see why these attitudes and behaviours exist within the contemporary sport. The following chapter continues this discussion of how performance has come to be prioritised over health within competitive cycling by examining doping practices and the notion of 'winning at all costs' in competitive cycling.

REFERENCES

Albert, E. (1999). Dealing with danger: The normalization of risk in cycling. *International Review for the Sociology of Sport, 34*(2), 157–171.

Anderson, E. D. (2009). The maintenance of masculinity among the stakeholders of sport. *Sport Management Review, 12*(1), 3–14.

Anderson, E. (2011). Masculinities and sexualities in sport and physical cultures: Three decades of evolving research. *Journal of Homosexuality, 58*(5), 565–578.

Anderson, E. (2014). *21st century jocks: Sporting men and contemporary heterosexuality.* Palgrave Macmillan.

Anderson, E., & White, A. (2018). *Sport, theory and social problems.* Routledge Taylor & Francis Group.

Atkinson, M. (2008). Triathlon, suffering and exciting significance. *Leisure Studies, 27*(2), 165–180. https://doi.org/10.1080/02614360801902216

Baron, D., Reardon, C., & Baron, S. H. (2013). *Clinical sports psychiatry: An international perspective.* John Wiley & Sons, Ltd.

Barrios, C., Bernardo, N. D., Vera, P., Laíz, C., & Hadala, M. (2015). Changes in sports injuries incidence over time in world-class Road cyclists. *International Journal of Sports Medicine, 36*(3), 241–248. Available at: https://www.thieme-connect.de/products/ejournals/abstract/10.1055/s-0034-1389983

BBC Sport. (2013). *Thomas rides with fractured pelvis.* [online] Available at: https://www.bbc.co.uk/sport/wales/23114057. Accessed 12 October 2020.

British Cycling. (2019). British Cycling reaches 150,000 members milestone for first time. Available at: https://www.britishcycling.org.uk/campaigning/article/20190502-campaigning-BRITISH-CYCLING-REACHES-150-000-MEMBERS-MILESTONE-FOR-FIRST-TIME-0

Coakley, J. J. (2002). Using sports to control deviance and violence among youths. In *Paradoxes of youth and sport* (pp. 13–30). State University of New York Press.

Connell, R. W., & Messerschmidt, J. W. (2005). Hegemonic masculinity: Rethinking the concept. *Gender & Society, 19*(6), 829–859.

Coverdale, D. (2020, December 10). *Brain injury charity chief warns cycling "lagging miles behind other sports" in concussion protocols.* Mail Online. https://www.dailymail.co.uk/sport/sportsnews/article-9035629/Brain-injury-charity-chief-warns-cycling-lagging-miles-sports-concussion-protocols.html

Curry, T. J. (1993). The effects of receiving a college letter on the sport identity. *Sociology of Sport Journal, 10*(1), 73–87.

Curry, T., & Strauss, R. H. (1994). A little pain never hurt anyone: A photo-essay on the normalization of sports injury. *Sociology of Sport Journal, 11*, 195–208.

Cycling Weekly. (2020, September 12). *Scan reveals Romain Bardet suffered "small haemorrhage" following concussion in Tour de France crash.* cycling-weekly.com. https://www.cyclingweekly.com/news/racing/tour-de-france/scan-reveals-romain-bardet-suffered-small-brain-haemorrhage-in-tour-de-france-crash-467917

Daly, E., White, A., Blackett, A. D., & Ryan, L. (2021). Pressure. A qualitative analysis of the perception of concussion and injury risk in retired professional Rugby players. *Journal of Functional Morphology and Kinesiology, 6*(3), 78. MDPI AG. Retrieved from https://doi.org/10.3390/jfmk6030078

Davidson, J. A. (2005). Epidemiology and outcome of bicycle injuries presenting to an emergency department in the United Kingdom. *European Journal of Emergency Medicine: Official Journal of the European Society for Emergency Medicine, 12*(1), 24–29. https://doi.org/10.1097/00063110-200502000-00007

De Bernardo, N., Barrios, C., Vera, P., Laiz, C., & Hadala, M. (2012). Incidence and risk for traumatic an overuse injury in top-level road cyclists. *Journal of Sports Science, 30*(10), 1047–1053. https://doi.org/10.1080/0264041 4.2012.687112

Dean, N., & Bundon, A. (2020). 'You're only falling into water!': Exploring surfers' understandings of concussion in Canadian surf culture. *Qualitative Research in Sport, Exercise and Health, 12*(4), 579–596. https://doi.org/1 0.1080/2159676X.2019.1657930

Decock, M., De Wilde, L., Van den Bossche, L., Steyaert, A., & Van Tongel, A. (2016). Incidence and aetiology of acute injuries during competitive road cycling. *British Journal of Sports Medicine, 50*, 669–672. Available at: https://bjsm. bmj.com/content/50/11/669

Doty, J. (2006). Sports build character?! *Journal of College and Character, 7*(3), 1–9.

Elliott, J., Anderson, R., Collins, S., & Heron, N. (2019). Sports-related concussion (SRC) assessment in road cycling: A systematic review and call to action. *BMJ Open Sport & Exercise Medicine, 5*(1). https://doi.org/10.1136/ bmjsem-2019-000525

Esterov, D., & Greenwald, B. (2017). Autonomic dysfunction after mild traumatic brain injury. *Brain Sciences, 7*(12), 100. https://doi.org/10.3390/ brainsci7080100

Farrell, M., Aherne, S., O'Riordan, S., O'Keeffe, E., Greene, C., & Campbell, M. (2019). Blood-brain barrier dysfunction in a boxer with chronic traumatic encephalopathy and schizophrenia. *Clinical Neuropathology, 38*(03), 51–58. https://doi.org/10.5414/np301130

Farrell, K. C., Reisinger, K. D., & Tillman, M. D. (2003). Force and repetition in cycling: Possible implications for iliotibial band friction syndrome. *The Knee, 10*(1), 103–109. https://doi.org/10.1016/s0968-0160(02)00090-x

Gatz, M., Messner, M. A., & Ball-Rokeach, S. (Eds.). (2002). *Paradoxes of youth and sport.* SUNY Press.

Greve, M. W., & Modabber, M. R. (2012). An epidemic of traumatic brain injury in professional Cycling. *Clinical Journal of Sport Medicine, 22*(2), 81–82. https://doi.org/10.1097/jsm.0b013e318243bf32

Haeberle, H. S., Navarro, S. M., Power, E. J., Schickendantz, M. S., Farrow, L. D., & Ramkumar, P. N. (2018). Prevalence and epidemiology of injuries among elite cyclists in the tour de France. *Orthopaedic Journal of Sports Medicine,* 6(9), 2325967118793392. https://doi.org/10.1177/2325967118793392

Hardwicke, J. (2022). Inside the peloton: An exploration into the culture of competitive road cycling with reference to masculinity, risk and injury, with a principle focus on concussion (Doctoral dissertation, University of Winchester).

Hardwicke, J., Batten, J., Anderson, E., & Hurst, H. T. (2022). Twitter discourse around competitive cycling and sport-related concussion. *Journal of Science and Cycling,* 11, 59–69. https://doi.org/10.28985/1322.jsc.02

Hardwicke, J., Baxter, B. A., Gamble, T., & Hurst, H. T. (2022). An investigation into helmet use, perceptions of sports-related concussion, and seeking medical care for head injury amongst competitive cyclists. *International Journal of Environmental Research and Public Health,* 19(5), 2861.

Hardwicke, J., & Hurst, H. T. (2020). Concussion knowledge and attitudes amongst competitive cyclists. *Journal of Science and Cycling,* 9, 53–66.

Harmon, K., Drezner, J., Gammons, M., et al. (2013). American medical society for sports medicine position statement. *Clinical Journal of Sport Medicine,* 23(1), 1–18. https://doi.org/10.1097/jsm.0b013e31827f5f93

Heron, N., Sarriegui, I., Jones, N., & Nolan, R. (2020). International consensus statement on injury and illness reporting in professional road cycling. *The Physician and Sportsmedicine,* 49, 130–136. https://doi.org/10.1080/00913847.2020.1830692

Hind, K., Konerth, N., Entwistle, I., Hume, P., Theadom, A., Lewis, G., et al. (2022). Mental health and wellbeing of retired elite and amateur rugby players and non-contact athletes and associations with sports-related concussion: The UK Rugby health project. *Sports Medicine,* 52(6), 1419–1431.

Howe, D. (2003). *Sport, professionalism and pain: Ethnographies of injury and risk.* Routledge.

Howe, P. D. (2004). *Sport, professionalism, and pain: Ethnographies of injury and risk.* Psychology Press.

Hughes, R., & Coakley, J. (1991). Positive deviance among athletes: The implications of overconformity to the sport ethic. *Sociology of Sport Journal,* 8(4), 307–325.

Hurst, H., & Hardwicke, J. (2020, September 22). *Cycling: Head injuries ignored because of entrenched macho culture.* The Conversation. https://theconversation.com/cycling-head-injuries-ignored-because-of-entrenched-macho-culture-146374

Hurst, H. T., Hannock, S., Hardwicke, J., & Anderson, E. (2020). Does participation in Downhill mountain biking affect measures of executive function? *Journal of Science and Cycling,* 9(3), 83–93.

Jafari, S., Etminan, M., Aminzadeh, F., & Samii, A. (2013). Head injury and risk of Parkinson disease: A systematic review and meta-analysis. *Movement Disorders, 28*(9), 1222–1229. https://doi.org/10.1002/mds.25458

Kiernan, P., Montenigro, P., Solomon, T., & McKee, A. (2015). Chronic traumatic encephalopathy: A neurodegenerative consequence of repetitive traumatic brain injury. *Seminars in Neurology, 35*(01), 020–028. https://doi.org/10.1055/s-0035-1545080

Krause, J., & Priest, R. (1993). *Sport value choices of U.S. military cadets—A longitudinal study of the class of 1993.* Unpublished manuscript, Office of Institutional Research, U.S. Military Academy, West Point, NY.

Kulkarni, P., Morrison, T. R., Cai, X., Iriah, S., Simon, N., Sabrick, J., Neuroth, L., & Ferris, C. F. (2019). Neuroradiological changes following single or repetitive mild TBI. *Frontiers in Systems Neuroscience, 13*, 1–12. https://doi.org/10.3389/fnsys.2019.00034

Langlois, J., Rutland-Brown, W., & Wald, M. (2006). The epidemiology and impact of traumatic brain injury. *Journal of Head Trauma Rehabilitation, 21*(5), 375–378.

Liston, K., McDowell, M., Malcolm, D., Scott-Bell, A., & Waddington, I. (2018). On being 'head strong': The pain zone and concussion in non-elite Rugby union. *International Review for the Sociology of Sport, 53*(6), 668–684.

Liston, K., Reacher, D., Waddington, I., & Smith, A. (2006). Managing pain and injury in non-elite Rugby union and Rugby league: A case study of players at a British university. *Sport in Society, 9*(3), 388–402.

Malcom, D. (2017). *Sport, medicine and health: The medicalization of sport?* (Abingdon and New York: Routledge, 2017), isbn: 978-1-138-82645-8. *Medical History, 62*(2), 247–248.

Malcom, D. (2019). *The concussion crisis in sport.* Routledge.

Matthews, C. R., Hurrell, A., Oliver, T. B., & Channon, A. (2022). Boxing, myths and reality building in sport for development programmes. *International Review for the Sociology of Sport.* https://doi.org/10.1177/10126902221112878

McGannon, K. R., Cunningham, S. M., & Schinke, R. J. (2013). Understanding concussion in socio-cultural context: A media analysis of A National Hockey League Star's concussion. *Psychology of Sport and Exercise, 14*(6), 891–899. https://doi.org/10.1016/j.psychsport.2013.08.003

Messner, M. A. (1990). When bodies are weapons: Masculinity and violence in sport. *International Review for the Sociology of Sport, 25*(3), 203–220. https://doi.org/10.1177/101269029002500303

Miracle, A., Jr., & Rees, C. R. (1994). *Lessons of the locker room: The myth of school sports.* Prometheus Books.

Montgomery, S., Hiyoshi, A., Burkill, S., Alfredsson, L., Bahmanyar, S., & Olsson, T. (2017). Concussion in adolescence and risk of multiple sclerosis. *Annals of Neurology, 82*(4), 554–561. https://doi.org/10.1002/ana.25036

Moore, R., Lepine, J., & Ellemberg, D. (2017). The independent influence of concussive and sub-concussive impacts on soccer players' neurophysiological and neuropsychological function. *International Journal of Psychophysiology, 112*, 22–30. https://doi.org/10.1016/j.ijpsycho.2016.11.011

Nixon, H. L. (1993). Accepting the risks of pain and injury in sport: Mediated cultural influences on playing hurt. *Sociology of Sport Journal, 10*(2), 183–196. https://doi.org/10.1123/ssj.10.2.183

Parry, K. D., Storr, R., Kavanagh, E. J., & Anderson, E. (2021). Conceptualising organisational cultural lag: Marriage equality and Australian sport. *Journal of Sociology, 57*(4), 986–1008.

Pinker, S. (2012). *The better angels of our nature: Why violence has declined* (Illustrated ed.). Penguin Books.

Pringle, R., & Markula, P. (2005). No pain is sane after all: A Foucauldian analysis of masculinities and men's rugby experiences of fear, pain, and pleasure. *Sociology of Sport Journal, 22*(4), 472–497.

Pro Cycling Statistics, Results and Rankings|ProCyclingStats.com. Pro Cycling Stats. 2022. Available online: https://www.procyclingstats.com/ (accessed on 15 December 2021).

Rawlings, S., Takechi, R., & Lavender, A. P. (2020). Effects of sub-concussion on neuropsychological performance and its potential mechanisms: A narrative review. *Brain Research Bulletin, 165*, 56–62.

Rees, A., Gibbons, T., & Dixon, K. (2014). The surveillance of racing cyclists in training: A bourdieusian perspective. *Surveillance & Society, 11*(4), 466–480.

Road CC. (2020, September 13). Team boss lauds Romain Bardet's "admirable courage" – But should someone have stopped Frenchman riding to stage finish with concussion? road.cc. https://road.cc/content/news/bardet-diagnosed-concussion-after-battling-finish-277217

Roderick, M. (2006). Adding insult to injury: Workplace injury in English professional football. *Sociology of Health & Illness, 28*(1), 76–97.

Rooney, D., Sarriegui, I., & Heron, N. (2020). 'As easy as riding a bike': A systematic review of injuries and illness in road cycling. *BMJ Open Sport & Exercise Medicine, 6*(1), e000840. https://doi.org/10.1136/bmjsem-2020-000840

Sabo, D., Heywood, L., Miller, K. E., & Melnick, M. J. (2004). *Her life depends on it: Sport, physical activity and the health and well-being of American girls.* Women's Sports Foundation.

Sanchis-Gomar, F., Olaso-Gonzalez, G., Corella, D., Gomez-Cabrera, M. C., & Vina, J. (2011). Increased average longevity among the "tour de France" cyclists. *International Journal of Sports Medicine, 32*(08), 644–647. https://doi.org/10.1055/s-0031-1271711

Sanderson, J., Weathers, M., Snedaker, K., & Gramlich, K. (2016). "I Was Able to Still Do My Job on the Field and Keep Playing": An Investigation of Female and Male Athletes' Experiences With (Not) Reporting Concussions. *Communication & Sport, 5*(3), 267–287. https://doi.org/10.1177/2167479515623455

Schlosser, A. J. (2016). *Concussion knowledge and attitudes: The impact of hegemonic masculinity.* The University of North Dakota.

Silberman, M. (2013). Bicycling injuries. *Current Sports Medicine Reports, 12*(5), 337–345. https://doi.org/10.1249/JSR.0b013e3182a4bab7

Taghdiri, F., Multani, N., Tarazi, A., Naeimi, S. A., Khodadadi, M., Esopenko, C., Green, R., Colella, B., Wennberg, R., Mikulis, D., Davis, K. D., Goswami, R., Tator, C., Levine, B., & Tartaglia, M. C. (2019). Elevated cerebrospinal fluid total tau in former professional athletes with multiple concussions. *Neurology, 92*(23), e2717–e2726. https://doi.org/10.1212/wnl.0000000000007608

Waddington, I. (2000). Sport and health: A sociological perspective. In *Handbook of sports studies* (pp. 408–421). Sage.

White, A. J., Parry, K. D., Humphries, C., Phelan, S., Batten, J., & Magrath, R. (2020). Duty of Karius: Media framing of concussion following the 2018 UEFA champions league final. *Communication & Sport.* https://doi.org/10.1177/2167479520948048

Wilson, L., Stewart, W., Dams-O'Connor, K., et al. (2017). The chronic and evolving neurological consequences of traumatic brain injury. *The Lancet Neurology, 16*(10), 813–825. https://doi.org/10.1016/s1474-4422(17)30279-x

Young, K., McTeer, W., & White, P. (1994). Body talk: Male athletes reflect on sport, injury, and pain. *Sociology of Sport Journal, 11*(2), 175–194. https://doi.org/10.1123/ssj.11.2.175

Young, K., & White, P. (1995). Sport, physical danger, and injury: The experiences of elite women athletes. *Journal of Sport and Social Issues, 19*(1), 45–61.

CHAPTER 7

Winning at All Costs: The Intersects of Doping, Hypercompetition and Masculinity in Cycling

INTRODUCTION

As much as I wanted to draft a book on cycling that did not include doping, it is difficult to ignore, and it foregrounds a lot of the discussion on competitive cycling culture, risk and health more broadly. Thus, this chapter offers a multifaceted discussion which is largely centred around doping. However, I take a broad approach to this discussion through considering the notion of 'winning at all costs' in cycling and how the hypermasculine and hypercompetitive culture of road cycling can lead to health-compromising behaviours in favour of performance enhancement, with doping being one example of this.

This chapter will not engage in moral discussions around doping in sport. As a sport steeped in a history of doping, strong views come to the fore on this issue in cycling. One side of this view, the most common, is that doping is an individual act of moral failing and is thus stigmatised. From this perspective, the practice is seen as 'unnatural', unhealthy and challenges the 'fairness' of sport and its ability to produce role models (Moller, 2010). This view is often portrayed in the media, held by the general public and present amongst sport fans.

However, another, more critical view, is that doping in cycling (and sport more broadly) is simply a product of the way sport has been structured and socially organised. In other words, it is a necessary part of

© The Author(s), under exclusive license to Springer Nature Switzerland AG 2023
J. Hardwicke, *Masculinities and the Culture of Competitive Cycling*, Palgrave Studies in Masculinity, Sport and Exercise, https://doi.org/10.1007/978-3-031-26975-2_7

performance in elite-level sport. Smith (2015) discusses doping practices in cycling as a result of the social environment a cyclist occupies and that it represents a form of approved deviance and rule breaking which are replete in the sport. For example, drafting team cars to return to the peloton, using a 'sticky bottle' (when a rider receives a bottle from a team car and holds tight as to gain a tow from the car) and race fixing where podium positions within a final breakaway are agreed before the finish line are all forms of accepted deviance in the sport (Christiansen & Hjorngard, 2013). As such, this chapter adopts a critical approach to understanding doping as a cultural phenomenon to better understand the arguments made throughout this book and reflect on the utility of understanding doping through the lens of masculinity.

To achieve this, the chapter begins with a discussion on the foundations of competitive sport within a capitalist society and how this led to an emphasis on competition and winning and a reminder of the role masculinity played in this development of sport. With this foundation set, I then work through the relationship between sport, masculinities and doping before applying it specifically to cycling. There is limited academic literature on this topic, but I present the argument that the orthodox masculine foundations on which competitive road cycling was developed was a significant factor, amongst others I discuss, leading to the environment in which doping became a logical option for cyclists, and thus was consumed into the culture.

Sport, Competition and Winning at All Costs

As discussed at various points throughout this book, organised and competitive sport was developed and institutionalised throughout the nineteenth century, the period in which Western societies were transitioning from a feudal society towards a capitalist system (Coakley, 2016a, 2016b). As such, the development of modern competitive sports was based upon the logic of industrial capitalism where competition and achievement were emphasised. This was true for competitive cycling, too, with the sport being influenced by social practices and ideologies predicated on the rational criterion of competition, domination and performance being the key tenets to shape the sport and its participants (Ritchie, 1975; Durry, 1977; Williams, 1989).

Whilst I outlined in Chap. 3 the role of masculinity in the development of competitive sport in the West, this was one of several socio-cultural forces that shaped sport. It is important to note other large-scale social and cultural changes during the late nineteenth century and how they intersected to shape modern sport. Importantly, this was a period in which notions of a nation state emerged in Britain and increasing importance was placed on national patriotism, which was reinforced by the imperialist expansion of Britain and expansion of economic capital to beyond boundaries of national markets, leading to more defined international rivalries and tensions (Budd, 2001).

Sport was used in this climate as a political project to instil the nationalist ideology into the working classes of Britain (Budd, 2001). I discussed the political utility of sport to develop orthodox masculinity amongst boys in Chap. 2, and this increased emphasis on the nation also served to reinforce the utility of sport to serve military interests (Coakley, 1990). Furthermore, with the transition to capitalism and increased emphasis on profit-making, the ideological tenets of capitalist business, such as aggressive individualism, competition and elitism, were mirrored in early competitive sport (Hargreaves, 1982; Budd, 2001; Anderson & White, 2018).

It is through these macro socio-political forces that the social structure of sport was organised around competition, and the Western cultural obsession with winning was born. In this environment, the purpose of sport was structured around notions of competition and winning being the core reason for participation. Much of this is still applicable to modern sport, which exhibits many facets of residual culture from the nineteenth century, and the emphasis on winning has been accelerated with the increased professionalism, commercialism and financial investment into sport in the twenty-first century (Smart, 2018).

Indeed, the very nature of traditional competitive sports is competitive by definition. Winners are determined by the constitutive rules and competition structurally built into sport, as the whole structure is predicated on determining a winner(s) (Cudd, 2007). In competitive team sport, participants are pitted against one another with the aim of winning. In more individual sports, participants are often pitted against an extremely difficult criteria for success that can only be achieved by few. This leads to a zero-sum game; one person or team can only win at the detriment of another person or team losing (Cudd, 2007; Anderson & White, 2018). This over-emphasis on competition can create a psychological environment of intensity and self-perfection, which often borders on narcissism and egotism (Cudd, 2007). Anderson and White (2018, p. 168) comment on the persistence of this ideology in sport:

126   J. HARDWICKE

> Unfortunately, the existing sport competition structure is so powerful in its influence, basked in decades of "tradition," that many maintain that without winning there is no purpose to sport. This ethos moves sport further from the field of leisure and recreation, and closer to the act of war.

This sentiment is echoed in the infamous quote from Vince Lombardi, an American football coach, that 'winning isn't everything; it's the only thing'. The narrow focus on winning being the sole purpose of sport is to the detriment of valuing qualities of skill development, companionship, having fun, decency, aesthetic beauty of bodily performance, amongst many others. Furthermore, with such high financial stakes in modern sport and the Western cultural obsession with winning, an environment is created where seeking advantages (doping, cheating, bending rules, whatever it is) becomes a logical option for athletes (Cudd, 2007; English, 2017; Anderson & White, 2018).

When considering a range of macro socio-cultural influences on the development of competitive sport, it can be understood as an institution that has been structurally defined upon strict ideological tenets of competition and winning at all costs. This has been shaped by the cultural influence of capitalism, imperialism, the nation state and the perceived crisis of masculinity throughout the nineteenth and twentieth centuries in Britain. The purpose of this discussion is to provide a foundation to further understand socio-negative consequences of sport, such as those discussed in previous chapters, and the focus of this chapter, doping practices.

Sport, Masculinity and Doping

Interestingly, the relationship between doping, sport and masculinities has received limited academic attention. Much of the literature regarding drug use and masculinity in physical activity settings is concerned with the use of performance/image-enhancing substances (PES) in gym and fitness contexts. Here, drug use has largely been theorised and understood through men's desires to gain muscle mass and construct a masculine identity (Andreasson, 2015). In this chapter, I am not concerned with drug use in this setting, rather, the focus is on understanding doping in competitive sport as a cultural process and its relationship to masculinity.

Important to note is that the use of performance-enhancing drugs is not new or novel to modern sport. Historical research reports the use of substances, such as mushrooms and mixtures of wine, dating back as far as

776 BC in ancient Greek Olympic athletes and Roman gladiators (Yesalis, 2002). Substances with stimulant properties were used to improve speed and endurance, and opiate-laced drinks to mask pain, allowing athletes to continue in competition when injured (Landry & Kokotailo, 1994). This phenomenon has been a constant throughout sports history, however, as modern sport was institutionalised during the late nineteenth and early twentieth centuries, the stakes increased and the professionalisation and commercialisation of sport increased the appeal of performance enhancement as prize money and rewards (fame, prestige, status) increased.

Concurrently, the science of performance-enhancing techniques also developed (Baron et al., 2007, p. 119). As such, the core structure of sport being centred around competition, winning and the spectacle of testing the boundaries of human physiology creates an environment in which participants are always going to seek performance advantages. This only becomes problematic in the world of sport when boundaries are drawn. For example, a substance is not inherently good or bad, it is constructed as so depending on sporting governing bodies classification of substances. Indeed, drug use in sport only became problematised during the 1960s as availability increased and national prestige became synonymous with sporting success, leading to countries developing doping regimes to ensure their athletes success on the world stage as sporting performances became symbolic of a nation's success (Dimeo, 2007, 2008; Waddington, 2005; Smith, 2015). Subsequent high-profile and publicised deaths of athletes attributed to the use of drugs led to increased regulation and concerns over athlete health. The International Olympic Committee (IOC) published its first banned list of substances as a response to these, and to protect the image of sport, in 1967 (Møller, 2010). Since, doping in sport remains an issue and multiple governing bodies work on regulating and restricting drug use, with the largest being the World Anti-Doping Agency (WADA) which formed in 1999.

Putting moral discussions of doping and regulation in sport aside, we can take this environment where the use of performance-enhancing drugs became a logical option and understand the influence masculinity also had on these processes. The structural emphasis on competition in sport outlined above also compliments the (re)production of orthodox masculinity. Building on the discussion outlined in Chaps. 2 and 3 regarding the influence of masculinity on the development of competitive sport, we can see how core tenets of orthodox masculinity reinforce the structures of sport. English (2017) notes how a key defining characteristic of orthodox masculinity, particularly in sport, is a win-at-all-costs attitude. This can lead to socio-negative consequences amongst athletes such as hyper-aggression, playing through injury, dehumanising competitors and team-mates, sexism and violence (Coakley, 2016a, 2016b; Anderson & White, 2018).

This process is aided by sport operating within a hierarchical structure with an excessive emphasis on winning (Messner, 1992). As a result, boys and men are conditioned to compete amongst each other for self-worth, and intra-male acceptance is dependent upon being a 'winner' (Messner, 1992, p. 34). As Anderson and White note 'Sport is an arena in which men can literally battle for supremacy' (2018, p. 110). This intrinsically reciprocal link between orthodox masculinity and hypercompetitive atti-tudes in sport is at the core of many socio-negative processes within con-temporary sport (English, 2017; Anderson, 2009). As I explicated in Chaps. 2 and 3, competitive sports development has been deeply influ-enced by notions of orthodox masculinity. As such, the institution of sport has been organised around the celebration and (re)production of an intense win-at-all-costs attitude. On this, English (2017, p. 188) comments:

> These attitudes are those that not only feature victory as the primary value, but also encourage all measures to be taken in pursuing the win. This includes viewing skill development and other excellences as instrumental to victory and not as intrinsically valuable, seeing opponents as enemies, risking physical injury, inflicting injury upon others, and when taken to the extreme, cheating and engaging in other immoral practices.

As such, sporting masculinities overly emphasise the notion of being a 'winner' in order to gain intra-male acceptance (Messner, 1992, p. 34). Greater athletic ability is also associated with greater masculine capital, creating a fraternal system in which boys and men compete to 'be the best' which in turn increases an individual's status. An environment is then cre-ated in which there is pressure to perform, and this increases the appeal of using performance-enhancing drugs to adhere to this culture and access the perceived benefits of dominant athletic performance.

An extension of the win-at-all-cost attitude on which much perfor-mance sport is built upon is the acceptance and presence of risk (a feature of orthodox masculinity). Here, performance is favoured over health as athletes align with the structural demands of sport being focused on competition and winning. In Chap. 5, I put forward the argument that competitive road cycling operates in a 'culture of risk' (Nixon, 1992), and this is true for many popular Western sports. To remind the reader, a culture of risk can be understood as an environment in which acceptance of risk and risk-taking is encouraged and forms a normalised behaviour and attitude. Cultures of risk also work to normalise violence and glorify an individual's ability to tolerate pain and injury.

An extension of this theorising is the notion of risky body cultures, which centres the body in understanding risk taking in sport. This makes sense since it is the body which the consequences of risk taking will mostly be experienced by an athlete. The adoption of risky attitudes towards the body by athletes is largely directed by a will to succeed (and win), but this comes with the increased risk of acute, subacute and chronic physical injury to the body. Safai (2003, p. 129) comments on this, 'as the body is built up to move through the competitive hierarchies of modern sport, the body is increasingly worn down – in essence, an athletic career also becomes a "pain career"'. As such, performance athletes can be understood to put their bodies 'on the line' in order to meet the demands of competitive sport.

The origins of this attitude can be mapped onto the development of modern sport, including the influence of masculinity in constructing a sporting environment with such strong emphasis on winning, not showing weakness and exhibiting stoicism. In this environment, we can use the lens of masculinity to understand doping practices in sport more broadly as a cultural practice and product of the way sport has been structured. Within risky body cultures that exist within many performance sports, use of substances may be sought for reasons such as to deal with injury, compete whilst injured and endure suffering, to gain a competitive advantage over others and to adhere to the sporting culture and the 'sport ethic' (Hughes & Coakly, 1991). Some of these factors will be considered in more detail below as applied to competitive road cycling.

Understanding Doping in Professional Road Cycling

Doping in the sport of road cycling has always existed. The purpose of this section is to consider doping practices in the sport as they relate to wider socio-cultural forces that have shaped the sport. In Chap. 3, I detailed the development of the sport and the role masculinity played in shaping a sport predicated on hypercompetition, risk and the requirement to deal

130   J. HARDWICKE

with injury, pain and suffering (all of which are glorified). It is in this environment that early doping practices were established in road cycling. This section will explore significant historical influences on the shaping of a doping culture in cycling and then consider matters in the contemporary sport.

Doping practices first entered cycling as a means of survival. As competitive cycling practices developed to distance the activity from a leisure pursuit and the increasing feminine coding of the bicycle, a strong emphasis was placed on pushing the limits of participants. Competitive bicycle racing was first established with 'track' racing, where participants would race around an oval circuit, usually on fields or prepared tracks (Ritchie, 1999). It was on these tracks the famous 'Six-day racing' was born, with the first documented race being held at the Agricultural Hall in Islington, London, in 1878 (Sporting Cyclist, 1967, p. 12). These events involved riders racing continuously around a track for six days, trying to reach the maximum distance possible, or until fatigue and exhaustion forced withdrawal. The events were hugely popular in Victorian Britain, with the focus of physical suffering being an appeal. The event quickly spread to the US also, and it was reported in The New York Times that such events were 'An athletic contest in which participants "go queer" in their heads and strain their powers until their faces become hideous with the tortures that rack them, is not sport. It is brutality' (New York Times, 1897 cited in Cycling, UK, 30 November 1982).

The event was quickly adapted based on humanitarian and safety grounds, with laws passed in 1898 which limited riders to 12 hours riding a day (Broughton, 2016). To combat this, it was re-organised into a team event where the workload could be shared between two riders, and this gained popularity across Europe and North America. Although track racing remained popular in Europe, it was road racing that elevated the status of bicycle racing. Following traditions of the Six-Day Races, early road races were also developed on notions of suffering and pushing absolute limits. For example, Paris-Roubaix (one of the oldest professional road cycling races), which first ran in 1896, covered a distance of 280 km. From 1896 to 1926, the race was between 260 and 280 km and since 2001 it has been around 260 km (Procycling stats, 2022). The same variance in distances and demands can be seen with the sport's most famous race, the Tour de France. First run in 1903, it was branded as the ultimate sporting test of an individual and the 'race to end all races' (Sidwells, 2018). The first edition of the race demanded riders to complete 2438 km over just

6 days (for reference, the 2022 edition was 3328 km covered over 24 days). Unsurprisingly, only 21 out of 60 starters finished the 1903 Tour de France (BikeRaceInfo, 2022). The following 20 editions of the race throughout the first part of the twentieth century were similarly testing, with 5000+ km routes being covered over just 15 stages.

It is no surprise that in these early races the use of drugs was rife, which was largely motivated by just surviving the demands of the sport. A range of drugs were used to do this. To combat the tiredness and exhaustion experienced, cocaine was regularly used by cyclists (Sidwells, 2018). Another common substance was nitroglycerine, a drug used to stimulate the heart after a cardiac arrest and was used to improve riders' breathing (Novich, 1964). The highly toxic poison, strychnine, was also used which was believed to strengthen muscular contractions. So widespread was the use of strychnine that one rider of the era commented that he developed such a tolerance to the drug that the doses he took could kill a smaller man (Dimeo, 2008).

Sports historian Alain Lunzenfichter (2007) comments that the use of such drugs was so normalised at the time that they were viewed as a necessity, and every-day practice, to survive the demands of the sport. Hallucinations were commonly reported in competitive cyclists from the sheer exhaustion of competition and effects of the cocktail of drugs consumed. Major Taylor, an American champion cyclist, withdrew from one race stating that "I cannot go on with safety, for there is a man chasing me around the ring with a knife in his hand" (Ritchie 1988).

Another influence on doping in cycling concerns the commercialisation of the sport and increasing financial rewards for winning. From the 1890s, competitive cycling was increasingly gaining popularity as a spectator sport which was largely directed by bike manufacturers' and the press' interest in arranging races as marketing strategies to increase sales of bikes and newspapers, respectively (Christiansen, 2010). Indeed, the Tour de France was created by the newspaper L'Auto as an advertising campaign (Edwardes-Evans et al., 2021). Christiansen (2010, p.92) comments on this:

> The point is that cycle sport, from the beginning, was surrounded with an aura of entrepreneurship, as it was linked to and rose from early modernity. This is so not only because of the fact that bike riders from the beginning collaborated with physicians and physiologists, but also because cycle sport from its birth was commercialised and ruled by market forces.

With the increasing financial investments going into the sport, the rewards for winning became more significant. Sidwells (2018) notes how good money could be earned by doing well in cycling competitions and, similar to boxing, it was alluring to working-class men as a route out of the mines and factories. As such, doping practices took hold to gain a competitive edge over others to increase the chances of reaping such rewards. And given these were within the rules at the time and there was very little regulation, it is unsurprising performance-enhancing drugs were widely used in competitive cycling during the late nineteenth and early twentieth centuries.

These two influences, the demands of the sport and the commercialisation of it, are still largely the influential factors on doping in the contemporary professional sport. (There are of course many other factors, but it is not in the scope of the book to explore these in depth.) Whilst not accounting for this process in its entirety, the culture of doping in the sport can be understood through the influence of masculinity on the early development of the sport, where an ethos of suffering and risk taking was central in the masculising of the bicycle (as discussed in Chap. 3). The second can be seen as a consequence of a range of macro socio-cultural processes, as discussed earlier in this chapter, which has led to a 'win-at-all-costs' attitude in the sporting environment. This attitude has also been influenced by notions of orthodox masculinity, where strong importance is placed on athletic ability and being the 'winner'.

Building on the above discussions, we can see how the foundations were laid to create a culture of doping in competitive cycling. Here, I will briefly consider the situation in the contemporary sport. Research into this area is problematic, and it is almost impossible to get a detailed insight to doping practices in cycling. Firstly, primary research on experiences of cyclists engaged in doping is a methodological minefield. What current competitive cyclist is going to be willing to discuss their doping practices, even with anonymity assured? Not many. This leaves much of our knowledge of the experiences of doping cyclists to come from those that have been caught. There is also the problem of false-consciousness, where individuals participating in research on doping in sport untruly report non-existent behaviours or falsely detail their experiences (Petroczi & Haugen, 2012). On top of this are practical barriers (gaining access to participants) and ethical issues around researcher knowledge of illegal activities. All of this therefore means we have no reliable epidemiology of drug use, limited understanding of reasons for doping and limited knowledge on the effects on cyclists' health, performance and career (Ohl et al., 2015).

However, some research has been conducted and useful materials such as online blogs, journalist interviews and auto-biographies can help us understand doping practices in cycling. I find Smith's (2015) work on doping in cycling particularly useful. Through an analysis of 112 doping cyclists' confessions in the media, an interactionist perspective is used to understand the reasons and meanings behind doping. The reasons are presented under three over-arching themes of maintaining their performance to themselves, presenting their performance to their team and supporting the grand spectacle of cycling (Smith, 2015).

Firstly, it was reported that doping was used to avoid damaging bodies, as a means to deal with injury and survive the physical toll of the sport (Smith, 2015). With injury, pain and suffering being core features of cycle racing (Hardwicke, 2022), and the culture of risk in which the sport operates, use of certain substances to deal with this are understood as a legitimate 'coping mechanism'. Use of medical discourse in doping cyclists accounts framed the drug use as something that cycling team medical staff deemed necessary (Smith, 2015). As such, from this angle, the presence of doping can be seen as a result of the culture of risk (Nixon, 1991) in which the sport operates and a mechanism to allow a cyclist's body to deal, physiologically, with such risks and demands.

Second, Smith (2015) reports on the role of the team and how doping practices become a necessary part of a team's operation. Here, individual and team performance is crucial, and cyclists reported an expectation within the team that they would engage in doping. Not doing so would lead to ostracisation and possible threat to their position in a team. Excerpts from professional cyclists highlighting this include (from Smith, 2015):

> It became obvious that if I wanted to stay competitive and be selected to do all the big races, I had to participate in a team-doping program. (Stephen Hodge)
> The pressure not to let myself and my team down saw to it that I took refuge in EPO. (Tom Lotz)
> Because of my career and the team I ended-up on, if I wasn't willing to do that (dope), I wasn't going to be there. (Floyd Landis)

134   J. HARDWICKE

Finally, it is regularly reported by cyclists that doping is a response to the demands of the sport (Smith, 2015). This was the first reason the practice entered the sport and pervades in the sport today. This is influenced by the perception that doping is necessary to participate in the sport, and especially so to be competitive. Comments from professional cyclists used by Smith (2015) to highlight this phenomenon include:

> But without EPO you can ride only ten stages at a very high level. Afterwards the fire is out. (Rolf Jarmann)
> In cycling, you get dropped in 99 out of 100 races, even when you give it everything. It hurts all the time; but you still are successful only a few times. (Jorg Jaksche)
> I started using stimulants, steroids and EPO. I heard in the peloton around me what was happening. I did it to remain competitive, even as a helper. (Marc Lotz)
> Well it's hard to imagine the endurance demanded by the Tour de France – 21 days, 2000 miles and a vicious vertical climb totaling some 50,000 feet in all. This ordeal is one reason that cycling became a dirty sport. (Tyler Hamilton)
> My experiences during that first week made me question whether it was even possible to compete in a race like that without doping. (Michael Barry)
> You don't understand, this is the only way I can even finish the Tour. (Frankie Andreu)

In summary, the reasons for doping in cycling are multifaceted. However, they can be best understood through a socio-cultural analysis of the sport to highlight how the social environment in which this practice becomes commonplace is constructed. The purpose of this section, and chapter, is to outline this process and place the practice in the context of how the sport developed and the socio-cultural influences on this. Before exploring this further, amateur cycling is briefly considered.

DOPING IN AMATEUR CYCLING

With the discussion so far in this chapter, the existence of, and rationale for, doping in professional cycling is clear. But what about amateur competitive cycling? The amateur cyclist does not face the same pressures that come with the professional sport, nor is winning races at this level going to bring money, fame and prestige (beyond the local environment). Yet, doping exists in amateur cycling (Ohl et al., 2015) and multiple concerns have been raised on this (Henning & Dimeo, 2018), providing a fascinating phenomenon for social analysis.

This is driven by cultural factors in the sport that leads to amateur participants to engage in doping practices. Dimeo and Henning (2015) quote one amateur cyclist that had doped, 'It was about being relevant in the group, which was pretty addicting ... The sport is all-consuming ... I was only involved in it for four years, and it took over most of my energy'. This echoes the discussion in Chap. 5, where I presented the argument that the sport operates within a strong subculture in which cyclists compete amongst each other for subcultural capital and status. This behaviour is interesting and aligns with previous discussions in this book where I have considered why amateur competitive cyclists seem to display the same attitudes towards the management of injury as professional cyclists, despite not having the same pressures or provision of medical support. It appears to be a display of adherence to the 'sport ethic' (Hughes & Coakley, 1991), where sporting success is prioritised over anything else.

Another interesting example comes from the UK, where a junior rider was banned from competition for taking EPO (Cycling Weekly, 2015). Speaking with the news outlet, the rider comments 'I got beaten by a lot, and when you get beaten by a lot you start questioning things. You question other people. I'm not trying to justify it, but when there is that much media exposure, about EPO, it is easy to be tempted. A big factor was losing that title' (Cycling Weekly, 2015). The title referred to was the British National 25 mile Junior Time Trial, a fairly small-scale event. This case study highlights the discussion earlier in the chapter on the sole focus of sport on winning and what the consequences of that can be.

DOPING AS DEVIANT OVERCONFORMITY TO THE CYCLING SUBCULTURE

As has been discussed, doping in cycling is a cultural behaviour that occurs across all levels of the sport. In order to appropriately theorise this phenomenon, considering material and symbolic factors (such as money, status and prestige) and approaches conceptualising sport-as-work (at the professional level) are not sufficient. Rather, the practice can be better understood through the culture of the sport (which has been strongly shaped around notions of orthodox masculinity, see Chap. 3).

136   J. HARDWICKE

More broadly, athletes that compete when injured, are seen to 'put in the hours' training, rapidly lose weight or increase muscle mass (depending on the sport) alongside other potentially harmful practices are praised by sport stakeholders (such as coaches, teammates, fans, media) (Coker-Cranney et al., 2018). Whilst policy modifications to manage and regulate such behaviours have been developed across sport, athletes of all levels continue to engage in behaviours believed to improve performance but to the detriment of health and wellbeing. For example, disordered eating, disordered exercise, overtraining, chronic pain management, use of PEDS and engaging in hazing rituals (Waldron & Krane, 2005; Coakley, 2009; Waldron & Kowalski, 2009).

All of the above can be understood through Hughes and Coakleys' (1991) concept of the sport ethic, which has been discussed earlier in the book. As a brief reminder, the sport ethic can be understood as (a) striving for distinction, or seeking perfection, (b) prioritising 'The Game' over one's personal life, (c) accepting risks and playing through pain and injury and (d) accepting no limits in the pursuit of excellence (Hughes & Coakley 1991). Athletes that overconform to this ethic are glorified within the sporting world (and broader culture). This behaviour has been referred to as 'deviant overconformity', which denotes athletes uncritically accepting sporting norms and adherence to them by doing things to an extreme (Coakley, 2015). This theorising allows us to understand behaviours across sport (amateur to professional) as the motivation to engage in such behaviours does not come from making money, fame or prestige but to gain the identity of an athlete and assimilate into a sporting culture (Hughes & Coakley, 1991).

As I discussed in Chap. 5, the sport of cycle racing involves significant commitment and sacrifice. It is also a sport with a strong subculture replete with informal social norms in which its members must learn and adhere to in order to gain acceptance. Therefore, cyclists are socialised into a social environment with a strong sporting ethic where taking risks are normalised and part of the 'every-day' experience in the sport (as argued over the previous chapters). A facet of this is engagement in doping practices, which can be understood as overconformity to the norms and values embodied in the sport of road cycling. Of course, not all cyclists dope. But this theorising helps understand the large proportion that do, as well as other health compromising practices that are common in cycling such as competing when injured (Hardwicke, 2022), over training (Kreher et al., 2012) and disordered eating (Riebl et al., 2007; Roberts et al., 2022).

CHAPTER SUMMARY

The purpose of this chapter was to further extend the discussion of health-compromising behaviours seen in cycling and understanding these from a socio-cultural perspective. The notion of 'winning at all costs' was used to frame this discussion, as well as doping practices providing a case study to focus on. It has been highlighted that such practices must be understood within the social context they occur, and not as an individual choice and behaviour. The historical development of sport, and cycling specifically, must be scrutinised and considered when developing an analysis to explain and understand health-compromising behaviours that occur in the contemporary sport. As detailed already throughout this book, the development of competitive cycling culture is tied to masculinity, and this has contributed to an environment where performance and winning are highly valued assets. This chapter has furthered an overall thesis of this book on the power of sporting subcultures to influence behaviours by providing another example of a health-compromising behaviour that can be understood through adherence to the sports culture. The following chapter moves away from a focus on health and considers how masculinity has impacted women in the sport.

REFERENCES

Anderson, E. (2009). *Inclusive Masculinity: The Changing Nature of Masculinities* (Routledge Research in Gender and Society) (1st ed.). Routledge.

Anderson, E., & White, A. (2018). *Sport, theory and social problems*. Routledge Taylor & Francis Group.

Andreasson, J. (2015). Reconceptualising the gender of fitness doping: Performing and negotiating masculinity through drug-use practices. *Social Sciences, 4*(3), 546–562. MDPI AG. Retrieved from https://doi.org/10.3390/socsci4030546

Baron, D. A., Martin, D. M., & Abol Magd, S. (2007). Doping in sports and its spread to at-risk populations: An international review. *World Psychiatry: Official Journal of the World Psychiatric Association (WPA), 6*(2), 118–123.

BikeRaceInfo. (2022). *Bicycle race results*. https://bikeraceinfo.com/annual/race2022.html

Broughton, E. (2016, February 4). The history of the six day races - magazine. RideVelo.http://www.ridevelo.cc/blog/2016/2/3/the-history-of-the-six-day-races.

Budd, A. (2001). Capitalism, sport and resistance: Reflections. *Sport in Society, 4*(1), 1–18.

Christiansen, A. V. (2010). "We are not sportsmen, we are professionals": Professionalism, doping and deviance in elite sport. *International Journal of Sport Management and Marketing, 7*(1/2), 91–103.

Christiansen, A. V., & Hjørngard, M. W. (2013). You can't buy something you aren't. On fixing results in cycling. *FairPlay, Revista de Filosofia, Ética y Derecho del Deporte*, (2), 64–84.

Coakley, J. J. (1990). *Sport in society: Issues and controversies* (No. Ed. 4). CV Mosby Company.

Coakley, J. (2009). From the outside in: Burnout as an organizational issue. *Journal of Intercollegiate Sport, 2*(1), 35–41.

Coakley, J. (2015). Drug use and deviant overconformity. In *Routledge handbook of drugs and sport* (pp. 379–392). Routledge.

Coakley, J. (2016a). Positive youth development through sport: Myths, beliefs, and realities. In *Positive youth development through sport* (pp. 21–33). Routledge.

Coakley, J. (2016b). Youth sports in the United States. In K. Green & A. Smith (Eds.), *Routledge handbook of youth sport*. Routledge.

Coker-Cranney, A., Watson, J. C., 2nd, Bernstein, M., Voelker, D. K., & Coakley, J. (2018). How far is too far? Understanding identity and overconformity in collegiate wrestlers. *Qualitative Research in Sport, Exercise and Health, 10*(1), 92–116. https://doi.org/10.1080/2159676X.2017.1372798

Cudd, A. E. (2007). Sporting metaphors: Competition and the ethos of capitalism. *Journal of the Philosophy of Sport, 34*(1), 52–67.

Cycling Weekly. (2015, December 10). *Junior time trial champion Gabriel Evans admits EPO use.* cyclingweekly.com. https://www.cyclingweekly.com/news/latest-news/junior-time-trial-champion-gabriel-evans-admits-epo-use-203450

Dimeo, P. (2007). A history of drug use in sport 1876–1976: Beyond good and evil. *Journal of Sports Science & Medicine, 6*(3), 382–382.

Dimeo, P. (2008). *A history of drug use in sport: 1876-1976: Beyond good and evil.* Routledge.

Dimeo, P., & Henning, A. (2015, January 27). *Forget lance Armstrong, the next big cycling doper could be your dad.* The Conversation. https://theconversation.com/forget-lance-armstrong-the-next-big-cycling-doper-could-be-your-dad-36734

Durry, J. (1977). *The Guinness guide to bicycling* (J. B. Wadley ed.). Guiness Superlatives Ltd.

Edwardes-Evans, L., Laget, S., McGrath, A., & Hinault, B. (2021). *The official history of the tour De France* (Updated ed.). Welbeck Publishing.

English, C. (2017). Toward sport reform: Hegemonic masculinity and reconceptualizing competition. *Journal of the Philosophy of Sport, 44*(2), 183–198.

Hardwicke, J. (2022). Inside the peloton: An exploration into the culture of competitive road cycling with reference to masculinity, risk and injury, with a principle focus on concussion (Doctoral dissertation, University of Winchester).

Hargreaves, J. (1982). Sport, culture and ideology. In J. Hargreaves (Ed.), *Sport, culture and ideology* (p. 41). Routledge and Kegan Paul.

Henning, A. D., & Dimeo, P. (2018). The new front in the war on doping: Amateur athletes. *International Journal of Drug Policy, 51*, 128–136. https://doi.org/10.1016/j.drugpo.2017.05.036

Hughes, R., & Coakley, J. (1991). Positive deviance among athletes: The implications of overconformity to the sport ethic. *Sociology of Sport Journal, 8*(4), 307–325.

Kreher, J. B., & Schwartz, J. B. (2012). Overtraining Syndrome: A Practical Guide. *Sports Health, 4*(2), 128–138. https://doi.org/10.1177/1941738111434406

Landry, G. L., & Kokotailo, P. K. (1994). Drug screening in the athletic setting. *Current Problems in Pediatrics, 24*(10), 344–359.

Lunzenfichter, A. (2007, 10 December). C'est pas du jeu!, L'Équipe, France.

Messner, M. A. (1992). Like family: Power, intimacy, and sexuality in male athletes' friendships. In P. M. Nardi (Ed.), *Men's friendships* (pp. 215–237). Sage Publications. https://doi.org/10.4135/9781483325736.n12

Møller, V. (2010). *The ethics of doping and anti-doping: Redeeming the soul of sport?* Routledge.

Nixon, H. L. (1991). Sport sociology that matters: Imperatives and challenges for the 1990s. *Sociology of Sport Journal, 8*(3), 281–294.

Nixon, H. L. (1992). A social network analysis of influences on athletes to play with pain and injuries. *Journal of Sport and Social Issues, 16*(2), 127–135. https://doi.org/10.1177/019372359201600208

Novich, Max M., Abbotempo, UK, 1964.

Ohl, F., Fincoeur, B., Lentillon-Kaestner, V., Defrance, J., & Brissonneau, C. (2015). The socialization of young cyclists and the culture of doping. *International Review for the Sociology of Sport, 50*(7), 865–882.

Petroczi, A., & Haugen, K. (2012). The doping self-reporting game: The paradox of a 'false-telling' mechanism and its potential research and policy implications. *Sport Management Review, 15*, 513–517.

Pro Cycling Statistics, Results and Rankings|ProCyclingStats.com. Pro Cycling Stats. 2022. Available online: https://www.procyclingstats.com/ (accessed on 15 December 2021).

Riebl, S. K., Subudhi, A. W., Broker, J. P., Schenck, K., & Berning, J. R. (2007). The prevalence of subclinical eating disorders among male cyclists. *Journal of the American Dietetic Association, 107*(7), 1214–1217. https://doi.org/10.1016/j.jada.2007.04.017

Ritchie, A. (1975). *King of the road*. Wildwood House.

Ritchie, A. (1988). Bearings, US. Andrew, Major Taylor, Bicycle Books, US.

Ritchie, A. (1999). The origins of bicycle racing in England: Technology, entertainment, sponsorship and advertising in the early history of the sport. *Journal of Sport History, 26*(3), 489–520.

Roberts, C. J., Hurst, H. T., & Hardwicke, J. (2022). Eating disorders and disordered eating in competitive Cycling: A scoping review. *Behavioral Sciences, 12*(12), 490.

Safai, P. (2003). Healing the body in the "culture of risk": Examining the negotiation of treatment between sport medicine clinicians and injured athletes in Canadian intercollegiate sport. *Sociology of Sport Journal, 20*(2), 127–146.

Sidwells, C. (2018). *The Call of the Road: The History of Cycle Road Racing.* William Collins.

Smart, B. (2018). Consuming Olympism: Consumer culture, sport star sponsorship and the commercialisation of the Olympics. *Journal of Consumer Culture, 18*(2), 241–260. https://doi.org/10.1177/1469540517747146

Smith, C. (2015). Tour du dopage: Confessions of doping professional cyclists in a modern work environment. *International Review for the Sociology of Sport, 52*(1), 97–111.

Sporting Cyclist, UK. (1967, October), p. 12.

Waddington, I. (2005). Changing patterns of drug use in British sport from the 1960s. *Sport in History, 25*(3), 472–496.

Waldron, J. J., & Kowalski, C. L. (2009). Crossing the line: Rites of passage, team aspects, and ambiguity of hazing. *Research Quarterly for Exercise and Sport, 80*(2), 291–302.

Waldron, J. J., & Krane, V. (2005). Motivational climate and goal orientation in adolescent female softball players. *Journal of Sport Behavior, 28*(4), 378.

Williams, T. (1989). Sport, hegemony and subcultural reproduction: The process of accommodation in bicycle road racing. *International Review for the Sociology of Sport, 24*(4), 315–333.

Yesalis, C. E. (2002). History of doping in sport. In M. S. Bahrke & C. E. Yesalis (Eds.), *Performance enhancing substances in sport and exercise* (pp. 1–20). Human Kinetics.

CHAPTER 8

Out in the Peloton: Sexual Minorities in Road Cycling

INTRODUCTION

In January 2021, Justin Laevens, a Belgian U23 professional cyclist, came out as the world's first openly gay male professional cyclist (Cycling News, 2021). Competitive road cycling has very little visible engagement with positive gay discourses and anecdotal reports of homophobia are common in the sport. The purpose of this chapter is to discuss why this might be the case, or indeed if it is the case. Through drawing on my own research in the area, as well as the arguments made throughout this book, an overview of the state of sexual minorities' experiences in road cycling is provided with a consideration for the role that masculinity may play in this. First, the relationship between masculinities, sexualities and sport is discussed before considering road cycling, specifically.

THE RELATIONSHIP BETWEEN MASCULINITIES, SEXUALITIES AND SPORT

Gender and sexuality are fundamentally linked concepts which are important to the study of sport. From the inception of organised competitive sport, in the mid-nineteenth century, through to sport played today, it is a highly gendered institution in society. Indeed, it is one of the few cultural locations where sex-segregation is normalised and mandated. The use of

© The Author(s), under exclusive license to Springer Nature
Switzerland AG 2023
J. Hardwicke, *Masculinities and the Culture of Competitive Cycling*,
Palgrave Studies in Masculinity, Sport and Exercise,
https://doi.org/10.1007/978-3-031-26975-2_8

141

gender as an organising principle for the study of sport reveals essential knowledge about the fundamental structures and character of sport (Hargreaves & Anderson, 2014). As such, gender has often been used as a conceptual principle for the study of all manners of areas, issues and contentions in sport. Indeed, it is the over-arching unit of analysis for this book.

When discussing gender, it is important to acknowledge that it is a very complex and fluctuating social category to analyse (McCormack et al., 2021). This is both in relation to the 'opposite' sex and amongst sexual categories. An extension of this is gender's close relationship to sexuality, which can be seen through cultural practices and behaviours, as well as specifically in sport. As such, they are relational concepts that cannot be discussed in isolation and thus both are included for the analysis in this chapter.

Gender is very influential on our life experiences. In Western societies, the dominant approach to understanding gender is through a dichotomy between males and females (the gender binary), which has been socially constructed in line with essentialist conceptions of gender based on biological sex differences. This book is concerned with men and masculinities, so that is the focus. However, the same relation and influence of gender is true for women and femininities.

There exists a strong association between the male (sex) and masculinity (gender), and even though 'sex' (a biological category) and 'gender' (a cultural category) are not synonymous, they are often viewed as such, and used interchangeably. Combined, they present dominant conceptions of males and masculinities. Essentially what it means to 'be a man'. Throughout the early development of sport, these gendered ideals were fundamentally structured into the institution to present societies dominant ideals of males and masculinity. But things are more complex, and gender is not innately connected to biological sex (Anderson & Magrath, 2019). Rather, there is an interplay between sex and gender dependent on what is socially ascribed in the socio-cultural context. The same is true for sexuality, where things are more complex than common narratives depict. The common ascription is a heterosexual-homosexual dichotomy, where the binary is rigid and fixed, but in reality this is not often the case (Magrath & McCormack, 2022).

Sport is one social context that is highly influential on the construction of masculinities and sexualities, and the (re)production of certain archetypes of each. Key to understanding this relationship is the evolution of research that focuses on the intersections of sport, masculinities and homosexuality. During the early development of sport sociology as a discipline, research focused on the relationship between sport, masculinities and homosexuality during the late twentieth century was characterised by the homophobic culture which existed during this time. Indeed, few studies examined openly gay athletes as they were so sparse in the Western world (Anderson, 2011).

In this era, the late twentieth century, sport was an institution that structurally promoted heterosexuality over homosexuality, and homophobia was rife (Anderson, 2011). Indeed, from data collected during interviews with heterosexual male athletes, Messner (1992) comments 'The extent of homophobia in the sports world is staggering. Boys (in sport) learn early that to be gay, to be suspected of being gay, or even to be unable to prove one's heterosexual status is not acceptable' (p. 34). This was true of recreational sport too, where Hekma (1998, p. 2) posits that gay males were systematically structured out of sport, which was considered a 'masculine preserve and a macho enterprise'.

The story of Professor Eric Anderson's coming out as Americas first openly gay high school coach in 1994 depicts the zeitgeist of the era (see Anderson, 2000 for an engaging and accessible insight on this). In his book *Trailblazing*, Anderson's story highlights the rampant homophobia that characterised sport and its associated institutions during the late twentieth century. Clearly this environment was detrimental to homosexual athletes, where most remained closeted due to the assumption the high levels of homophobia, and vocal opposition to homosexuality amongst sportsmen, suggested that coming out would be an unpleasant experience (Woog, 1998). Unfortunately, this assumption was largely true. Some of sports first openly gay athletes, such as Justin Fashanu, highlight this hostile environment.

An important phenomenon here, which highlights the relationship between masculinities and sexualities, is the influence this homophobic culture had on heterosexual male athletes. This consideration forms the basis of an 'Andersonian' (Borkowska, 2020) approach to understanding masculinities, as outlined in Chap. 2. Men's competitive sport was built on the premise of homophobia and functioned as a social institution with the political project of defining certain archetypes of heterosexual masculinity as acceptable, whilst ostracising others (Crosset, 1990; Messner, 2002). As such, cultural homophobia acted as a policing mechanism for heterosexual male gender expression (Anderson, 2009). As a culturally cherished and esteemed social institution, sport was a location where orthodox notions of masculinity were (re)produced, as outlined in Chaps. 2 and 3.

However, in recent years, and most starkly in the West, acceptance and tolerance of homosexuality have rapidly increased in wider society (McCormack, 2012). Resultantly, sport too has seen a relative decline in homophobia (Anderson, 2009), bisexual phobia (Ripley et al., 2011) and LGB athletes report far more positive experiences of coming out than seen in the late twentieth century (Bush et al., 2012; Anderson et al., 2016; White et al., 2021). There is a growing body of academic research suggesting sport, like broader society, is increasingly becoming a more inclusive space for sexual minorities. Yet, much of this research has been conducted in popular team-based sports and, at the time of writing, there has been no such investigation into the sport of road cycling to indicate the experiences of sexual minorities in the sport and if the culture has shifted in line with the broader culture.

A Background to Sexual Minorities in Competitive Road Cycling

Due to the lack of formal literature on the topic, informal reports in the media provide the only insight to sexual minorities in competitive road cycling. Firstly, an interesting discussion from one of road cycling's only openly transgender figures (she transitioned post retirement from the sport) helps understand the situation in the sport. Phillipa York, who competed as Robert Millar, is one of Britain's most successful cyclists. Talking to the Guardian on the culture within professional cycling, she discusses how 'the [macho] culture in professional cycling is preventing riders from coming out as gay' (Kelner, 2018). She depicts how, within the competitive cycling culture, being homosexual is still coded as a weakness and a detriment to an athlete's masculinity. She comments how athletes in cycling must hide any weaknesses because of the brutality of not only the demands of the sport, but the culture of roadside fans.

Whilst there remain, at the time of writing, no openly gay male professional cyclists at the very top level of the sport, Justin Laevens, came out as the world's first openly gay male professional cyclist in early January 2021 (Cycling News, 2021). All previous gay male professional cyclists have come out after retirement from the sport. On coming out, Justin commented 'I didn't find it difficult to express myself, but I did in sport, because I don't know any [cyclist] who is gay', (Outsports, 2021a, 2021b). Later in 2021, Clay Davies publicly came out making him the first elite male competitive road cyclist to do so in the UK (Outsports, 2021a, 2021b). His story provides some insight to the level and context of road cycling largely examined in this book. I spoke with Clay on this experience (having previously raced with him we were already connected), and his experiences more broadly in cycling. What was clear in our conversations is that it was not so much that cyclists, writ large, are homophobic but rather the culture of the sport and the institutions responsible for cycle sports lack the support for positive gay discourses. Furthermore, we spoke at length about the seemingly macho culture of the sport and how this does not lend itself to an environment conducive for coming out (Private communication). In a media interview, Davies commented:

> There's this perception – whether it's true or not, and I think it is to some degree – that serious amateur cyclists, pro cyclists, semi-pro, elite riders, whatever, are quite a funny bunch. That they're not quite as socially dynamic as others, that there's a bit of a closed mindset, a not-quite-as-worldly type of approach. That they might behave strangely if they knew you were gay. (The British Continental, 2021a, 2021b)

Whilst the problem is seemingly more cultural, Davies did report hearing anti-gay slurs in the sport with negative intent as well as having a previous roommate that would not shower while he was in the room (The British Continental, 2021a, 2021b). Further, whilst the response to his public coming out has been reported to be 'entirely positive', which fits with academic research into the subject of coming out (Anderson et al., 2016; White et al., 2021), he has been very publicly critical of British Cycling for their lack of support around the issue (Outsports, 2021a, 2021b).

Shortly after Clay Davies publicly came out, a UK male junior rider reached out to the cycling news outlet *The British Continental* which published the original story on Clay. Asking to remain anonymous, the junior rider shared his experiences of being a gay male cyclist and why he has chosen to remain closeted (The British Continental, 2021a, 2021b). In speaking with the cycling news outlet, the anonymous rider commented:

> It was also around this time [turning 14 and racing at the youth level] where the laddish behaviour from fellow riders started to appear. This manifested

itself with homophobic slurs, insulting other riders in a homophobic way, and even talking about girls in a derogatory way.

As a young lad who had just started getting top results in the youth national series, this was demoralising. It made me question if it was the right sport, a safe sport, for people like me. In fact, I still question how much things have changed when I hear juniors and under-23s using the same homophobic language they did half a decade ago. I could easily name and shame, but I won't.

In my experience, British Cycling does not care about this issue. Countless times I have been at British Cycling-run sessions – like Regional Schools of Racing (RSRs), and even on Great Britain Cycling Team apprentice camps and the Junior Academy – and a rider has said something homophobic, transphobic or used a slur in front of the coaches, in front of commissaires, and none of them has reacted in the slightest.

This story reflects much of the sentiments made by Clay and seems to point towards the same problems, particularly the lack of institutional support from the cycling governing bodies. The above discussions and prima facie evidence perhaps explain why there are no openly gay male athletes in the World Tour cycling ranks, despite it being highly statistically likely that some athletes are gay in this cohort. This is, however, unproven, and it may be the case that there are few gay male professional cyclists as they are simply not interested or overly represented in the sport.

Anderson and colleagues (2005, 2016) provide two hypotheses to account for this possible phenomenon: the homophobia hypothesis and the non-participation hypothesis. The homophobia hypothesis posits that gay men may not disclose their sexuality in fear of homophobia within the sporting culture. This hypothesis seemingly aligns with the comments from Phillipa York previously discussed, that professional cyclists fear disclosing their sexuality (Kelner, 2018). However, increasing academic research is reporting the widespread acceptance of gay teammates across sports and declining homophobic environments (see; Adams, 2011; Adams & Kavanagh, 2018; Magrath, 2019; White et al., 2021). Yet, as previously mentioned, this academic inquiry has not reached competitive cycling, so the attitudes and environment are not known.

The non-participation hypothesis posits that gay men are not proportionally represented in many sports because they chose not to participate in them. Here, common narratives predict that the percentage of gay men in the general population must be matched within sporting populations. Anderson et al. (2016) outline this approach as reductionist and offer a more balanced perspective. Research shows that in net grouping, gay men's bodies are slightly different to straight men (Anderson et al., 2016), being more feminised than straight males (Bailey, 2003). Because of this, on net average, gay men may not be drawn to typically masculinised domains found in competitive sports such as Rugby, Football or American football. Rather, we see an over-representation of gay men in theatre, music, dance and feminised sports that explain the statistical deficit in competitive team sports (Anderson et al., 2016).

Competitive road cycling offers an interesting sport to observe both these hypotheses. The environment of the sport values orthodox masculine values, with research showing the demonstration of this through harmful injury management behaviours (O'Reilly et al., 2020; Hardwicke & Hurst, 2020) and competitive male road cyclists identifying more closely with stricter archetypes of masculinity than the general population (Powell et al., 2005; Hardwicke, 2022). Yet, the anatomy required to excel in the sport requires thin bodies that would typically be socially coded as feminine. Furthermore, cultural practices of shaving legs and lycra clothing required in the sport adds to the feminine coded behaviours (Brittain, 2022). With lack of academic research, only speculation into this aspect of competitive cycling culture can be posited and we must caution against using single case studies from media reports. However, in order to start addressing this gap in knowledge I conducted empirical research into the topic which is reported on below.

OUT IN THE PELOTON STUDY

The remainder of this chapter will report the results from my research into this area which sought to investigate the experiences of, and attitudes towards, sexual minorities in cycling. A self-report survey was used which contained a range of questions for LGBTQ+ identifying participants and a separate set of questions for straight identifying participants. Questions for LGBTQ+ cyclists covered areas such as experiences within the sport, experiences of homophobic abuse, views on governing bodies' inclusion policies and any perceived barriers for sexual minorities in cycling.

Questions for straight cyclists covered areas such as experiences of witnessing or using homophobic abuse as well as own self-rated beliefs on the topic. Two validated scales were also used to measure attitudes: The Attitudes Toward Lesbians and Gay Men Scale (ATLG) (Herek, 1984) and the Attitudes Toward Transgender Men and Women (ATTMW) scale

148   J. HARDWICKE

(Billard, 2018). This data is currently under review for publication in academic journal article format where more detail is provided on the study. However, the data set is publicly available where all questions and participant responses can be seen (Source: Hardwicke, 2022). For the purpose of this book, a descriptive overview of the findings is provided and discussion of these.

A total of 359 cyclists completed the survey, of which 148 identified as LGBTQ+. Table 8.1 presents a demographic breakdown of the survey respondents. Importantly, this research included a range of cyclists and not just competitive cyclists. Grous (2012) typology of cyclists was used to stratify participant's engagement with cycling. These are broken into: (1). Enthusiast: Cycling is a sport or a passion; (2). Recreational User: Cycles for enjoyment, sightseeing, and light exercise; (3). Commuter: Utilises cycling as a principal or additional mode of transport for work; (4). Other. For clarity in the context of this book, competitive cyclists fall under 'enthusiast'. The sample was predominately made up of enthusiast cyclists and of the 189 enthusiast cyclists, 129 participated in road cycling.

The sample was international, but mainly Western focused with most participants from the UK and US. The importance of considering 'serious leisure' cyclists alongside competitive road cyclists was outlined in Chap. 1. Due to the paucity of the literature in this specific area, data from all groups of cyclists are presented here. Considerations (and reservations) are offered for the generalisability of the data to the competitive sport.

EXPERIENCES OF SEXUAL MINORITIES IN CYCLING

Of the 148 LGBTQ+ cyclists, most reported being open about their sexuality within their immediate cycling group or community. Results were as follows, out to all (33.9%), out to some (18.2%), out to most (16.2%), out to none (5.4%), out to one (2.7%). Thirty-five of the participants (23.6%) responded 'N/A' to this due to not being in a cycling group or community. The majority of the participants reported being publicly open about their sexuality to cycling peers, and the survey asked these participants to respond on a Likert-scale to a number of statements about their experiences and feelings towards coming out. The results of these are displayed in Table 8.2.

Most of the LGBTQ+ cyclists reported positively on their experiences and felt comfortable coming out in the cycling community, as well as feeling welcomed. Statistical analysis of the data presented in Table 8.2 found

8 OUT IN THE PELOTON: SEXUAL MINORITIES IN ROAD CYCLING 149

Table 8.1 Demographic breakdown of survey respondents ($N = 359$)

Self-reported characteristic	Responses	
	N	%
Sex		
Male	236	65.7
Female	114	31.8
Intersex	1	0.3
Other	5	1.4
Prefer not to say	3	0.8
Age (years)		
<18	4	1.1
18–24	35	9.7
25–34	96	26.7
35–44	88	24.5
45–54	89	24.8
55–64	37	10.3
65>	10	2.8
Self-selected identity to best describe oneself		
Straight male	158	44.0
Straight female	51	14.2
Bisexual male	14	3.9
Bisexual female	51	14.2
Gay male	61	17.0
Gay female	29	8.1
Trans male	3	0.8
Trans female	11	3.1
Asexual female	2	0.6
Non-binary	5	1.4
Prefer not to say	2	0.6
Other	5	1.4
Category of cyclist		
Enthusiast	189	52.6
Recreational	104	29.0
Commuter	53	14.8
Other	13	3.6

Cycling Type (Enthusiast, Recreational, Commuter or Other), Age and Sexuality (Gay, Lesbian, Bisexual, Transgender) had no significant effect on responses to the statements. Participants were also asked to rate their overall experiences within cycling compared to other sports or organised exercise. Responses were as follows, experiences have been equal across sports (37.8%), best in cycling (9.5%), better in other sports (9.5%) and

150   J. HARDWICKE

Table 8.2   Frequency of Likert survey responses (n =148)

	Frequency of Likert survey responses				
Statement	Strongly disagree	Disagree	Neutral	Agree	Strongly agree
'I felt comfortable coming out amongst the cycling community'	5.0%	18.8%	23.8%	37.6%	14.9%
'I feel that my sexuality is welcome in the cycling community'	1.0%	16.8%	31.7%	40.6%	9.9%
'I feel that my gender identity is welcome in the cycling community'	5%	12.9%	18.8%	35.6%	27.7%
'I felt more comfortable coming out amongst my cycling community than in other areas of my life'	9.9%	36.6%	32.7%	13.9%	6.9%

not sure (9.5%). Fifty of the participants (33.8%) responded 'N/A' to this due to only having experiences within cycling.

Participants were also asked about their experiences of anti-LGBTQ+ discourse in the form of verbal harassment and physical hostility. Responses are displayed in Table 8.3. Most participants reported not experiencing direct harassment or hostility due to their sexual identity. However, more participants reported hearing anti-LGBTQ+ language but when intent to personally harm was not present. Of those that reported experiencing such language, either direct or indirect, they were asked what their perception of intent was. Participants mostly reported that intent of the language use was 'humour/banter'. This is important to consider as language can change at a slower rate than attitudes (McCormack, 2011), with research in sport highlighting that presence of homophobic language is not always synonymous with homophobic attitudes (Cleland et al., 2021; Magrath, 2018). As such, homosexually themed language must be considered in terms of intent, context and effect (McCormack, 2011). In this sample, only a small number of participants reported experiencing anti-LGBTQ+ language with intent of direct abuse. Further research on this area is required.

Finally, participants were asked about their views on cycling more broadly. Participants were asked if they felt cycling governing bodies and organisations were doing enough to accommodate LGBTQ+ cyclists. Responses were as follows, no (64.9%), not sure (29.1%) and yes (6.1%). The majority of participants (60.1%) either Agreed or Strongly Agreed

8 OUT IN THE PELOTON: SEXUAL MINORITIES IN ROAD CYCLING   151

Table 8.3 Frequency of responses to experiences anti-LGBTQ+ discourse (n = 148)

Question	Responses (%)				
	Experienced none	Experienced one or a few incidents	Experienced this on a monthly basis	Experienced this on a weekly basis	Prefer not to say
In the last five years, have you experienced direct verbal harassment as a result of being known, or suspected, as LGBTQ+?	62.8%	31.8%	2.0%	2.0%	1.4%
In the last five years, have you experienced direct physical hostility as a result of being known as LGBTQ+?	84.5%	13.5%	1.3%	0.8%	0.0%
In the last five years, how often have you heard slurs, or word usage that might convey LGBTQ+ prejudice, but without intent to harm you personally?	23.6%	56.1%	12.8%	7.4%	0.0%

that there were barriers for the inclusion of LGB participants in cycling, and 81.1% for transgender participants. Lack of representation, homophobic environment and discriminatory policies were the main barriers to inclusion cited by participants. Participants were asked how they thought cycling compared to other sports efforts to encourage LGBTQ+ inclusion. Responses were as follows, behind on other sports (39.9%), not sure (31.1%), equal to other sports (20.9%) and better than other sports (8.1%).

ATTITUDES TOWARDS SEXUAL MINORITIES IN CYCLING

Of the 211 straight-identifying participants, most displayed positive attitudes towards sexual minorities in cycling. Table 8.4 displays responses to the statements assessing general attitudes which highlights this finding.

152   J. HARDWICKE

Table 8.4   Frequency of Likert survey responses (n =211)

	Frequency of Likert survey responses				
Statement	Strongly disagree	Disagree	Neutral	Agree	Strongly agree
Knowing that a teammate/cycling friend was LGB would negatively change my opinion on them	89.1%	9%	0.9%	2.4%	0.5%
Knowing that a teammate/cycling friend was transgender would negatively change my opinion on them	78.7%	13.3%	5.2%	2.4%	0.5%
I would be comfortable if one of my teammates/cycling friends comes out as LGBTQ+	8.1%	0.5%	2.4%	10.9%	78.2%
It's common in cycling for men to make jokes about being feminine/girly	12.8%	23.7%	26.1%	30.3%	7.1%

However, it was found that a considerable number (37.4%) of the participants reported that it was common in cycling for men to make jokes about being feminine/girly. Most participants (65.9%) reported having never witnessed anti-LGBTQ+ or homophobic language used as direct abuse in cycling, and 29.9% only witnessing one or a few incidents in the last five years.

The two validated scales used to assess attitudes towards lesbian and gay people (ATLG Scale) and transgender (ATTMF Scale) are rated on a possible scale of 10–50, with a higher score indicating more negative attitudes. Mean scores in the sample for the ATLG scale were 13.7 (standard deviation= 5.8) and ATTMF scale was 21.1 (standard deviation= 10.7). Mostly positive attitudes towards sexual minorities were found within this sample, with scores consistent with previous research in sporting contexts (Rooper & Halloran, 2007; Mullen et al., 2020; Magrath et al., 2022). There were no statistical differences found for effect of age, sex or cyclist type on ATLG or ATTMF scores. However, a significant difference in scores on the ATLG scale vs. ATTMF scale was found, with results suggesting participants held greater positive attitudes towards Gay Males and Lesbian Females than Transgender Men and Transgender Females.

Discussion of the Data

In summary, the above data details the first empirical study into sexual minorities in cycling. The findings suggest cycling, broadly speaking, is reflecting the trend seen in sport and society of increasing liberalisation and positive attitudes towards sexual diversity, in support of Inclusive Masculinity Theory. Further, the mostly positive experiences reported by sexual minorities in cycling is consistent with academic research on the topic (Bush et al., 2012; Anderson et al., 2016; White et al., 2021). However, it interesting to note that liberal attitudes towards LGB were greater than towards transgender individuals. This discrepancy has been reported in previous research (Norton & Herek, 2013), and likely presents a cultural lag in attitudes as transgender discourse and activism is a more recent social phenomenon compared to LGB.

Importantly, generalisability to the professional and competitive level of the sport cannot be made from this data alone. Research is needed at this level of the sport to make any inferences towards the presence of homophobia and experiences of homosexual athletes at top levels of the sport. Within this sample, most of the participants engaged with the sport in a competitive or 'serious leisure' capacity which is the focus of this book. Whilst mostly positive attitudes and experiences were found amongst this group, issues were reported at the institutional level of the sport and the view that governing bodies in cycling are not placing visible efforts into promoting positive LGBTQ+ discourses. This has been reported on previously and conceptualised as 'Organisational cultural lag' in that sporting institutions lag behind individual and broader societal attitudes towards sexual diversity (Letts, 2021; Parry et al., 2021).

As discussed throughout this book, masculinity is a complex and fluctuating social category. Whilst prominent features of orthodox masculinity are evident within competitive cycling culture, it may be that subscription to orthodox masculinity does not correlate with attitudes towards sexual minorities. Whilst orthodox masculinity in part developed on the rejection of femininity and homosexuality, as discussed in Chaps. 2 and 3, it may be that this aspect of orthodox masculinity has shifted due to larger cultural changes and decreasing homophobia.

However, absolute claims based on this data cannot be made and it only exists as a preliminary insight and departure point for future research. With the prima facie evidence presented earlier in this chapter that points towards the competitive sport and professional sport having issues with homophobia, more academic research on this topic is needed before any claims of inference can be made with confidence. I propose the hypothesis that the idolisation of orthodox masculinity in competitive cycling culture is a significant contributing factor for the lack of openly gay male cyclists across the competitive sport. As the data above suggests, this may not be an issue with individual attitudes, but a cultural issue that is embedded within the structure of the sport of road cycling.

Briefly, the limitations of the data must also be highlighted. As with all self-reported data, we must interpret the findings with caution. There is the potential problem of a self-selection bias whereby those that participated in the survey had a personal interest or investment in the research area. There is also the concern of social desirability, whereby respondents may select responses that align with what would be deemed socially desirable and not what reflects their personal beliefs. This is particularly prominent when considering attitudes towards sexual minorities. Finally, considerations for the context of experiences of sexual minorities cannot be made based on this data. This is where future research using qualitative methodologies is required to build a deeper understanding of the area.

CHAPTER SUMMARY

In summary, this chapter has presented an overview of sexual minorities in cycling. It has been highlighted as an area in need of academic research with very limited data available at current to provide any detailed or valid insight. However, when considered in light of the discussion throughout this book and the thesis put forward that competitive road cycling culture is predicated on a valuing of orthodox masculinity, some insight can be gained. It appears that individual attitudes towards sexual minorities may not be an issue, but rather the hyper-masculine culture of the competitive sport creates an environment in which sexual minorities (particularly gay males) may feel unwelcome. Furthermore, at an institutional level, the sport is notably behind compared to other sports in promoting positive sexual minority discourses. Yet, this chapter serves as a point of discussion only and due to the lack of data, insight is limited. Future research is required, and a starting point may be to investigate the relationship between masculinity and the sports subculture and how this may influence the experience of gay males in the sport.

REFERENCES

Adams, A. (2011). "Josh wears pink cleats": Inclusive masculinity on the soccer field. *Journal of Homosexuality, 58*(5), 579–596.

Adams, A., & Kavanagh, E. (2018). Inclusive ideologies and passive performances: Exploring masculinities and attitudes toward gay peers among boys in an elite youth football academy. *Journal of Gender Studies, 27*(3), 313–322.

Anderson, E. (2000). *Trailblazing: America's first openly gay track coach.*

Anderson, E. (2005). Orthodox and inclusive masculinity: Competing masculinities among heterosexual men in a feminized terrain. *Sociological Perspectives, 48*(3), 337–355.

Anderson, E. (2009). *Inclusive Masculinity: The Changing Nature of Masculinities* (Routledge Research in Gender and Society) (1st ed.). Routledge.

Anderson, E. (2011). Masculinities and sexualities in sport and physical cultures: Three decades of evolving research. *Journal of Homosexuality, 58*(5), 565–578.

Anderson, E., & Magrath, R. (2019). *Men and masculinities* (1st ed.). Routledge.

Anderson, E., Magrath, R., & Bullingham, R. (2016). *Out in sport* (1st ed.). Routledge.

Bailey, M. J. (2003). *The man who would be queen: The science of gender-bending and transsexualism.* Joseph Henry Press.

Billard, T. J. (2018). Attitudes toward transgender men and women: Development and validation of a new measure. *Frontiers in Psychology, 9*, 387.

Borkowska, K. (2020). Approaches to studying masculinity: A nonlinear perspective of theoretical paradigms. *Men and Masculinities, 23*(3–4), 409–424.

Brittain, J. J. (2022). Atrophying masculinity within professional Road Cycling. In *The Routledge handbook of gender politics in sport and physical activity.* Routledge.

Bush, A., Anderson, E., & Carr, S. (2012). The declining existence of men's homophobia in British sport. *Journal for the Study of Sports and Athletes in Education, 6*(1), 107–120.

Cleland, J., Cashmore, E., Dixon, K., & MacDonald, C. (2021). Analyzing the presence of homosexually-themed language among association football fans in the United Kingdom. *Communication & Sport.* https://doi.org/10.1177/21674795211005838

Crosset, T. (1990). Masculinity, sexuality, and the development of early modern sport. In *Sport, men and the gender order: Critical feminist perspectives* (pp. 45–54). Human Kinetics.

Cyclingnews. (2021, January 7). Belgian U23' cross racer Justin Laevens comes out as gay. cyclingnews.com. https://www.cyclingnews.com/news/belgian-u23-cross-racer-justin-laevens-comes-out-as-gay/

Grous, A. (2012). *The 'Olympic cycling effect': A report prepared for sky and British Cycling.* London School of Economics and Political Science.

156   J. HARDWICKE

Hardwicke, J. (2022). Inside the peloton: An exploration into the culture of competitive road cycling with reference to masculinity, risk and injury, with a principle focus on concussion (Doctoral dissertation, University of Winchester).

Hardwicke, J., & Hurst, H. T. (2020). Concussion knowledge and attitudes amongst competitive cyclists. *Journal of Science and Cycling, 9,* 53–66.

Hargreaves, J., & Anderson, E. (Eds.). (2014). *Routledge handbook of sport, gender and sexuality.* Routledge.

Hekma, G. (1998). "As long as they don't make an issue of it…" gay men and lesbians in organized sports in The Netherlands. *Journal of Homosexuality, 35*(1), 1–23.

Herek, G. M. (1984). Attitudes toward lesbians and gay men: A factor-analytic study. *Journal of Homosexuality, 10*(1–2), 39–51.

Kelner, M. (2018, May 1). Philippa York says macho culture prevents cyclists coming out. *The Guardian.* https://www.theguardian.com/sport/2018/apr/30/philippa-york-macho-culture-cyclistscoming-out

Letts, D. (2021). Sexual minority prevalence and attitudes within the British horseracing industry. *International Review for the Sociology of Sport, 56*(6), 823–841.

Magrath, R. (2018). 'To try and gain an advantage for my team': Homophobic and homosexually themed chanting among English football fans. *Sociology, 52*(4), 709–726.

Magrath, R. (2019). 'To try and gain an advantage for my team': Homophobic and homosexually themed chanting among English football fans. *Sociology, 52*(4), 709–726.

Magrath, R., Batten, J., Anderson, E., & White, A. J. (2022). Five-year cohort study of White-British male student-athletes' attitudes toward gay men. *Journal for the Study of Sports and Athletes in Education, 16*(3), 262–276.

Magrath, R., & McCormack, M. (2022). Friendship dynamics of young men with non-exclusive sexual orientations: Group diversity, physical intimacy and emotionality. *Journal of Social and Personal Relationships.* https://doi.org/10.1177/02654075221127232

McCormack, M. (2011). Mapping the terrain of homosexually-themed language. *Journal of Homosexuality, 58*(5), 664–679.

McCormack, M. (2012). *The declining significance of homophobia.* Oxford University Press.

McCormack, M., Anderson, E., Jamie, K., & David, M. (2021). *Discovering sociology.* Bloomsbury Publishing.

Messner, M. A. (1992). Like family: Power, intimacy, and sexuality in male athletes' friendships. In P. M. Nardi (Ed.), *Men's friendships* (pp. 215–237). Sage Publications. https://doi.org/10.4135/9781483325736.n12

Messner, M. A. (2002). *Taking the field: Women, men, and sports* (Vol. 4). U of Minnesota Press.

Norton, A. T., & Herek, G. M. (2013). Heterosexuals' attitudes toward transgender people: Findings from a national probability sample of US adults. *Sex Roles, 68*(11), 738–753.

O'Reilly, M., Mahon, S., Reid, D., Hume, P., Hardaker, N., & Theadom, A. (2020). Knowledge, attitudes, and behavior toward concussion in adult cyclists. *Brain Injury, 34*(9), 1175–1182. https://doi.org/10.1080/02699052.2020.1793386

Outsports. (2021a, August 25). *Cyclist clay Davies comes out, calls out his sport for homophobia.* Outsports. https://www.outsports.com/homophobia/2021/8/25/22641481/clay-davies-british-cycling-gay-homophobia

Outsports. (2021b, January 8). *Gay cyclist Justin Laevens is one of first pro male riders to come out.* Outsports. https://www.outsports.com/2021/1/8/22220390/justin-laevens-cyclist-gay-belgium

Parry, K. D., Storr, R., Kavanagh, E. J., & Anderson, E. (2021). Conceptualising organisational cultural lag: Marriage equality and Australian sport. *Journal of Sociology, 57*(4), 986–1008.

Powell, D., Stiles, B., Haff, G., & Kilgore, L. (2005). The notion of masculinity in male collegiate road cyclists. *Creative Sociology, 33*(2), 153. https://ojs.library.okstate.edu/osu/index.php/FICS/article/view/1558

Ripley, M., Anderson, E., McCormack, M., Adams, A., & Pitts, R. (2011). The decreasing significance of stigma in the lives of bisexual men: Keynote address, bisexual research convention, London. *Journal of Bisexuality, 11*(2–3), 195–206.

The British Continental. (2021a, July 29). *Clay Davies interview: Free spirit.* The British Continental. https://thebritishcontinental.co.uk/2021/07/23/clay-davies-interview-free-spirit/

The British Continental. (2021b, July 31). *Being gay in cycle sport: A junior rider's experience.* The British Continental. https://thebritishcontinental.co.uk/2021/07/29/being-gay-in-cycle-sport-a-junior-riders-experience/

White, A. J., Magrath, R., & Emilio Morales, L. (2021). Gay male athletes' coming-out stories on Outsports.com. *International Review for the Sociology of Sport, 56*(7), 1017–1034.

Woog, D. (1998). *Jocks: True stories of America's gay male athletes.* Alyson.

CHAPTER 9

Women on Wheels: Orthodox Masculinity and the Marginalisation of Women in Competitive Cycling

INTRODUCTION

From the inception of modern sport in the West as an organised and codified institution from the mid-nineteenth century, it has been distinctly shaped by gender relations (Hargreaves & Anderson, 2014). In short, sports were largely created by men, for men (and boys) (Matthews & Channon, 2019), leading to Dunning's (1986) thesis of sport being a 'male preserve'. This was certainly the case in the development of competitive cycling, as detailed in Chap. 3 and will be revisited in this chapter. The intersects of men, masculinity and sport developed as a key research area in the sociology of sport, where the over-arching thesis was that sport served to sustain hegemonic male power, normalise the marginalisation of women and sexual minorities, and reinforce intra-male status hierarchies (Dunning, 1986; Messner, 1992; Messner and Sabo, 1990; Pronger, 1990). Researchers have highlighted that girls, and women, face multiple barriers and issues in sport, and that the hegemonic masculinity of sport influenced women's strive for gender parity with regard to legitimacy, recognition and resources in sport (Taylor et al., 2022). As such, the historical and contemporary marginalisation of women in sport, and its relation to masculinity, has been a central concern to much research and commentary in the sociology of sport (Mansfield et al., 2017).

© The Author(s), under exclusive license to Springer Nature Switzerland AG 2023
J. Hardwicke, *Masculinities and the Culture of Competitive Cycling*, Palgrave Studies in Masculinity, Sport and Exercise, https://doi.org/10.1007/978-3-031-26975-2_9

160   J. HARDWICKE

The purpose of this chapter is to examine these influences of gender relations on the development of competitive sport, and specifically road cycling. The aim is to provide an understanding of how a sporting subculture in which orthodox masculinity is idolised may lead to women being marginalised. To do this, a discussion of orthodox masculinity and gender segregation in sport is first offered to provide a theoretical foundation. The remainder of the chapter then reviews the literature on women in competitive cycling and considers the role of the culture of road cycling in producing socio-negative consequences for women.

ORTHODOX MASCULINITY AND WOMEN IN SPORT

Organised, competitive, male team sports have traditionally been theorised as an institution which (re)produces an orthodox form of masculinity that promotes socio-negative (sexist, misogynistic and anti-feminine) attitudes towards women (Bryson, 1987; Burstyn, 1999; Burton-Nelson, 1995; Crosset, 1990; Curry, 1991; Hughes & Coakley, 1991; Messner, 1992, 2002; Muir & Seitz, 2004; Nixon, 1994; Robidoux, 2001; Sabo & Panepinto, 1990; Schacht, 1996; Anderson, 2005). As a result, women's exclusion in sport has a long history (Hargreaves, 2002), where women were structurally excluded from organised sport, creating an environment for behaviours aligning with orthodox masculinity to flourish (Ferez, 2012; Theberge, 1985). Whilst we have seen a decline in sexism in sport (and broader society) (Bryant, 2003), it remains a substantive social problem, particularly in competitive sport (Olgive & McCormack, 2021).

Of interest is that sport is one of the few institutions in which participants continue to be segregated by gender in ways that would be considered unacceptable in other social institutions (Pfister, 2010). Whilst segregation in sport is supported by many women athletes who wish to be distanced from the hypermasculine culture of violence and aggression in many male sporting cultures (Hargreaves, 1994; Smith, 1983), gender segregation can limit gender equity through reinforcing gender differences, reproducing male privilege over women and supporting the gender binary (Fielding-Lloyd & Meân, 2008; McDonagh & Pappano, 2008). Gendered segregation in sport is a lively discussion and of course includes considerations for physiological advantages between sexes being a rationale for segregation. However, it is not in the scope of this book to explore this further here (see Anderson, 2008, Joseph & Anderson, 2015 and

Olgive & McCormack, 2021 for some thought-provoking research on the issue).

Traditional sport can be understood as an institution that can contribute to a homophobic, sexist, and misogynistic gender regime (Anderson, 2008), as well as reproducing orthodox forms of masculinity. Tenets of orthodox masculinity explored in previous chapters included risk-taking, self-sacrifice, willingness to inflict bodily damage, and the acceptance of pain and injury. Of concern here, however, is the marginalisation of others and antipathy towards femininity which is also a feature of orthodox masculinity (Anderson, 2005). Competitive team sports have been argued to play a role in the promotion of anti-feminine, sexist and misogynistic attitudes among male athletes (Anderson, 2008). Indeed, the objectification and sexualising of female athletes by male athletes and sport stakeholders is a persistent issue (Daniels et al., 2020).

Much of the previous research and theorising on the reproduction of orthodox masculinity in competitive sport has been done on traditional men's team-based sports, such as football, basketball and hockey. These are sports Messner (2002) describes as the institutional centre of sports, and Anderson (2009) has described these sports as primary domains for studying shifts in masculinity because they have been theorised to be social locations of men steeped in orthodox understandings of gender. It is argued that male athletes are socialised into a homophobic, sexist, anti-feminine and misogynistic gender regime through the cultures associated with these sports (Anderson, 2008).

However, theorising of more individualised sports and their associated masculine cultures is limited. This is particularly the case with competitive road cycling, with this book offering the first comprehensive discussion of masculinity in competitive road cycling. As McDonald (2014) notes, forms of masculinity must be understood within the context of specific sports. Following this, in Chap. 3, I presented a socio-historical discussion of the development of competitive cycling which can be seen to share many characteristics with traditional team sports that emerged in the industrial era. As such, the early theorising discussed above is relevant to the analysis here, as specific sports reflect the culture from which they emerge (Anderson & White, 2018). Competitive cycling can be considered in similar terms to sports such as football (soccer) and rugby, as they all emerged in the late nineteenth century and exhibit a cultural footprint from this period.

162   J. HARDWICKE

Sports from this era, that are steeped in notions of orthodox masculinity, are also the leading sports that have historically excluded women, continue to marginalise women and have problems with sexism. It is here we see the relationship between orthodox masculinity and the influence this can have on women's experiences in sport. The remainder of this chapter will consider the situation of women's cycling more specifically by first providing a historical overview before discussing the contemporary sport.

HISTORICAL OVERVIEW OF WOMEN IN COMPETITIVE CYCLING

Women have a rich history with competitive cycling that has been largely overlooked in writings on sports history, women's history and specifically bicycle history (Giles, 2018). Whilst it is not in the scope of this book to go into depth here, both Giles (2018) and Kiersnowska (2019) provide excellent detailed accounts of women in competitive cycling. In this section, a brief historical overview is provided to give context to the following discussion on women's experiences in the sport and relations of this to notions of masculinity.

Following the invention of the Rover Safety bicycle, women were riding bikes for leisure, recreation, transport and racing. Whilst accounts of women's racing pre-dates the invention of the safety bicycle, with the earliest documented account of women racing being in 1868 (Simpson, 2007), it was not until the late 1880s and early 1890s women's racing began developing with emphasis (Ryder et al., 2021). Important to note is that women's races did gain traction in this time, and in some cases, women were able to earn more money than male cyclists (Simpson, 2007). However, this initial promising growth was stymied by increasing social barriers such as ridicule and threats, public criticism, concerns over conflicts with Victorian notions of femininity, and concerns for health (Rubinstein, 1977; Vertinsky 1990, Mackintosh & Norcliffe, 2007; McCrone 2014). These were discussed in more depth in Chap. 3, and I detailed how these were wedded to notions of masculinity in the Victorian era.

The culmination of this was a significant institutional barrier in the form of a half century ban of women's racing (Simpson, 2007). Whilst women kept racing in various forms, it was not until 1958 that the Union Cycliste Internationale (UCI), the international governing body of cycling, officially sanctioned a women's world championship (Ryder et al., 2021). It was not until 1984 that a women's road race was introduced to the Olympic Games (Simpson, 2007, p. 51). Furthermore, the women's Tour de France only saw its first edition in 2022. Whilst issues persist, the women's sport is in a much better place in the twenty-first century. There is now an international competition supported by the UCI called the Women's World Tour. This has been in place since 2016 and was created with aims to reach parity with the World Tour for men by increased racing days, increased television coverage and exposure and a larger social media presence (Huyett, 2015).

WOMEN IN CONTEMPORARY COMPETITIVE CYCLING

The gender disparity of participation across cycling contexts has been an ongoing concern in the literature (Heesch et al., 2012; Aldred et al., 2016), particularly in competitive cycling (Ayala et al., 2021). Whilst limited data exists, what is available points towards cycle sports being largely a male dominated sport. For example, only 15% to 17.5% of athletes in officially sanctioned bicycle races were registered in women's fields in Australia, the UK and the US (Australian Human Rights Commission, 2006; British Cycling, 2017; Larson, 2013). Certain disciplines of cycle sports see significantly lower participation rates, for example in ultra-endurance mountain bike races in Europe, women represent approximately 2–4% of the total participants (Gloor et al., 2013).

With limited data on competitive cycling from the UK, USA Cycling reported females only accounted for 15% of licensed competitive cyclists nationally in 2015, which was just a 2% increase since 2009 (USA Cycling, 2015). A similar trend is seen in recreational and leisure cycling in the UK, with data suggesting that 69% of frequent cyclists in Britain are men (British Cycling, 2021). With participation rates considerably low, women in competitive cycling also typically have shorter course lengths and race durations, fewer opportunities to race and significantly smaller prize pools compared to men in the sport (Forrest, 2010; Lucas, 2012; Ryder et al., 2021).

EXPERIENCES OF WOMEN IN ROAD CYCLING

Some of the structural issues within the women's sport have been outlined and this section is concerned with the individual negative experiences of women within the sport and its relationship to masculinity. Important to note is that this does not mean *all* women have negative experiences in the sport. Rather, this section highlights that issues have been reported in the literature and many are related to notions of masculinity.

Firstly, a common theme in the literature focused on women's experiences in competitive cycling is sexism. Indeed, Ryder et al. (2021) suggest that women competitive cyclists are deeply embedded in gendered struggles for rewards and legitimation which has been shaped by sexism which is structured into traditional sports. Competitive road cycling has had a long, and enduring, problem with sexism (Slappendel, 2018). Whilst academic research is limited, issues of financial control, psychological and physical abuse and unfair pay structures have been reported in the cycling community via popular press articles (O'Donnell, 2020; Slappendel, 2018). Dellanebbia (2020) reported women competitive cyclists often felt on the receiving end of patronising and condescending comments largely centred around assumptions about strength, speed and capabilities. Similarly, this experience of casual sexism was reported by Ryder et al. (2021) with a professional women cyclist suggesting:

> I hear a lot of stuff from guys, like: 'oh women's cycling isn't exciting, oh women are slower so it's not as exciting.' It's bullshit, like, haha, it's just something I've heard my whole life because that's what they say…Like men telling me I didn't know what I was doing or trying to tell me how to go faster or trying to tell me how to fix my bike or men commenting on my body shape or how I look in lycra or talking about other female cyclists or using 'riding like a girl' as an insult. (Extract from Ryder et al., 2021)

A similar finding was reported by Ayala et al. (2021) whereby stereotypes around women in cycling were reported to negatively influence women's experiences in the sport. Assumptions around skill level, speed and strength were also reported with participants suggesting that 'riding like a girl' was a common insult used amongst cycling communities. Indeed, my research discussed in Chap. 8 supports this by highlighting that cyclists reported it was fairly common in cycling for men to make jokes about being feminine/girly. Experiences of this type of language have been reported as barriers and deterrents for women participating in competitive cycling (Dixon et al., 2017; Ayala et al., 2021; Ryder et al., 2021).

Another interesting finding from the literature is centred around aggression. Dellanebbia (2020) reported that male competitive cyclists were perceived to display more aggressive behaviours when cycling than women cyclists. This occurred in training and competition settings, and were reported as mostly occurring between men, but also towards women. For example, one participant in the study suggested:

> Men can get really, really, really aggressive... I've seen men punch each other in the middle of a ride (laughs) going 20-something miles per hour, grab each other's jersey, get in a fist fight riding their bike. (Extract from Dellanebbia, 2020)

This is an under-explored area in the academic literature. However, when considered in light of the findings from my own research presented in Chap. 3 it provides some understanding of this through the lens of masculinity. As detailed throughout the book, the sports culture is predicated on notions of orthodox masculinity and research suggests male cyclists appear to identify with a stricter notion of masculinity than the general population (Powell et al., 2005; Hardwicke, 2022). A feature of orthodox masculinity is hyper-aggression (Anderson, 2009), and this may in part explain findings from the above studies on women's experiences in road cycling where a culture exists in which orthodox masculinity is idolised.

Another reported issue is that of harassment and feelings of an unsafe environment. Indeed, women cycling in the nineteenth and early twentieth century were regularly victims of harassment and physical abuse in public due to the perceived cultural aversion to women cycling at the time (Rubinstein, 1977). Unfortunately, this is not only an historical issue. Ayala et al. (2021) reported that women competitive cyclists highlighted feelings of being threatened, receiving verbal threats and being physically and sexually harassed or assaulted. More academic research is required in this area, which can be problematic due to sensitivities around the nature of harassment, particularly of a sexual nature. Furthermore, Anderson and White (2018) suggest sexual harassment and/or assault may be under-reported because of athletes fears over complaints not being taken seriously, or that doing so may hinder their careers.

166   J. HARDWICKE

However, reports in the popular press suggest there are persistent issues in cycling. Sports journalist, Chennaoui, reported on an anonymous report of sexual abuse from a top women professional cyclist as well as others that have come forward as a result (Rouler, 2021). The report, titled 'Cycling's #metoo movement', details explicit experiences of female cyclists being sexually harassed by male staff on the team and highlights the problem as a 'hidden' problem in the sport in which the prevalence and scale is not fully known, but is concerning. Further, a report by the Dutch Cycling Federation in 2018 suggested that more than a quarter of top female Dutch riders reported feeling unsafe in the sport, and 13% said they had been on the receiving end of inappropriate sexual behaviour, including 'touching' and comments (Cycling News, 2017). Whilst this is of course deeply concerning, such findings must be interpreted tentatively as the methodology and sample size are not clearly detailed, nor is the report publicly available. British Cycling has also been under scrutiny for issues regarding sexism, with one prominent event in recent times being Shane Sutton's resignation from his position as the British Cycling technical director after allegations of sexism and discrimination towards women (Cycling News, 2016).

The above discussion highlights that while academic evidence is sparse, there appears to be persistent issues within women's competitive cycling leading to an argument that women have historically been marginalised in the sport and largely remain so, despite advances being made (Ryder et al., 2021). A large proportion of this phenomenon can be understood through the lens of masculinity, and hegemony of orthodox masculinity in many sporting cultures. In the following section, I will discuss this in more detail and provide some theoretical frameworks for making sense of the findings reported of negative experiences of women in competitive cycling.

Negotiating an Orthodox Masculine Culture

With the preceding discussion, it can be seen that women's sport has been trivialised and marginalised by a sexist culture for decades (Coakley & Donnelly, 1999), and cycling has not escaped this. Whilst advances have been made through legislation, such as Title IX, the advocacy work of the Women's Sports Foundation and the increasingly inclusive culture we now live in, issues persist for women in sport and they are still subject to multiple types of abuse, much of which is by men (and mostly by male coaches) (Anderson & White, 2018). Much of this has been as a result of organised and competitive sports being an institution where an orthodox form of masculinity that promotes socio-negative (sexist, misogynistic and anti-feminine) attitudes towards women has thrived (Hughes & Coakley, 1991; Anderson, 2005).

This chapter has discussed these matters in the context of the sport of competitive road cycling. Current research suggests the sport continues to have issues with sexism entrenched in the sport, and that women are marginalised within road cycling. I outlined research that reported on the experiences of women with some key themes of sexism, harassment and witnessing aggression being highlighted. With these in mind, the discussion so far throughout this book on the tenets of orthodox masculinity and the presence, and idolisation, of this archetype within road cycling culture provides some explanation to why such behaviours and experiences are seen within the sport.

With the argument put forward in Chap. 5, competitive road cycling can be understood as a sport with a strong subculture which is present across all levels of the sport. Many facets of this subculture have been predicated on, and shaped by, notions of orthodox masculinity. As such, if an individual finds themselves in this culture and they do not align with it (e.g. women) then they may face marginalisation through the various means highlighted above. This is also compounded by institutional problems in the sport in that men still disproportionately occupy the positions of power across the sport, for example sitting on the boards of governing bodies and in coaching and managerial roles. Taken together, women competitive cyclists can be in a position in which they must negotiate an orthodox masculine culture and may suffer marginalisation due to the anti-feminine notions associated with orthodox masculinities.

Limitations and Considerations

As highlighted throughout this chapter, much more research is needed in this area. The discussion and arguments I have put forward have been grounded in the available data, but this is working from a very limited pool of empirical data. As women's competitive cycling continues to grow and develop, hopefully academic interest will do so in tandem. Important here, is that discussions of women's cycling culture is limited and how this may diverge from traditional competitive cycling culture which is deeply tied to masculinity, thus impacting both men and women. As women's cycling grows, as well as younger generations coming through that have grown up in an era of inclusivity, the dominant structuring of traditional competitive cycling may be increasingly met with resistance and begin to be reshaped and restructured.

Furthermore, as highlighted with the participation data presented in this chapter, the lower levels of women competitive cyclists lead to a situation in which women are often a minority amongst men when joining in on group training rides or even in competitive settings. Indeed, the research on women's experiences in cycling (Dellanebbia, 2020; Ayala et al., 2021; Ryder et al. 2021) largely reports on women's experiences with male cyclists, likely due to these cyclists being a minority in their respective geographic locations and thus being in closer contact with male cyclists. This may change if the sport exponentially grows, with more women-only clubs, training rides and races. The theoretical and empirical arguments made throughout this book will hopefully act as a point of departure for future research into the sport where women competitive cyclists' experiences and views on masculinity in the sport are explored, a gap in the current literature.

CHAPTER SUMMARY

This chapter has turned the focus away from male cyclists and onto the experiences of women, whilst keeping the lens of masculinity as the analytical framework. The key problem put forward in this chapter is that issues remain in the sport regarding women's experiences. I have suggested that a large proportion of this can be understood through the culture of competitive cycling being predicated on notions of orthodox masculinity and understanding the historical development of the sport shines further light on the issue. However, there is hope and signs that things are improving which aligns with the increasingly liberal and inclusive culture within the West. With that said, more research into the area is needed and specifically the relationship between masculinity, women and cycling needs further exploration, and indeed, cycling femininities and women's identities in the sport. Following the trend of what the future of the sport may look like, and if the culture being predicated on orthodox masculinity will change, the following concluding chapter picks up this discussion offering directions for the future and a summary of the arguments made throughout the book.

REFERENCES

Aldred, R., Woodcock, J., & Goodman, A. (2016). Does more cycling mean more diversity in cycling? *Transport Reviews, 36*(1), 28–44.

Anderson, E. (2005). Orthodox and inclusive masculinity: Competing masculinities among heterosexual men in a feminized terrain. *Sociological Perspectives, 48*(3), 337–355.

Anderson, E. (2008). Inclusive masculinity in a fraternal setting. *Men and Masculinities, 10*(5), 604–620.

Anderson, E. (2009). *Inclusive Masculinity: The Changing Nature of Masculinities* (Routledge Research in Gender and Society) (1st ed.). Routledge.

Anderson, E., & White, A. (2018). *Sport, theory and social problems.* Routledge Taylor & Francis Group.

Australian Human Rights Commission. (2006). *What's the score? A survey of cultural diversity and racism in Australian sport.* Retrieved from https://www.humanrights.gov.au/sites/default/files/content/racial_discrimination/whats_the_score/pdf/cycling.pdf

Ayala, E. E., Riley-Schmida, A., Faulkner, K. P., & Maleski, K. (2021). Microaggressions experienced by women and gender diverse athletes in competitive cycling. *Women in Sport and Physical Activity Journal, 29*(1), 59–67.

British Cycling. (2017). *British Cycling 2017: A year in review.* Retrieved December 2, 2019, from http://www.ourstory.britishcycling.org.uk/

British Cycling. (2021). *British cycling backs diversity in cycling report.* https://www.britishcycling.org.uk/road/article/20190617-Home-Page-Why-we-re-supporting-the-Diversity-in-Cycling-report-0

Bryant, A. N. (2003). Changes in attitudes toward women's roles. *Sex Roles, 48*(3–4), 131–142.

Bryson, L. (1987, January). Sport and the maintenance of masculine hegemony. In *Women's studies international forum* (Vol. 10, No. 4, pp. 349–360). Pergamon.

Burstyn, V. (1999). *The rites of men: Manhood, politics and the culture of sport.* University of Toronto Press.

Burton-Nelson, M. (1995). *The Stronger Women Get, the More Men Love Football: Sexism and the American Culture of Sports.* Perfect Bound.

Coakley, J. J., & Donnelly, P. (Eds.). (1999). *Inside sports.* Routledge.

Crosset, T. (1990). Masculinity, sexuality, and the development of early modern sport. In *Sport, men and the gender order: Critical feminist perspectives* (pp. 45–54). Human Kinetics.

Curry, T. J. (1991). Fraternal bonding in the locker room: A profeminist analysis of talk about competition and women. *Sociology of Sport Journal, 8*(2), 119–135.

Cycling News. (2016, April 27). *Shane Sutton resigns amid sexism and discrimination claims.* cyclingnews.com. https://www.cyclingnews.com/news/shane-sutton-resigns-amid-sexism-and-discrimination-claims/

Cycling News. (2017, December 12). Philippa York: Cycling's conservative culture suppresses LGBT issues. Cyclingnews.Com. https://www.cyclingnews.com/news/philippa-york-cyclings-conservative-culture-suppresses-lgbt-issues/

Daniels, E. A., Hood, A., LaVoi, N. M., & Cooky, C. (2020). Sexualized and athletic: Viewers' attitudes toward sexualized performance images of female athletes. *Sex Roles, 84*, 112–124.

Dellanebbia, A. M. (2020). *The experiences of women competitive road cyclists: A qualitative study* (Doctoral dissertation, Texas Woman's University).

Dixon, M. A., Graham, J. A., Hartzell, A. C., & Forrest, K. (2017). Enhancing women's participation and advancement in competitive cycling. *Journal of Applied Sport Management, 9*(4), 6.

Dunning, E. (1986). Sport as a male preserve: Notes on the social sources of masculine identity and its transformations. *Theory, Culture & Society, 3*(1), 79–90.

Ferez, S. (2012). From women's exclusion to gender institution: A brief history of the sexual categorisation process within sport. *The International Journal of the History of Sport, 29*(2), 272–285.

Fielding-Lloyd, B., & Meân, L. J. (2008). Standards and separatism: The discursive construction of gender in English soccer coach education. *Sex Roles, 58*(1–2), 24–39.

Forrest, K. E. (2010). *Gender disparities in competitive cycling: An analysis of the structural, socio-cultural, and individual factors affecting female participation in Texas* (doctoral dissertation).

Giles, R. (2018). *Women on the move: The forgotten era of Women's bicycle racing.* Nebraska University Press.

Gloor, R. U., Knechtle, B., Knechtle, P., Rust, C. A., Haupt, S., Rosemann, T., & Lepers, R. (2013). Sex-related trends in participation and performance in the 'Swiss bike masters' from 1994–2012. *Perceptual and Motor Skills, 116*(2), 640–654. https://doi.org/10.2466/30.pms.116.2.640-654

Hardwicke, J. (2022). Inside the peloton: An exploration into the culture of competitive road cycling with reference to masculinity, risk and injury, with a principle focus on concussion (Doctoral dissertation, University of Winchester)

Hargreaves, J. (1994). *Sporting females: Critical issues in the history and sociology of Women's sport.* Routledge.

Hargreaves, J. (2002). *Sporting females: Critical issues in the history and sociology of women's sport.* Routledge.

Hargreaves, J., & Anderson, E. (Eds.). (2014). *Routledge handbook of sport, gender and sexuality.* Routledge.

Heesch, K. C., Sahlqvist, S., & Garrard, J. (2012). Gender differences in recreational and transport cycling: A cross-sectional mixed-methods comparison of cycling patterns, motivators, and constraints. *International Journal of Behavioral Nutrition and Physical Activity, 9*(1), 1–12.

Hughes, R., & Coakley, J. (1991). Positive deviance among athletes: The implications of overconformity to the sport ethic. *Sociology of Sport Journal, 8*(4), 307–325.

Huyett, E. (2015, August 14). UCI women get upgraded to WorldTour status for 2016.https://www.bicycling.com/racing/a20043057/uci-women-get-upgraded-to-worldtour- status-for-2016/.

Joseph, L. J., & Anderson, E. (2015). The influence of gender segregation and teamsport experience on occupational discrimination in sportbased employment. *Journal of Gender Studies, 25*(5), 586–598.

Kiersnowska, B. (2019). Female cycling and the discourse of moral panic in late Victorian Britain. *Atlantis, 41*(2), 85–104.

Larson, D. (2013). 2013 membership survey and analysis: Prepared for USA Cycling, Inc. Retrieved from https://s3.amazonaws.com/USACWeb/forms/encyc/2013-USAC-Membership-Surv ey-Report.pdf

Lucas, S. (2012). Women's cycle racing: Enduring meanings. *Journal of Sport History, 39*(2), 227–242.

Mackintosh, P. G., & Norcliffe, G. (2007). Gender and social geography of Cycling in the late nineteenth-century. In *Cycling and society* (p. 153). Ashgate.

Mansfield, L., Caudwell, J., Wheaton, B., & Watson, B. (Eds.). (2017). *The Palgrave handbook of feminism and sport, leisure and physical education.* Palgrave Macmillan UK.

Matthews, C. R., & Channon, A. (2019). The 'male preserve' thesis, sporting culture, and men's power. In *Routledge international handbook of masculinity studies* (pp. 373–383). Routledge.

McCrone, K. (2014). Individual sports: Lawn tennis, golf and Cycling. In *Sport and the physical emancipation of English women (RLE sports studies)* (pp. 184–221). Routledge.

McDonagh, E., & Pappano, L. (2008). *Playing with the boys: Why separate is not equal in sports.* Oxford University Press.

McDonald, I. (2014). Portraying Sporting masculinity through film: Reflections on Jorgen Leth's A Sunday in hell. In *Routledge handbook of sport, gender and sexuality* (pp. 480–487). Routledge.

Messner, M. A. (1992). Like family: Power, intimacy, and sexuality in male athletes' friendships. In P. M. Nardi (Ed.), *Men's friendships* (pp. 215–237). Sage Publications. https://doi.org/10.4135/9781483325736.n12

Messner, M. A. (2002). *Taking the field: Women, men, and sports* (Vol. 4). U of Minnesota Press.

Messner, M. A., & Sabo, D. F. (1990). *Sport, men, and the gender order: Critical feminist perspectives* (Vol. 10). Human Kinetics.

Muir, K. B., & Seitz, T. (2004). Machismo, misogyny, and homophobia in a male athletic subculture: A participant-observation study of deviant rituals in collegiate rugby. *Deviant Behavior, 25*(4), 303–327.

Nixon, H. L. (1994). Social pressure, social support, and help seeking for pain and injuries in college sports networks. *Journal of Sport and Social Issues, 18*(4), 340–355. https://doi.org/10.1177/019372394018004004

O'Donnell, B. (2020, December 28). *Abuse of power in women's cycling, an all too familiar story: Bridie O'Donnell.* CyclingTips. https://cyclingtips. com/2017/02/abuse-of-power-in-womens-cycling-an-all-too-familiar-story-bridie-odonnell/

Ogilvie, M. F., & McCormack, M. (2021). Gender-collaborative training in elite university sport: Challenging gender essentialism through integrated training in gender-segregated sports. *International Review for the Sociology of Sport, 56*(8), 1172–1188.

Pfister, G. (2010). Women in sport – Gender relations and future perspectives. *Sport in Society, 13*(2), 234–248.

Powell, D., Stiles, B., Haff, G., & Kilgore, L. (2005). The notion of masculinity in male collegiate road cyclists. *Creative Sociology, 33*(2), 153. https://ojs. library.okstate.edu/osu/index.php/FICS/article/view/1558

Pronger, B. (1990). *The arena of masculinity: Sports, homosexuality, and the meaning of sex.* Macmillan.

Robidoux, M. A. (2001). *Men at play: A working understanding of professional hockey.* McGill-Queen's Press-MQUP.

Rouler. (2021). *Cycling's #MeToo moment.* Rouleur. https://www.rouleur.cc/ blogs/the-rouleur-journal/cycling-s-metoo-moment-part-one

Rubinstein, D. (1977). Cycling in the 1890s. *Victorian Studies, 21*(1), 47–71.

Ryder, S., McLachlan, F., & McDonald, B. (2021). Riding in a Man's world: Gendered struggles in professional Women's Road Cycling. In *The Professionalisation of Women's Sport.* Emerald Publishing Limited.

Sabo, D., & Panepinto, J. (1990). Football ritual and the social reproduction of masculinity. In *Sport, men, and the gender order: Critical feminist perspectives* (pp. 115–126). Human Kinetics.

Schacht, S. P. (1996). Misogyny on and off the "pitch" the gendered world of male rugby players. *Gender & Society, 10*(5), 550–565.

Simpson, C. S. (2007). Capitalising on curiosity: women's professional cycle racing in the late-nineteenth century. In *Cycling and society* (pp. 47–65). Ashgate Publishing.

Slappendel, J. (2018, May 12). Op-Ed: The institutional sexism in cycling needs to end. Outside Online. https://www.outsideonline.com/culture/opinion/ op-ed-institutional-sexism-cycling-needs-end/.

Smith, M. (1983). *Violence in sport.* Butterworths.

Taylor, T., Fujak, H., Hanlon, C., & O'Connor, D. (2022). A balancing act: Women players in a new semi-professional team sport league. *European Sport Management Quarterly, 22*(4), 527–547.

Theberge, N. (1985). Toward a feminist alternative to sport as a male preserve. *Quest, 37*(2), 193–202.

USA Cycling. (2015, December 16). *Diversity, equity, & inclusion.* USA Cycling. https://usacycling.org/diversity-equity-inclusion

Vertinsky, P. A. (1990). *The eternally wounded woman: Women, doctors, and exercise in the late nineteenth century.* Manchester University Press.

CHAPTER 10

Crossing the Finish Line: Conclusions

This chapter brings the book to its finish line. A summary of the book's content is provided to remind the reader of what has been explored and argued throughout this work. I then offer a short consideration for the future of the sport and directions for future cycling research before a concise conclusion is presented.

BOOK SUMMARY

Throughout this book I have argued, and provided evidence, that the culture of competitive road cycling has been shaped by influences of masculinity during its development in the nineteenth century, and that the contemporary sports subculture is largely predicated on tenets of orthodox masculinity. Therefore, prominent features of orthodox masculinity remain valued amongst competitive male road cyclists and within road cycling culture. This becomes a 'problem' when considered through the examples used in this book such as risk-taking, injury management, doping practices and the exclusion of 'others' (sexual minorities and women). Previous authors have described road cycling masculinity as prioritising competition, risk, winning, speed and physicality (Barrie et al., 2019, p. 116). The aim of this book is to have picked this apart and provide a comprehensive insight to how the culture of the sport has been shaped to value and reproduce this notion of masculinity.

© The Author(s), under exclusive license to Springer Nature   173
Switzerland AG 2023
J. Hardwicke, *Masculinities and the Culture of Competitive Cycling*,
Palgrave Studies in Masculinity, Sport and Exercise,
https://doi.org/10.1007/978-3-031-26975-2_10

To achieve this aim, Chap. 2 first laid the theoretical foundations for the book by highlighting the scholarship on men and masculinities and situating this work within the theoretical framework of Inclusive Masculinity Theory. It was discussed that, across contemporary Western societies, masculinities are changing towards more inclusive forms, and this is increasingly the case in sporting settings also. However, all sports do not reflect this social change in even rates, and it was highlighted that the construction of masculinities differs across different sports, with each sport having to be understood in its specific context (McDonald, 2014). I went on to present Williams' (1977) theorising of cultural change and Ogburn's (1957) concept of cultural lag as frameworks to account for sporting subcultures that appear to deviate from the dominant culture in relation to the forms of masculinity valued.

In order to understand the specific context of cycling masculinities, I first presented a historical analysis due to the sociological emphasis that we must understand the past to understand the present. As such, Chap. 3 presented a detailed discussion of the early roots of competitive road cycling's development within Victorian Britain and across Western societies. Here, the development of the sport was mapped onto the broader social and cultural changes that were occurring at the time, and road cycling was identified as a sport that emerged in this area and thus shares the industrial footprint of other popular, highly gendered, sports such as rugby and football. The chapter put forward the argument that the early culture of cycling was shaped by notions of orthodox masculinity, and the behaviours and practices of cyclists in this era reflected this.

With the historical influence that gender relations had on the development of the sport explained, Chap. 4 progressed on to discuss contemporary road cycling. The sports development through the twentieth century and into the twenty-first century was presented through the lens of masculinity. It was highlighted that the gendered nature of the sport continued, and masculinity has had an enduring influence on the contemporary sport, which is regularly described as having a macho, hyper-masculine culture. In support of this notion, empirical data was presented showing competitive male cyclists to more closely identify with orthodox scriptures of masculinity compared to the general population.

Chapter 5 then combined the lens of masculinity with a subcultural analysis to explore the culture of competitive road cycling. It was highlighted that the subculture of road cycling has a cult-like environment with numerous cultural practices, nuances and unwritten rules that new

10 CROSSING THE FINISH LINE: CONCLUSIONS 175

members must learn and adhere to in order to gain membership. The notion of risk was presented, with an empirically informed thesis put forward that road cycling operates within a 'culture of risk'. Furthermore, the literature on 'serious leisure' sports was discussed with the argument put forward that road cycling should be considered in these terms, with the activity forming a significant part of participants' identity. Taken together, the overarching argument of the chapter was that the strong subculture of the sport must be studied and understood as it can explain the individual behaviours of cyclists, which set the scene of the following chapters.

With the theoretical and empirical grounding presented, Chaps. 6 and 7 applied this with a health focus. First, the injury management practices of competitive male cyclists were discussed in Chap. 6. The highly injurious nature of the sport was highlighted, and the lens of masculinity was used to explain empirical research findings that competitive road cyclists often chose to compete when injured and will under-report injury to remain competitive. Expanding on this, Chap. 7 explored doping practices through the notion of the 'winning at all costs' attitude within the sport, and this was also contextualised within the framework of masculinity and the culture of the sport. Taken together, the two chapters suggest that the culture of the sport reflects central tenets of orthodox masculinity, as well as Hughes and Coakley's (1991) notion of the 'sport ethic', whereby performance is prioritised over health.

Finally, Chaps. 8 and 9 moved away from a health focus and discussed the experiences of sexual minorities and women within competitive road cycling. Both of these groups have historically been considered 'others' and marginalised in relation to men and orthodox masculinity. With the subculture of the sport being shaped around orthodox masculinity, Chap. 8 discussed how this may influence the experiences of sexual minorities in the sport. Anecdotal reports of homophobia in the sport were highlighted and empirical research presented which suggested mostly positive experiences of sexual minorities in cycling (broadly, not just competitive cycling) and mostly positive attitudes amongst straight-identifying cyclists. It was suggested that individual attitudes may not be an issue, but rather the culture of the sport and institutional support which can marginalise sexual minorities. Chapter 9 continued this discussion by examining the experiences of women in the sport. This was explored on both an individual and an institutional level, with the problem of sexism within the sport highlighted. Importantly, both these areas were highlighted as areas in need of more research.

Future Directions for Cycling and Research

As contemporary Western society continues to transition towards inclusivity, and boys and men growing up in this zeitgeist continue to redefine and diversify their notions of masculinity from that of previous generations, the culture of road cycling may be challenged, resisted and/or reshaped. One key area associated with the softening of masculinities in the twenty-first century is a move away from a disregard for health, particularly in sport settings. As younger generations continue to move through the 'ranks' in competitive road cycling, the stubborn attitudes around injury and risk-taking may begin to be met with more resistance. An example of this comes from one of my younger research participants, a 19-year-old elite competitive cyclist. They can be quoted saying:

> Personally, I think nine times out of ten it's ridiculous to try and race after a crash. Chiefly because of the risk of concussion and its effects. I think cyclists can sometimes be a bit stupid and narrow minded around injury, all they want to do is race and they think that racing is more important than their wellbeing and not even thinking about long term potential damage.

Over the coming years, the 'old school' attitudes and traditions within competitive road cycling culture, particularly those related to injury management, may become what Williams (1977) has termed 'archaic' cultural facets that become extinct and lose value within this social context. However, as discussed throughout this book, many aspects of the sports culture remain entrenched in orthodox masculinity and there is not enough socio-cultural research into the sport to track any trends or changes here. This is particularly the case for understanding the experiences of women and sexual minorities, where much more research is required.

An alternative possibility is that participation rates within road cycling will drop if the sport does not adapt to align with the contemporary culture of inclusivity. New forms of cycling practices which are not so tied to a strong subculture predicated on tenets of orthodox masculinity may gain greater popularity. The example of gravel cycling highlights this hypothetical scenario. Gravel cycling is an ultra-endurance cycling discipline which is seeing a rapid increase in popularity over recent years (Mueller et al., 2019). One of the appeals of this new discipline is its inclusive culture that is distinctly different from road cycling. For example, it has been suggested that 'Road racing is old, storied, rigid, precise. Gravel racing is young, burgeoning, lax, loose' (Trek, 2022). As this sport develops, future academic research into the socio-cultural aspects of this emerging cycling practice will be interesting.

Furthermore, the emerging sport has been highlighted for its emphasis on diversity and inclusion (Price, 2022) and athletes of all gender categories race together on the same course (Opel & Rook, 2022). Much of the development of gravel cycling has been based on a divergence from the traditional culture associated with road cycling. As such, the developing culture around gravel cycling is distinctly different from the road cycling culture described throughout this book and it does not have such strict 'unwritten rules' new members must learn and abide by.

Within the critical sport literature, very little has been written on the socio-cultural aspects of competitive road cycling (Falcous, 2017; Hardwicke, 2022). This book offers the first comprehensive insight into the culture of competitive road cycling, and the use of masculinity as an analytical framework to investigate a range of areas within the sport. That being said, much more research is required to understand the cultural dimensions of cycling for sport. From working on this book, some key points of departure for future research may be:

- Women's experience in competitive road cycling
- The relationship between women and masculinity in competitive cycling
- Experiences of gender diverse and sexual minorities in cycling
- Injury and risk-taking in competitive road cycling using qualitative methodologies
- Socio-cultural research across the various disciplines within competitive cycling

CONCLUSION

Competitive sport, historically, acted as an institution that defined a conservative and orthodox form of gendered and sexual male that was idolised by society. But, as we have seen significant shifts in Western society, the performance of masculinity has changed in sport also (Anderson, 2009). However, sport should not be viewed as homogenous and the masculinities in subcultures across different sports must be contextually considered on their own terms. The evidence presented throughout this book has discussed competitive road cycling within this cultural nexus.

I have argued that the culture of the sport has been deeply shaped by influences of masculinity and that the contemporary sports subculture is largely predicated on tenets of orthodox masculinity. Furthermore, the social identities of competitive road cyclists are strongly influenced by their participation within the sport and an adherence to the culture. This is important to consider in the ways it can manifest in the behaviours of competitive cyclists, such as increased risk-taking, injury management and other health-compromising behaviours, as well as exclusive attitudes towards those that may deviate from orthodox masculinity.

Therefore, prominent features of orthodox masculinity remain valued amongst competitive male road cyclists and road cycling culture can be considered as a 'host' for residual cultural practices (Williams, 1977), which presents a cultural lag (Ogburn, 1957) behind broader society. Furthermore, this book extends the thesis of other socio-cultural research on road cycling that it is a sport with a strong subculture that can be hard to access for 'outsiders' (Williams, 1989; Albert, 1999; Rees et al. 2014; Hardwicke, 2022). I have explored the historical development of this culture, and the social factors that have contributed to the contemporary situation. This raises issues of inclusive participation in the sport and whether there are differing levels of access across groups in society which warrants further research.

As the sport continues to develop, there is hope that this culture will begin to be resisted and reshaped to better align with contemporary society. As the sport moves away from such a valuing of orthodox masculinity, we would expect to see road cyclists (of all levels) more readily withdraw themselves from races after crashing, prioritise health over performance, develop healthier habits in their athletic pursuits and not be so influenced by hyper-competition and a 'win at all costs' attitude. Furthermore, the sport may become more welcoming to a wider range of people and the stubborn trend of road cycling being a white male sport may begin to erode. Alternatively, the rise of new forms of cycling, such as gravel racing discussed above, may continue to grow in popularity and traditional road cycling and its strong subculture may reduce in cultural relevance to amateur participants—time will tell.

REFERENCES

Albert, E. (1999). Dealing with danger: The normalization of risk in cycling. *International Review for the Sociology of Sport, 34*(2), 157–171.

Anderson, E. (2009). *Inclusive Masculinity: The Changing Nature of Masculinities* (Routledge Research in Gender and Society) (1st ed.). Routledge.

Barrie, L., Waitt, G., & Brennan-Horley, C. (2019). Cycling assemblages, self-tracking digital technologies and negotiating gendered subjectivities of road cyclists on-the-move. *Leisure Sciences, 41*(1–2), 108–126.

Falcous, M. (2017). Why we ride: Road cyclists, meaning, and lifestyles. *Journal of Sport and Social Issues, 41*(3), 239–255.

Hardwicke, J. (2022). Inside the peloton: An exploration into the culture of competitive road cycling with reference to masculinity, risk and injury, with a principle focus on concussion (Doctoral dissertation, University of Winchester).

Hughes, R., & Coakley, J. (1991). Positive deviance among athletes: The implications of overconformity to the sport ethic. *Sociology of Sport Journal, 8*(4), 307–325.

McDonald, I. (2014). Portraying Sporting masculinity through film: Reflections on Jorgen Leth's A Sunday in hell. In *Routledge handbook of sport, gender and sexuality* (pp. 480–487). Routledge.

Mueller, J. T., Landon, A. C., & Graefe, A. R. (2019). Modeling the role of social identity in constraint negotiation for ultra-endurance gravel cycling. *Journal of Leisure Research, 50*(2), 81–106.

Ogburn, W. F. (1957). *Cultural lag as theory.* Sociology & Social Research.

Opel, M., & Rook, A. (2022, June 17). *Bike racing's newest frontier: As gravel racing defines itself, these riders are leading the charge.* cyclingweekly.com. https://www.cyclingweekly.com/racing/bike-racings-newest-frontier-as-gravel-racing-defines-itself-these-riders-are-leading-the-charge

Price, J. (2022, August 16). *Focusing on diversity and inclusion, gravel bike racing welcomes all to this sport.* NPR.org. https://www.npr.org/2022/08/16/1117440946/gravel-bike-racing-welcomes-everyone-to-fast-growing-sport

Rees, A., Gibbons, T., & Dixon, K. (2014). The surveillance of racing cyclists in training: A bourdieusian perspective. *Surveillance & Society, 11*(4), 466–480.

Trek. (2022). *The beginners guide to racing gravel.* Retrieved form https://blog.trekbikes.com/en_UK/2022/03/20/the-beginners-guide-to-racing-gravel/

Williams, R. (1977). *Marxism and literature* (Vol. 392). Oxford Paperbacks.

Williams, T. (1989). Sport, hegemony and subcultural reproduction: The process of accommodation in bicycle road racing. *International Review for the Sociology of Sport, 24*(4), 315–333.

REFERENCES

Aboim, S. (2016). *Plural masculinities: The remaking of the self in private life.* Routledge.

Abramson, C. M., & Modzelewski, D. (2011). Caged morality: Moral worlds, subculture, and stratification among middle-class cage-fighters. *Qualitative Sociology, 34*(1), 143–175.

Adams, A. (2011). "Josh wears pink cleats": Inclusive masculinity on the soccer field. *Journal of Homosexuality, 58*(5), 579–596.

Adams, A., & Kavanagh, E. (2018). Inclusive ideologies and passive performances: Exploring masculinities and attitudes toward gay peers among boys in an elite youth football academy. *Journal of Gender Studies, 27*(3), 313–322.

Adams, A., Anderson, E., & McCormack, M. (2010). Establishing and challenging masculinity: The influence of gendered discourses in organized sport. *Journal of Language and Social Psychology, 29*(3), 278–300.

Albert, E. (1984). Equipment as a feature of social control in the sport of bicycle racing. *Sport and the Sociological Imagination,* 318–338.

Albert, E. (1990). Constructing the order of finish in the sport of bicycle racing. *Journal of Popular Culture, 23*(4), 145–154.

Albert, E. (1991). Riding a line: Competition and cooperation in the sport of bicycle racing. *Sociology of Sport Journal, 8*(4), 341–361.

Albert, E. (1997). Bicycle racing and the social construction of place. In P. De Nardis, A. Mussino, & N. Porro (Eds.), *Sport: Social problems, social movements.* Edizioni Seam.

Albert, E. (1999). Dealing with danger: The normalization of risk in cycling. *International Review for the Sociology of Sport, 34*(2), 157–171.

© The Author(s), under exclusive license to Springer Nature Switzerland AG 2023
J. Hardwicke, *Masculinities and the Culture of Competitive Cycling,* Palgrave Studies in Masculinity, Sport and Exercise, https://doi.org/10.1007/978-3-031-26975-2

182 REFERENCES

Aldred, R., Woodcock, J., & Goodman, A. (2016). Does more cycling mean more diversity in cycling? *Transport Reviews, 36*(1), 28–44.

Anderson, E. (2000). *Trailblazing: America's first openly gay track coach.*

Anderson, E. (2002). Openly gay athletes: Contesting hegemonic masculinity in a homophobic environment. *Gender & Society, 16*(6), 860–877.

Anderson, E. (2005a). *In the game: Gay athletes and the cult of masculinity.* SUNY Press.

Anderson, E. (2005b). Orthodox and inclusive masculinity: Competing masculinities among heterosexual men in a feminized terrain. *Sociological Perspectives, 48*(3), 337–355.

Anderson, E. (2008a). 'I used to think women were weak': Orthodox masculinity, gender segregation, and sport. *Sociological Forum, 23*(2), 257–280.

Anderson, E. (2008b). Inclusive masculinity in a fraternal setting. *Men and Masculinities, 10*(5), 604–620.

Anderson, E. (2009a). *Inclusive masculinity: The changing nature of masculinities (Routledge research in gender and society)* (1st ed.). Routledge.

Anderson, E. D. (2009b). The maintenance of masculinity among the stakeholders of sport. *Sport Management Review, 12*(1), 3–14.

Anderson, E. (2011). Masculinities and sexualities in sport and physical cultures: Three decades of evolving research. *Journal of Homosexuality, 58*(5), 565–578.

Anderson, E. (2014). *21st century jocks: Sporting men and contemporary heterosexuality.* Palgrave Macmillan.

Anderson, E., Adams, A., & Rivers, I. (2012). "I kiss them because I love them": The emergence of heterosexual men kissing in British institutes of education. *Archives of Sexual Behavior, 41*(2), 421–430.

Anderson, E., & Fidler, C. O. (2018). Elderly British men: Homohysteria and orthodox masculinities. *Journal of Gender Studies, 27*(3), 248–259. https://doi.org/10.1080/09589236.2017.1391690

Anderson, E., & Magrath, R. (2019). *Men and masculinities* (1st ed.). Routledge.

Anderson, E., Magrath, R., & Bullingham, R. (2016). *Out in sport* (1st ed.). Routledge.

Anderson, E., & McCormack, M. (2015). Cuddling and spooning: Heteromasculinity and homosocial tactility among student-athletes. *Men and Masculinities, 18*(2), 214–230. https://doi.org/10.1177/1097184X14523433

Anderson, E., & McCormack, M. (2018). Inclusive masculinity theory: Overview, reflection and refinement. *Journal of Gender Studies, 27*(5), 547–561.

Anderson, E., McCormack, M., & Lee, H. (2012). Male team sport hazing initiations in a culture of decreasing Homohysteria. *Journal of Adolescent Research, 27*, 427–448.

Anderson, E., & McGuire, R. (2010). Inclusive masculinity theory and the gendered politics of men's rugby. *Journal of Gender Studies, 19*(3), 249–261.

REFERENCES   **183**

Anderson, E., Ripley, M., & McCormack, M. (2019). A mixed-method study of same-sex kissing among college-attending heterosexual men in the US. *Sexuality & Culture, 23*(1), 26–44.

Anderson, E., & White, A. (2018). *Sport, theory and social problems.* Routledge Taylor & Francis Group.

Andreasson, J. (2015). Reconceptualising the gender of fitness doping: Performing and negotiating masculinity through drug-use practices. *Social Sciences, 4*(3), 546–562. MDPI AG. Retrieved from https://doi.org/10.3390/socsci4030546

Arxer, S. L. (2011). Hybrid masculine power: Reconceptualizing the relationship between homosociality and hegemonic masculinity. *Humanity and Society, 35*(4), 390–422.

Atencio, M., Beal, B., & Wilson, C. (2009). The distinction of risk: Urban skateboarding, street habitus and the construction of hierarchical gender relations. *Qualitative Research in Sport and Exercise, 1*(1), 3–20. https://doi.org/10.1080/19398440802567907

Atkinson, M. (2008). Triathlon, suffering and exciting significance. *Leisure Studies, 27*(2), 165–180. https://doi.org/10.1080/02614360801902216

Atkinson, M. (2010). *Deconstructing men & masculinities (themes in Canadian sociology).* Oxford University Press.

Atkinson, M., & Young, K. (2008). *Deviance and social control in sport.* Human Kinetics.

Australian Human Rights Commission. (2006). *What's the score? A survey of cultural diversity and racism in Australian sport.* Retrieved from https://www.humanrights.gov.au/sites/default/files/content/racial_discrimination/whats_the_score/pdf/cycling.pdf

Ayala, E. E., Riley-Schmida, A., Faulkner, K. P., & Maleski, K. (2021). Microaggressions experienced by women and gender diverse athletes in competitive cycling. *Women in Sport and Physical Activity Journal, 29*(1), 59–67.

Bailey, M. J. (2003). *The man who would be queen: The science of gender-bending and transsexualism.* Joseph Henry Press.

Bailey, P. (2014). *Leisure and class in Victorian England: Rational recreation and the contest for control, 1830–1885.* Routledge.

Balkmar, D. (2018). Violent mobilities: Men, masculinities and road conflicts in Sweden. *Mobilities, 13*(5), 717–732. https://doi.org/10.1080/1745010 1.2018.1500096

Baron, D. A., Martin, D. M., & Abol Magd, S. (2007). Doping in sports and its spread to at-risk populations: An international review. *World Psychiatry: Official Journal of the World Psychiatric Association (WPA), 6*(2), 118–123.

Baron, D., Reardon, C., & Baron, S. H. (2013). *Clinical sports psychiatry: An international perspective.* John Wiley & Sons, Ltd.

184 REFERENCES

Barrie, L., Waitt, G., & Brennan-Horley, C. (2019). Cycling assemblages, self-tracking digital technologies and negotiating gendered subjectivities of road cyclists on-the-move. *Leisure Sciences, 41*(1–2), 108–126.

Barrios, C., Bernardo, N. D., Vera, P., Laíz, C., & Hadala, M. (2015). Changes in sports injuries incidence over time in world-class Road cyclists. *International Journal of Sports Medicine, 36*(3), 241–248. Available at: https://www.thieme-connect.de/products/ejournals/abstract/10.1055/s-0034-1389983

Bartleet, H. W. (1931). *Bartleet's bicycle book.* Edward J. Burrow & Co.

BBC Sport. (2013). *Thomas rides with fractured pelvis.* [online] Available at: https://www.bbc.co.uk/sport/wales/23114057. Accessed 12 October 2020.

Becker, H. (1963). *Outsiders: Studies in the sociology of deviance.* The Free Press.

Becker, H. (1967). History, culture, and subjective experience. *Journal of Health and Social Behavior, 8,* 163–176.

Bem, S. L. (1981). Bem sex role inventory. *Journal of Personality and Social Psychology.*

BikeRaceInfo. (2022). *Bicycle race results.* https://bikeraceinfo.com/annual/race2022.html

Billard, T. J. (2018). Attitudes toward transgender men and women: Development and validation of a new measure. *Frontiers in Psychology, 9,* 387.

Borkowska, K. (2020). Approaches to studying masculinity: A nonlinear perspective of theoretical paradigms. *Men and Masculinities, 23*(3–4), 409–424.

Bosson, J. K., & Vandello, J. A. (2011). Precarious manhood and its links to action and aggression. *Current Directions in Psychological Science, 20*(2), 82–86.

Bourdieu, P. (1986). The Forms of Capital. In H. Lauder, P. Brown, J.-A. Dillabough & A. H. Halsey (eds.), *Education, globalisation and social change.* Oxford: Oxford University Press.

Brannon, R., & David, D. (1976). The male sex role: Our culture's blueprint of manhood, and what it's done for us lately. In *The forty-nine percent majority: The male sex role* (pp. 1–48). Addison-Wesley.

Bridges, T. (2014). A very "gay" straight? Hybrid masculinities, sexual aesthetics, and the changing relationship between masculinity and homophobia. *Gender & Society, 28*(1), 58–82.

British Cycling. (2017). *British Cycling 2017: A year in review.* Retrieved December 2, 2019, from http://www.ourstory.britishcycling.org.uk/

British Cycling. (2019). British Cycling reaches 150,000 members milestone for first time. Available at: https://www.britishcycling.org.uk/campaigning/article/20190502-campaigning-BRITISH-CYCLING-REACHES-150-000-MEMBERS-MILESTONE-FOR-FIRST-TIME-0

British Cycling. (2021). *British cycling backs diversity in cycling report.* https://www.britishcycling.org.uk/road/article/20190617-Home-Page-Why-we-re-supporting-the-Diversity-in-Cycling-report-0

REFERENCES   185

British Cycling reaches 150,000 members milestone for first time. British Cycling. https://www.britishcycling.org.uk/campaigning/article/20190502-campaigning-BRITISH-CYCLING-REACHES-150-000-MEMBERS-MILESTONE-FOR-FIRST-TIME-0. Published 2020. Accessed June 26, 2020.

Brittain, J. J. (2022). Atrophying masculinity within professional Road Cycling. In *The Routledge handbook of gender politics in sport and physical activity*. Routledge.

Broughton, E. (2016, February 4). The history of the six day races - magazine. Ride Velo. http://www.ridevelo.cc/blog/2016/2/3/the-history-of-the-six-day-races.

Brown, T. D., O'Connor, J. P., & Barkatsas, A. N. (2009). Instrumentation and motivations for organised cycling: The development of the Cyclist Motivation Instrument (CMI). *Journal of Sports Science & Medicine, 8*(2), 211.

Bryant, A. N. (2003). Changes in attitudes toward women's roles. *Sex Roles, 48*(3–4), 131–142.

Bryson, L. (1987, January). Sport and the maintenance of masculine hegemony. In *Women's studies international forum* (Vol. 10, No. 4, pp. 349–360). Pergamon.

Budd, A. (2001). Capitalism, sport and resistance: Reflections. *Sport in Society, 4*(1), 1–18.

Burstyn, V. (1999). *The rites of men: Manhood, politics and the culture of sport*. University of Toronto Press.

Burton-Nelson, M. (1995). *The Stronger Women Get, the More Men Love Football: Sexism and the American Culture of Sports*. Perfect Bound.

Bush, A., Anderson, E., & Carr, S. (2012). The declining existence of men's homophobia in British sport. *Journal for the Study of Sports and Athletes in Education, 6*(1), 107–120.

Cancian, F. M. (1987). *Love in America: Gender and self-development*. Cambridge University Press.

Carrillo, H., & Hoffman, A. (2017). 'Straight with a pinch of bi': The construction of heterosexuality as an elastic category among adult US men. *Sexualities, 21*(1–2), 90–108.

Chandler, T. J., & Nauright, J. (2013). *Making the rugby world: Race, gender, commerce*. Routledge.

Chang, H. (2016). *Autoethnography as method*. Routledge.

Chauncey, G. (1994). *Gay New York: Gender, urban culture, and the making of the gay male world, 1890–1940* (Illustrated ed.). Basic Books.

Chavez, C. (2008). Conceptualizing from the inside: Advantages, complications, and demands on insider positionality. *The Qualitative Report, 13*(3), 474–494.

Christiansen, A. V. (2010). "We are not sportsmen, we are professionals": Professionalism, doping and deviance in elite sport. *International Journal of Sport Management and Marketing, 7*(1/2), 91–103.

186 REFERENCES

Christiansen, A. V., & Hjørngard, M. W. (2013). You can't buy something you aren't. On fixing results in cycling. *FairPlay, Revista de Filosofia, Ética y Derecho del Deporte, 2,* 64–84.

Chvatík, V., Hardwicke, J., & Anderson, E. (2022). Inclusive masculinity and Czechia youth. *International Sociology, 37*(1), 124–142.

Clarsen, B., Krosshaug, T., & Bahr, R. (2010). Overuse injuries in professional Road cyclists. *The American Journal of Sports Medicine, 38*(12), 2494–2501. https://doi.org/10.1177/0363546510376816

Cleland, J., Cashmore, E., Dixon, K., & MacDonald, C. (2021). Analyzing the presence of homosexually-themed language among association football fans in the United Kingdom. *Communication & Sport.* https://doi.org/10.1177/21674795211005838

Clements, B., & Field, C. D. (2014). Public opinion toward homosexuality and gay rights in Great Britain. *Public Opinion Quarterly, 78*(2), 523–547.

Clyde, L., & Franklin, W. (2012). *The changing definition of masculinity (perspectives in sexuality) (softcover reprint of the original 1st ed. 1984th ed.).* Springer.

Coakley, J. J. (1990). *Sport in society: Issues and controversies* (No. Ed. 4). CV Mosby Company.

Coakley, J. J. (2002). Using sports to control deviance and violence among youths. In *Paradoxes of youth and sport* (pp. 13–30). State University of New York Press.

Coakley, J. (2009). From the outside in: Burnout as an organizational issue. *Journal of Intercollegiate Sport, 2*(1), 35–41.

Coakley, J. (2015). Drug use and deviant overconformity. In *Routledge handbook of drugs and sport* (pp. 379–392). Routledge.

Coakley, J. (2016a). Positive youth development through sport: Myths, beliefs, and realities. In *Positive youth development through sport* (pp. 21–33). Routledge.

Coakley, J. (2016b). Youth sports in the United States. In K. Green & A. Smith (Eds.), *Routledge handbook of youth sport.* Routledge.

Coakley, J. J., & Donnelly, P. (Eds.). (1999). *Inside sports.* Routledge.

Coakley, J., Hallinan, C., & McDonald, B. (2011a). *Sports in society 2: Sociological issues & controversies.* McGraw-Hill.

Coakley, J., Hallinan, C. J., & McDonald, B. (2011b). *Sports in society: Sociological issues and controversies.* McGraw Hill.

Coker-Cranney, A., Watson, J. C., 2nd, Bernstein, M., Voelker, D. K., & Coakley, J. (2018). How far is too far? Understanding identity and overconformity in collegiate wrestlers. *Qualitative Research in Sport, Exercise and Health, 10*(1), 92–116. https://doi.org/10.1080/2159676X.2017.1372798

Connell, R. W. (1987). *Gender and power: Society, the person, and sexual politics.* Stanford University Press.

Connell, R. W. (1995). *Masculinities.* University of California Press.

Connell, R. W., & Messerschmidt, J. W. (2005). Hegemonic masculinity: Rethinking the concept. *Gender & Society, 19*(6), 829–859.

REFERENCES 187

Cooky, C., Messner, M. A., & Musto, M. (2015). It's dude time!: A quarter century of excluding women's sports in televised news and highlight shows. *Communication & Sport, 3*(3), 261–287.

Courtenay, W. H. (2000). Constructions of masculinity and their influence on men's well-being: A theory of gender and health. *Social Science & Medicine, 50*(10), 1385–1401.

Coverdale, D. (2020, December 10). *Brain injury charity chief warns cycling "lagging miles behind other sports" in concussion protocols.* Mail Online. https://www.dailymail.co.uk/sport/sportsnews/article-9035629/Brain-injury-charity-chief-warns-cycling-lagging-miles-sports-concussion-protocols.html

Cowan, D., & Taylor, I. M. (2016). 'I'm proud of what I achieved; I'm also ashamed of what I done': A soccer coach's tale of sport, status, and criminal behaviour. *Qualitative Research in Sport, Exercise and Health, 8*(5), 505–518.

Cox, P. (2005, May). Conflicting agendas in selling cycling. In *Proceedings of the Velo-City 2005 Conference*, Dublin, UK.

Crosset, T. (1990). Masculinity, sexuality, and the development of early modern sport. In *Sport, men and the gender order: Critical feminist perspectives* (pp. 45–54). Human Kinetics.

Crosset, T., & Beal, B. (1997). The use of "subculture" and "subworld" in ethnographic works on sport: A discussion of definitional distinctions. *Sociology of Sport Journal, 14*(1), 73–85.

Cudd, A. E. (2007). Sporting metaphors: Competition and the ethos of capitalism. *Journal of the Philosophy of Sport, 34*(1), 52–67.

Cunningham, M. (2008). Changing attitudes toward the male breadwinner, female homemaker family model: Influences of women's employment and education over the lifecourse. *Social Forces, 87*(1), 299–323.

Curry, T. J. (1991). Fraternal bonding in the locker room: A profeminist analysis of talk about competition and women. *Sociology of Sport Journal, 8*(2), 119–135.

Curry, T. J. (1993). The effects of receiving a college letter on the sport identity. *Sociology of Sport Journal, 10*(1), 73–87.

Curry, T., & Strauss, R. H. (1994). A little pain never hurt anyone: A photo-essay on the normalization of sports injury. *Sociology of Sport Journal, 11*, 195–208.

Cycling, (1891–1900).

Cycling, UK, 30 November 1982.

Cycling News. (2016, April 27). *Shane Sutton resigns amid sexism and discrimination claims.* cyclingnews.com. https://www.cyclingnews.com/news/shane-sutton-resigns-amid-sexism-and-discrimination-claims/

Cycling News. (2017, December 12). Philippa York: Cycling's conservative culture suppresses LGBT issues. Cyclingnews.Com. https://www.cyclingnews.com/news/philippa-york-cyclings-conservative-culture-suppresses-lgbt-issues/

188 REFERENCES

Cycling News. (2018, May 16). *Report finds widespread bullying, intimidation and abuse in Dutch cycling.* cyclingnews.com. https://www.cyclingnews.com/news/report-finds-widespread-bullying-intimidation-and-abuse-in-dutch-cycling/

Cycling Statistics, *results and rankings | ProCyclingStats.com.* (2022). https://www.procyclingstats.com

Cycling Weekly. (2015, December 10). *Junior time trial champion Gabriel Evans admits EPO use.* cyclingweekly.com. https://www.cyclingweekly.com/news/latest-news/junior-time-trial-champion-gabriel-evans-admits-epo-use-203450

Cycling Weekly. (2020, September 12). *Scan reveals Romain Bardet suffered "small haemorrhage" following concussion in Tour de France crash.* cyclingweekly.com. https://www.cyclingweekly.com/news/racing/tour-de-france/scan-reveals-romain-bardet-suffered-small-brain-haemorrhage-in-tour-de-france-crash-467917

Cyclingnews. (2021, January 7). Belgian U23' cross racer Justin Laevens comes out as gay. cyclingnews.com. https://www.cyclingnews.com/news/belgian-u23-cross-racer-justin-laevens-comes-out-as-gay/

Dahlquist, M., Leisz, M. C., & Finkelstein, M. (2015). The club-level road cyclist: Injury, pain, and performance. *Clinical Journal of Sport Medicine: Official journal of the Canadian Academy of Sport Medicine, 25*(2), 88–94. https://doi.org/10.1097/JSM.0000000000000111

Daly, E., White, A., Blackett, A. D., & Ryan, L. (2021). Pressure. A qualitative analysis of the perception of concussion and injury risk in retired professional Rugby players. *Journal of Functional Morphology and Kinesiology, 6*(3), 78. MDPI AG. Retrieved from https://doi.org/10.3390/jfmk6030078

Daniels, E. A., Hood, A., LaVoi, N. M., et al. (2021). Sexualized and athletic: Viewers' attitudes toward sexualized performance images of female athletes. *Sex Roles, 84*, 112–124. https://doi.org/10.1007/s11199-020-01152-y

Davidson, J. A. (2005). Epidemiology and outcome of bicycle injuries presenting to an emergency department in the United Kingdom. *European Journal of Emergency Medicine: Official Journal of the European Society for Emergency Medicine, 12*(1), 24–29. https://doi.org/10.1097/00063110-200502000-00007

De Bernardo, N., Barrios, C., Vera, P., Laiz, C., & Hadala, M. (2012). Incidence and risk for traumatic an overuse injury in top-level road cyclists. *Journal of Sports Science, 30*(10), 1047–1053. https://doi.org/10.1080/02640414.2012.687112

Dean, N., & Bundon, A. (2020). 'You're only falling into water!': Exploring surfers' understandings of concussion in Canadian surf culture. *Qualitative Research in Sport, Exercise and Health, 12*(4), 579–596. https://doi.org/10.1080/2159676X.2019.1657930

REFERENCES 189

Decock, M., De Wilde, L., Van den Bossche, L., Steyaert, A., & Van Tongel, A. (2016). Incidence and aetiology of acute injuries during competitive road cycling. *British Journal of Sports Medicine, 50*, 669–672. Available at: https://bjsm.bmj.com/content/50/11/669

Dellanebbia, A. M. (2020). *The experiences of women competitive road cyclists: A qualitative study* (Doctoral dissertation, Texas Woman's University).

Denzin, N. K., Lincoln, Y. S., & Guba, E. G. (2005). *Paradigmatic controversies, contradictions, and emerging confluences. The sage handbook of qualitative research* (pp. 163–188). Sage Publications.

Derlega, V. J., Catanzaro, D., & Lewis, R. J. (2001). Perceptions about tactile intimacy in same-sex and opposite-sex pairs based on research participants' sexual orientation. *Psychology of Men & Masculinity, 2*(2), 124.

Dimeo, P. (2007). A history of drug use in sport 1876–1976: Beyond good and evil. *Journal of Sports Science & Medicine, 6*(3), 382–382.

Dimeo, P. (2008). *A history of drug use in sport: 1876-1976: Beyond good and evil.* Routledge.

Dimeo, P., & Henning, A. (2015, January 27). *Forget lance Armstrong, the next big cycling doper could be your dad.* The Conversation. https://theconversation.com/forget-lance-armstrong-the-next-big-cycling-doper-could-be-your-dad-36734

Ditz, T. L. (2004). The new Men's history and the peculiar absence of gendered Power: Some remedies from early American gender history. *Gender History, 16*(1), 1–35. https://doi.org/10.1111/j.0953-5233.2004.324_1.x

Dixon, M. A., Graham, J. A., Hartzell, A. C., & Forrest, K. (2017). Enhancing women's participation and advancement in competitive cycling. *Journal of Applied Sport Management, 9*(4), 6.

Donnelly, P. (1985). Sport subcultures. *Exercise and Sport Sciences Reviews, 13*(1), 539–578.

Donnelly, P. (2007). *Sport culture and subcultures.* The Blackwell Encyclopedia of Sociology.

Donnelly, P., & Young, K. (1988). The construction and confirmation of identity in sport subcultures. *Sociology of Sport Journal, 5*(3), 223–240.

Doty, J. (2006). Sports build character?! *Journal of College and Character, 7*(3), 1–9.

Drinkell, P. (2021). *The Road Cyclist's companion* (Revised PB edition) (Revised). Cicada Books.

Dunning, E. (1986). Sport as a male preserve: Notes on the social sources of masculine identity and its transformations. *Theory, Culture & Society, 3*(1), 79–90.

Dunning, E. G., & Sheard, K. G. (1973). The Rugby football Club as a type of 'male preserve': Some sociological notes. *International Review of Sport Sociology, 8*(3), 5–24. https://doi.org/10.1177/101269027300800301

Durkheim, E. (1933). *The division of labor in society.* Free Press.

Durry, J. (1977). *The Guinness guide to bicycling* (J. B. Wadley ed.). Guiness Superlatives Ltd.

Edwardes-Evans, L., Laget, S., McGrath, A., & Hinault, B. (2021). *The official history of the tour De France* (Updated ed.). Welbeck Publishing.

Eitzen, S. (2001). *Sport in contemporary society: An anthology.* MacMillian.

Elliott, J., Anderson, R., Collins, S., & Heron, N. (2019). Sports-related concussion (SRC) assessment in road cycling: A systematic review and call to action. *BMJ Open Sport & Exercise Medicine, 5*(1). https://doi.org/10.1136/bmjsem-2019-000525

English, C. (2017). Toward sport reform: Hegemonic masculinity and reconceptualizing competition. *Journal of the Philosophy of Sport, 44*(2), 183–198.

Esterov, D., & Greenwald, B. (2017). Autonomic dysfunction after mild traumatic brain injury. *Brain Sciences, 7*(12), 100. https://doi.org/10.3390/brainsci7080100

Falcous, M. (2017). Why we ride: Road cyclists, meaning, and lifestyles. *Journal of Sport and Social Issues, 41*(3), 239–255.

Farrell, M., Aherne, S., O'Riordan, S., O'Keeffe, E., Greene, C., & Campbell, M. (2019). Blood-brain barrier dysfunction in a boxer with chronic traumatic encephalopathy and schizophrenia. *Clinical Neuropathology, 38*(03), 51–58. https://doi.org/10.5414/np301130

Farrell, K. C., Reisinger, K. D., & Tillman, M. D. (2003). Force and repetition in cycling: Possible implications for iliotibial band friction syndrome. *The Knee, 10*(1), 103–109. https://doi.org/10.1016/s0968-0160(02)00090-x

Ferez, S. (2012). From women's exclusion to gender institution: A brief history of the sexual categorisation process within sport. *The International Journal of the History of Sport, 29*(2), 272–285.

Fielding-Lloyd, B., & Meân, L. J. (2008). Standards and separatism: The discursive construction of gender in English soccer coach education. *Sex Roles, 58*(1–2), 24–39.

Fine, G. A. (1979). Small groups and culture creation: The idioculture of little league baseball teams. *American Sociological Review,* 733–745.

Fine, G. A., & Kleinman, S. (1979). Rethinking subculture: An interactionist analysis. *American Journal of Sociology, 85*(1), 1–20.

Fleming, J. E. (2015). The bicycle boom and women's rights. *The Gettysburg Historical Journal, 14*(1), 3.

Fleming, P. J., Lee, J. G., & Dworkin, S. L. (2014). "Real men don't": Constructions of masculinity and inadvertent harm in public health interventions. *American Journal of Public Health, 104*(6), 1029–1035. https://doi.org/10.2105/AJPH.2013.301820

Floyd, K., & Morman, M. T. (2000). Affection received from fathers as a predictor of men's affection with their own sons: Tests of the modeling and compensation hypotheses. *Communications Monographs, 67*(4), 347–361.

REFERENCES 191

Forrest, K. E. (2010). *Gender disparities in competitive cycling: An analysis of the structural, socio-cultural, and individual factors affecting female participation in Texas* (doctoral dissertation).

Freud, S., Strachey, J., Marcus, S., & Chodorow, N. J. (1905). *Three essays on the theory of sexuality* (Revised ed.). Basic Books.

Gair, S. (2012). Feeling their stories: Contemplating empathy, insider/outsider positionings, and enriching qualitative research. *Qualitative Health Research, 22*(1), 134–143.

Gatz, M., Messner, M. A., & Ball-Rokeach, S. (Eds.). (2002). *Paradoxes of youth and sport.* SUNY Press.

Geertz, C. (1966). Religion as a cultural system. In M. Banton (Ed.), *Anthropological approaches to the study of religion* (pp. 1–46). Tavistock.

Geertz, C. (2000). Deep play: Notes on the Balinese cockfight. In *Culture and politics* (pp. 175–201). Palgrave Macmillan.

Giles, R. (2018). *Women on the move: The forgotten era of Women's bicycle racing.* Nebraska University Press.

Glackin, O. F., & Beale, J. T. (2018). 'The world is best experienced at 18 mph'. The psychological wellbeing effects of cycling in the countryside: An interpretative phenomenological analysis. *Qualitative Research in Sport, Exercise and Health, 10*(1), 32–46.

Gloor, R. U., Knechtle, B., Knechtle, P., Rust, C. A., Haupt, S., Rosemann, T., & Lepers, R. (2013). Sex-related trends in participation and performance in the 'Swiss bike masters' from 1994–2012. *Perceptual and Motor Skills, 116*(2), 640–654. https://doi.org/10.2466/30.pms.116.2.640-654

Goffman, E. (1959). *The presentation of self in everyday life.* Anchor Books.

Goffman, E. (1963). Embarrassment and Social Organization. In N. J. Smelser & W. T. Smelser (Eds.), *Personality and social systems* (pp. 541–548). John Wiley & Sons.

Goffman, E. (2002). The presentation of self in everyday life. 1959. Garden City, NY, 259.

Goldstone, J. A. (1996). Gender, work, and culture: Why the industrial revolution came early to England but late to China. *Sociological Perspectives, 39*(1), 1–21. https://doi.org/10.2307/1389340

Green, B. C., & Jones, I. (2005). Serious leisure, social identity and sport tourism. *Sport in Society, 8*(2), 164–181.

Greve, M. W., & Modabber, M. R. (2012). An epidemic of traumatic brain injury in professional Cycling. *Clinical Journal of Sport Medicine, 22*(2), 81–82. https://doi.org/10.1097/jsm.0b013e318243bf32

Grous, A. (2012). *The 'Olympic cycling effect': A report prepared for sky and British Cycling.* London School of Economics and Political Science.

Guardian. (2018, May 1). *Philippa York says macho culture prevents cyclists coming out.* The Guardian. https://www.theguardian.com/sport/2018/apr/30/philippa-york-macho-culture-cyclists-coming-out.

192 REFERENCES

Haeberle, H. S., Navarro, S. M., Power, E. J., Schickendantz, M. S., Farrow, L. D., & Ramkumar, P. N. (2018). Prevalence and epidemiology of injuries among elite cyclists in the tour de France. *Orthopaedic Journal of Sports Medicine, 6*(9), 2325967118793392. https://doi.org/10.1177/2325967118793392

Haines, C., Smith, T. M., & Baxter, M. F. (2010). Participation in the risk-taking occupation of skateboarding. *Journal of Occupational Science, 17*(4), 239–245. https://doi.org/10.1080/14427591.2010.9686701

Hall, S., & Jefferson, T. (Eds.). (2006). *Resistance through rituals: Youth subcultures in post-war Britain.* Routledge.

Hallenbeck, S. (2015). *Claiming the bicycle: Women, rhetoric, and technology in nineteenth-century America.* SIU Press.

Hamdan, A. (2009). Reflexivity of discomfort in insider-outsider educational research. *McGill Journal of Education/Revue des sciences de l'éducation de McGill, 44*(3), 377–404.

Hardwicke, J. (2022a). *An investigation into attitudes towards, and experiences of, sexual minorities in cycling.* University of Northampton. https://doi.org/1 0.24339/5011a1d2-7adb-4584-9373-de911f4d91cb

Hardwicke, J. (2022). An investigation into masculinity among competitive road cyclists. *Journal of Emerging Sport Studies, 7.*

Hardwicke, J. (2022c). *Inside the peloton: An exploration into the culture of competitive road cycling with reference to masculinity, risk and injury, with a principle focus on concussion* (Doctoral dissertation, University of Winchester).

Hardwicke, J., Batten, J., Anderson, E., & Hurst, H. T. (2022). Twitter discourse around competitive cycling and sport-related concussion. *Journal of Science and Cycling, 11,* 59–69. https://doi.org/10.28985/1322.jsc.02

Hardwicke, J., Baxter, B. A., Gamble, T., & Hurst, H. T. (2022). An investigation into helmet use, perceptions of sports-related concussion, and seeking medical care for head injury amongst competitive cyclists. *International Journal of Environmental Research and Public Health, 19*(5), 2861.

Hardwicke, J., & Hurst, H. T. (2020). Concussion knowledge and attitudes amongst competitive cyclists. *Journal of Science and Cycling, 9,* 53–66.

Hargreaves, J. (1982). Sport, culture and ideology. In J. Hargreaves (Ed.), *Sport, culture and ideology* (p. 41). Routledge and Kegan Paul.

Hargreaves, J. A. (1990). Gender on the sports agenda. *International Review for the Sociology of Sport, 25*(4), 287–307. https://doi.org/10.1177/101269029002500403

Hargreaves, J. (1994). *Sporting females: Critical issues in the history and sociology of Women's sport.* Routledge.

Hargreaves, J. (2002). *Sporting females: Critical issues in the history and sociology of women's sport.* Routledge.

REFERENCES   193

Hargreaves, J., & Anderson, E. (Eds.). (2014). *Routledge handbook of sport, gender and sexuality*. Routledge.

Harmon, K. (2013). American medical society for sports medicine position statement. *Clinical Journal of Sport Medicine, 23*(1), 1–18. https://doi.org/10.1097/jsm.0b013e31827f5f93

Harmon, K., Drezner, J., Gammons, M., et al. (2013). American medical society for sports medicine position statement. *Clinical Journal of Sport Medicine, 23*(1), 1–18. https://doi.org/10.1097/jsm.0b013e31827f5f93

Hasan, M. K., Aggleton, P., & Persson, A. (2018). The makings of a man: Social generational masculinities in Bangladesh. *Journal of Gender Studies, 27*(3), 347–361.

Hearn, J. (2004). From hegemonic masculinity to the hegemony of men. *Feminist Theory, 5*(1), 49–72.

Heesch, K. C., Sahlqvist, S., & Garrard, J. (2012). Gender differences in recreational and transport cycling: A cross-sectional mixed-methods comparison of cycling patterns, motivators, and constraints. *International Journal of Behavioral Nutrition and Physical Activity, 9*(1), 1–12.

Hekma, G. (1998). "As long as they don't make an issue of it..." gay men and lesbians in organized sports in The Netherlands. *Journal of Homosexuality, 35*(1), 1–23.

Henning, A. D., & Dimeo, P. (2018). The new front in the war on doping: Amateur athletes. *International Journal of Drug Policy, 51*, 128–136. https://doi.org/10.1016/j.drugpo.2017.05.036

Herek, G. M. (1984). Attitudes toward lesbians and gay men: A factor-analytic study. *Journal of Homosexuality, 10*(1–2), 39–51.

Heron, N., Sarriegui, I., Jones, N., & Nolan, R. (2020). International consensus statement on injury and illness reporting in professional road cycling. *The Physician and Sportsmedicine, 49*, 130–136. https://doi.org/10.1080/00913847.2020.1830692

Hill, J. (2010). *Sport in history: An introduction*. Bloomsbury Publishing.

Hill, T., & Dao, M. (2021). Personal pasts become academic presents: Engaging reflexivity and considering dual insider/outsider roles in physical cultural fieldwork. *Qualitative Research in Sport, Exercise and Health, 13*(3), 521–535.

Hill, J., & Metcalfe, A. (2003). Sport, leisure and culture in twentieth-century Britain. *Labour, 52*, 316.

Hind, K., Konerth, N., Entwistle, I., Hume, P., Theadom, A., Lewis, G., et al. (2022). Mental health and wellbeing of retired elite and amateur rugby players and non-contact athletes and associations with sports-related concussion: The UK Rugby health project. *Sports Medicine, 52*(6), 1419–1431.

Hodkinson, P. (2005). 'Insider research'in the study of youth cultures. *Journal of Youth Studies, 8*(2), 131–149.

194 REFERENCES

Holden, J. (2015). *The ecology of culture*. Available at: http://www.culturalmanagement.ac.rs/uploads/research_file_1/66134e4b60bbb5800408f992fa4d0 fe4e2ff6a31.pdf

Holt, R. (1990). *Sport and the British: A modern history*. Oxford University Press.

Howe, D. (2003). *Sport, professionalism, and pain: ethnographies of injury and risk*. Psychology Press.

Hu, L. (2018). Is masculinity 'deteriorating'in China? Changes of masculinity representation in Chinese film posters from 1951 to 2016. *Journal of Gender Studies, 27*(3), 335–346.

Hughes, R., & Coakley, J. (1991). Positive deviance among athletes: The implications of overconformity to the sport ethic. *Sociology of Sport Journal, 8*(4), 307–325.

Hurst, H., & Hardwicke, J. (2020, September 22). *Cycling: Head injuries ignored because of entrenched macho culture*. The Conversation. https://theconversation.com/cycling-head-injuries-ignored-because-of-entrenched-macho-culture-146374

Hurst, H., Novak, A., Cheung, S., & Atkins, S. (2019). Knowledge of and attitudes towards concussion in cycling: A preliminary study. *Journal of Science and Cycling, 8*(1), 11–17. Available at: http://www.jsc-journal.com/ojs/index. php?journal=JSC&page=article&op=view&path%5B%5D=10.2898 5%2F1906.jsc.03&path%5B%5D=534

Hurst, H. T., Hannock, S., Hardwicke, J., & Anderson, E. (2020). Does participation in Downhill mountain biking affect measures of executive function? *Journal of Science and Cycling, 9*(3), 83–93.

Hutchinson, M. (2018). *Re: Cyclists: 200 years on two wheels*. Bloomsbury Publishing.

Huyett, E. (2015, August 14). UCI women get upgraded to WorldTour status for 2016.https://www.bicycling.com/racing/a20043057/uci-women-get-upgraded-to-worldtour- status-for-2016/.

Ingham, A. (1975). Occupational subcultures in the work world of sport. In *Sport and social order* (pp. 333–389). Addison-Wesley.

Irwin, J. (1977). *Scenes*. Sage Publications.

Jafari, S., Etminan, M., Aminzadeh, F., & Samii, A. (2013). Head injury and risk of Parkinson disease: A systematic review and meta-analysis. *Movement Disorders, 28*(9), 1222–1229. https://doi.org/10.1002/mds.25458

Jenkins, R. (2002). Foundations of sociology. In *Foundations of sociology* (pp. 1–14). Palgrave.

Jones, T. (2022). Amateur sport cycling: The rise of the MAMIL. In *Routledge companion to Cycling* (pp. 287–297). Routledge.

Joseph, L. J., & Anderson, E. (2016). The influence of gender segregation and teamsport experience on occupational discrimination in sport-based employment. *Journal of Gender Studies, 25*(5), 586–598.

REFERENCES 195

Kelner, M. (2018, May 1). Philippa York says macho culture prevents cyclists coming out. *The Guardian*. https://www.theguardian.com/sport/2018/apr/30/philippa-york-macho-culture-cyclistscoming-out

Kern, L., Geneau, A., Laforest, S., Dumas, A., Tremblay, B., Goulet, C., Lepage, S., & Barnett, T. A. (2014). Risk perception and risk-taking among skateboarders. *Safety Science, 62*, 370–375. https://doi.org/10.1016/j.ssci.2013.08.009

Kidd, S. A., & Kral, M. J. (2005). Practicing participatory action research. *Journal of Counseling Psychology, 52*(2), 187.

Kiernan, P., Montenigro, P., Solomon, T., & McKee, A. (2015). Chronic traumatic encephalopathy: A neurodegenerative consequence of repetitive traumatic brain injury. *Seminars in Neurology, 35*(01), 020–028. https://doi.org/10.1055/s-0035-1545080

Kiersnowska, B. (2019). Female cycling and the discourse of moral panic in late Victorian Britain. *Atlantis, 41*(2), 85–104.

Kimmel, M. (1994a). Masculinity as homophobia: Fear, shame and silence in the construction of gender identity. In H. Brod & M. Kaufman (Eds.), *Theorizing masculinities* (pp. 119–141). Sage.

Kimmel, M. S. (1994b). Fear, shame, and silence in the construction of gender identity. In *Theorizing masculinities* (pp. 119–141). Sage.

Kimmel, M. (1995). *Manhood in American: A cultural history*. Free Press.

Kimmel, M. (1996). *Manhood in America* (4th ed.). Oxford University Press.

Kimmel, M. S., & Messner, M. A. (1992). *Men's lives*. Macmillan Publishing Co, Inc.

Klein, D. J. (1986). *Effects of systematic exercise and body building/weight lifting on self-esteem of female subjects* (Doctoral dissertation, Kean University).

Kolsrud, F. (2014). Exhaustion of leisure: Identity and cycling. NANO: New American Notes Online, (4). Retrieved from https://www.proquest.com/scholarly-journals/exhaustion-leisure-identity-cycling/docview/2326843084/se-2

Krause, J., & Priest, R. (1993). *Sport value choices of U.S. military cadets—A longitudinal study of the class of 1993*. Unpublished manuscript, Office of Institutional Research, U.S. Military Academy, West Point, NY.

Kreher, J. B., & Schwartz, J. B. (2012). Overtraining syndrome: A practical guide. *Sports Health, 4*(2), 128–138. https://doi.org/10.1177/1941738111434406

Kulkarni, P., Morrison, T. R., Cai, X., Iriah, S., Simon, N., Sabrick, J., Neuroth, L., & Ferris, C. F. (2019). Neuroradiological changes following single or repetitive mild TBI. *Frontiers in Systems Neuroscience, 13*, 1–12. https://doi.org/10.3389/fnsys.2019.00034

Landry, G. L., & Kokotaio, P. K. (1994). Drug screening in athletic settings. *Current Problems in Pediatrics, 24*, 344–359.

Langlois, J., Rutland-Brown, W., & Wald, M. (2006). The epidemiology and impact of traumatic brain injury. *Journal of Head Trauma Rehabilitation, 21*(5), 375–378.

196 REFERENCES

Larson, D. (2013). 2013 membership survey and analysis: Prepared for USA Cycling, Inc. Retrieved from https://s3.amazonaws.com/USACWeb/forms/encyc/2013-USAC-Membership-Surv ey-Report.pdf

Laurendeau, J. (2006). He didn't go in doing a skydive: Sustaining the illusion of control in an edgework activity. *Sociological Perspectives, 49*(4), 583–605.

Letts, D. (2021). Sexual minority prevalence and attitudes within the British horseracing industry. *International Review for the Sociology of Sport, 56*(6), 823–841.

Levant, R. F., & Wimer, D. J. (2014). Masculinity constructs as protective buffers and risk factors for Men's health. *American Journal of Men's Health, 8*(2), 110–120. https://doi.org/10.1177/1557988313494408

Liston, K. (2019, January 19). Concussion: Culture eats protocol for breakfast. In *Invited talk presented at the GAA Coaching Conference*, Dublin.

Liston, K., McDowell, M., Malcolm, D., Scott-Bell, A., & Waddington, I. (2018). On being 'head strong': The pain zone and concussion in non-elite Rugby union. *International Review for the Sociology of Sport, 53*(6), 668–684.

Liston, K., Reacher, D., Waddington, I., & Smith, A. (2006). Managing pain and injury in non-elite Rugby union and Rugby league: A case study of players at a British university. *Sport in Society, 9*(3), 388–402.

Lorber, J. (1994). *Paradoxes of gender*. Yale University Press.

Lucas, S. (2012). Women's cycle racing: Enduring meanings. *Journal of Sport History, 39*(2), 227–242.

Lunzenfichter, A. (2007, 10 December). C'est pas du jeu!, L'Équipe, France.

Lyng, S. (1990). Edgework: A social psychological analysis of voluntary risk taking. *American Journal of Sociology, 95*(4), 851–886. https://doi.org/10.1086/229379

Lyng, S. (2005). *Edgework: The sociology of risk-taking* (1st ed.). Routledge.

Mackintosh, P. G. (2005). Scrutiny in the Modern City: The domestic public and the Toronto local Council of Women at the turn of the twentieth century. *Gender, Place & Culture, 12*(1), 29–48. https://doi.org/10.1080/096636 90500082836

Mackintosh, P. G., & Norcliffe, G. (2007). Gender and social geography of Cycling in the late nineteenth-century. In *Cycling and society* (p. 153). Ashgate.

Maffesoli, M. (1996). *The time of the tribes: The decline of individualism in mass society* (Trans. D. Smith), Sage.

Magrath, R. (2016). *Inclusive masculinities in contemporary football: Men in the beautiful game*. Routledge.

Magrath, R. (2017). 'To try and gain an advantage for my team': Homophobic and homosexually themed chanting among English football fans. *Sociology, 52*(4), 709–726. https://doi.org/10.1177/0038038517702600

Magrath, R. (2018). 'To try and gain an advantage for my team': Homophobic and homosexually themed chanting among English football fans. *Sociology, 52*(4), 709–726.

Magrath, R., Batten, J., Anderson, E., & White, A. J. (2022). Five-year cohort study of White-British male student-athletes' attitudes toward gay men. *Journal for the Study of Sports and Athletes in Education, 16*(3), 262–276.

Magrath, R., & McCormack, M. (2022). Friendship dynamics of young men with non-exclusive sexual orientations: Group diversity, physical intimacy and emotionality. *Journal of Social and Personal Relationships.* https://doi.org/10.1177/02654075221127232

Majors, R. (1990). Cool pose: Black masculinity and sports. In M. A. Messner & D. F. Sabo (Eds.), *Sport, men and the gender order.* Human Kinetics.

Malcom, D. (2017). *Sport, medicine and health: The medicalization of sport?* (Abingdon and New York: Routledge, 2017), isbn: 978-1-138-82645-8. *Medical History, 62*(2), 247–248.

Malcom, D. (2019). *The concussion crisis in sport.* Routledge.

Manners, W. (2015). *Uncle, grandpa and the boys: Re-imagining relationships and masculinities within 1890s English Cycling clubs.* (Doctoral dissertation, University of York).

Manners, W. (2018). *Revolution: How the bicycle reinvented modern Britain.* Prelude Books.

Mansfield, L., Caudwell, J., Wheaton, B., & Watson, B. (Eds.). (2017). *The Palgrave handbook of feminism and sport, leisure and physical education.* Palgrave Macmillan UK.

Martin, P. Y., & Hummer, R. A. (1989). Fraternities and rape on campus. *Gender & Society, 3*(4), 457–473.

Matthews, C. R. (2016). The appropriation of hegemonic masculinity within selected research on men's health. *NORMA, 11*(1), 3–18.

Matthews, C. R. (2020). 'The fog soon clears': Bodily negotiations, embodied understandings, competent body action and 'brain injuries' in boxing. *International Review for the Sociology of Sport, 56*(5), 719–738. https://doi.org/10.1177/1012690220907026

Matthews, C. R., & Channon, A. (2019). The 'male preserve' thesis, sporting culture, and men's power. In *Routledge international handbook of masculinity studies* (pp. 373–383). Routledge.

Matthews, C. R., Hurrell, A., Oliver, T. B., & Channon, A. (2022). Boxing, myths and reality building in sport for development programmes. *International Review for the Sociology of Sport.* https://doi.org/10.1177/1012690 2221112878

McCormack, M. (2011). Mapping the terrain of homosexually-themed language. *Journal of Homosexuality, 58*(5), 664–679.

McCormack, M. (2012). *The declining significance of homophobia.* Oxford University Press.

McCormack, M. (2014). The intersection of youth masculinities, decreasing homophobia and class: An ethnography. *The British Journal of Sociology, 65*(1), 130–149.

198 REFERENCES

McCormack, M., & Anderson, E. (2014a). Homohysteria: Definitions, context and intersectionality. *Sex Roles, 71*(3), 152–158.

McCormack, M., & Anderson, E. (2014b). The influence of declining homophobia on men's gender in the United States: An argument for the study of homohysteria. *Sex Roles, 71*(3–4), 109–120.

McCormack, M., Anderson, E., Jamie, K., & David, M. (2021). *Discovering sociology*. Bloomsbury Publishing.

McCreary, D. R. (1994). The male role and avoiding femininity. *Sex Roles, 31*(9), 517–531.

McCrone, K. (2014). Individual sports: Lawn tennis, golf and Cycling. In *Sport and the physical emancipation of English women (RLE sports studies)* (pp. 184–221). Routledge.

McDevitt, P. (2004). *May the best man win: Sport, masculinity and nationalism in Great Britain and the empire, 1880–1935*. Palgrave Macmillan.

McDonagh, E., & Pappano, L. (2008). *Playing with the boys: Why separate is not equal in sports*. Oxford University Press.

McDonald, I. (2014). Portraying Sporting masculinity through film: Reflections on Jorgen Leth's A Sunday in hell. In *Routledge handbook of sport, gender and sexuality* (pp. 480–487). Routledge.

McGannon, K. R., Cunningham, S. M., & Schinke, R. J. (2013). Understanding concussion in socio-cultural context: A media analysis of A National Hockey League Star's concussion. *Psychology of Sport and Exercise, 14*(6), 891–899. https://doi.org/10.1016/j.psychsport.2013.08.003

Mecredy, R. J. (1891). Cycling. *Fortnightly review, 50*, 75–88.

Merton, R. K. (1972). Insiders and outsiders: A chapter in the sociology of knowledge. *American Journal of Sociology, 78*(1), 9–47.

Messner, M. A. (1990). When bodies are weapons: Masculinity and violence in sport. *International Review for the Sociology of Sport, 25*(3), 203–220. https://doi.org/10.1177/101269029002500303

Messner, M. A. (1992). Like family: Power, intimacy, and sexuality in male athletes' friendships. In P. M. Nardi (Ed.), *Men's friendships* (pp. 215–237). Sage Publications. https://doi.org/10.4135/9781483325736.n12

Messner, M. A. (2002). *Taking the field: Women, men, and sports* (Vol. 4). U of Minnesota Press.

Messner, M. A., & Sabo, D. F. (1990). *Sport, men, and the gender order: Critical feminist perspectives* (Vol. 10). Human Kinetics.

Messner, M. A., & Sabo, D. F. (1994). *Sex, violence & power in sports: Rethinking masculinity*. Crossing Press.

Michael, B. (2015). 'Just don't hit on me and I'm fine': Mapping high school wrestlers' relationship to inclusive masculinity and heterosexual recuperation. *International Review for the Sociology of Sport, 50*(8), 912–928. https://doi.org/10.1177/1012690213501168

REFERENCES   199

Miracle, A., Jr., & Rees, C. R. (1994). *Lessons of the locker room: The myth of school sports*. Prometheus Books.

Møller, V. (2010). *The ethics of doping and anti-doping: Redeeming the soul of sport?* Routledge.

Montgomery, S., Hiyoshi, A., Burkill, S., Alfredsson, L., Bahmanyar, S., & Olsson, T. (2017). Concussion in adolescence and risk of multiple sclerosis. *Annals of Neurology, 82*(4), 554–561. https://doi.org/10.1002/ana.25036

Moore, R., Lepine, J., & Ellemberg, D. (2017). The independent influence of concussive and sub-concussive impacts on soccer players' neurophysiological and neuropsychological function. *International Journal of Psychophysiology, 112*, 22–30. https://doi.org/10.1016/j.ijpsycho.2016.11.011

Morales, L., & Caffyn-Parsons, E. (2017). "I love you, guys" : A study of inclusive masculinities among high school cross-country runners. *Boyhood Studies, 10*(1), 66–87. https://doi.org/10.3167/bhs.2017.100105

Morioka, R. (2014). Gender difference in the health risk perception of radiation from Fukushima in Japan: The role of hegemonic masculinity. *Social Science & Medicine, 1982*(107), 105–112. https://doi.org/10.1016/j.socscimed.2014.02.014

Morris, M., & Anderson, E. (2015). 'Charlie is so cool like': Authenticity, popularity and inclusive masculinity on YouTube. *Sociology, 49*(6), 1200–1217.

Mueller, J. T., Landon, A. C., & Graefe, A. R. (2019). Modeling the role of social identity in constraint negotiation for ultra-endurance gravel cycling. *Journal of Leisure Research, 50*(2), 81–106.

Muggleton, D. (2000). *Inside subculture*. Berg Publishers.

Muir, K. B., & Seitz, T. (2004). Machismo, misogyny, and homophobia in a male athletic subculture: A participant-observation study of deviant rituals in collegiate rugby. *Deviant Behavior, 25*(4), 303–327.

Mullin, E. M., & Cook, S. (2021). Collegiate coach attitudes towards lesbians and gay men. *International Journal of Sports Science & Coaching, 16*(3), 519–527.

Murdock, G., & McCron, R. (1976). Youth and class: The career of a confusion. In *Working class youth culture* (pp. 10–26). Routledge and Kegan Paul.

Nash, J. E. (1977). Lying about running: The functions of talk in a scene. *Qualitative Sociology, 3*(2), 83–99.

Nauright, J., & Chandler, T. J. L. (Eds.). (1996). *Making men: Rugby and masculine identity* (Vol. 10). Psychology Press.

Nelson, M. B. (1995). *The stronger women get, the more men love football: Sexism and the American culture of sports*. PerfectBound.

Nixon, H. L. (1991). Sport sociology that matters: Imperatives and challenges for the 1990s. *Sociology of Sport Journal, 8*(3), 281–294.

Nixon, H. L. (1992). A social network analysis of influences on athletes to play with pain and injuries. *Journal of Sport and Social Issues, 16*(2), 127–135. https://doi.org/10.1177/019372359201600208

Nixon, H. L. (1993). Accepting the risks of pain and injury in sport: Mediated cultural influences on playing hurt. *Sociology of Sport Journal, 10*(2), 183–196. https://doi.org/10.1123/ssj.10.2.183

Nixon, H. L. (1994). Social pressure, social support, and help seeking for pain and injuries in college sports networks. *Journal of Sport and Social Issues, 18*(4), 340–355. https://doi.org/10.1177/019372394018004004

Nixon, H. L. (1996). Explaining pain and injury attitudes and experiences in sport in terms of gender, race, and sports status factors. *Journal of Sport and Social Issues, 20*(1), 33–44. https://doi.org/10.1177/019372396020001004

Noble, J., & Davies, P. (2009). Cultural capital as an explanation of variation in participation in higher education. *British Journal of Sociology of Education, 30*(5), 591–605.

Norcliffe, G. (2001a). *Ride to modernity: The bicycle in Canada, 1869–1900* (Illustrated ed.). University of Toronto Press, Scholarly Publishing Division.

Norcliffe, G. B. (2001b). *The ride to modernity: The bicycle in Canada, 1869–1900.* University of Toronto Press.

Norcliffe, G. (2006). Associations, modernity and the insider-citizens of a Victorian highwheel bicycle club. *Journal of Historical Sociology, 19*(2), 121–150. https://doi.org/10.1111/j.1467-6443.2006.00275.x

Norton, A. T., & Herek, G. M. (2013). Heterosexuals' attitudes toward transgender people: Findings from a national probability sample of US adults. *Sex Roles, 68*(11), 738–753.

Novich, Max M., Abbotempo, UK, 1964.

O'Conner, P. (2016). Skateboarding, helmets, and control: Observations from skateboard media and a Hong Kong skatepark. *Journal of Sport & Social Issues, 40*(6), 477–498.

O'Connor, J. P., & Brown, T. D. (2007). Real cyclists don't race: Informal affiliations of the weekend warrior. *International Review for the Sociology of Sport, 42*(1), 83–97.

O'Donnell, B. (2020, December 28). *Abuse of power in women's cycling, an all too familiar story: Bridie O'Donnell.* CyclingTips. https://cyclingtips.com/2017/02/abuse-of-power-in-womens-cycling-an-all-too-familiar-story-bridie-odonnell/

O'Reilly, M., Mahon, S., Reid, D., Hume, P., Hardaker, N., & Theadom, A. (2020). Knowledge, attitudes, and behavior toward concussion in adult cyclists. *Brain Injury, 34*(9), 1175–1182. https://doi.org/10.1080/02699052.2020.1793386

Ogburn, W. F. (1957). *Cultural lag as theory.* Sociology & Social Research.

Ogilvie, M. F., & McCormack, M. (2021). Gender-collaborative training in elite university sport: Challenging gender essentialism through integrated training in gender-segregated sports. *International Review for the Sociology of Sport, 56*(8), 1172–1188.

Ohl, F., Fincoeur, B., Lentillon-Kaestner, V., Defrance, J., & Brissonneau, C. (2015). The socialization of young cyclists and the culture of doping. *International Review for the Sociology of Sport, 50*(7), 865–882.

Oosterhuis, H. (2016). Cycling, modernity and national culture. *Social History, 41*(3), 233–248.

Opel, M., & Rook, A. (2022, June 17). *Bike racing's newest frontier: As gravel racing defines itself, these riders are leading the charge*. cyclingweekly.com. https://www.cyclingweekly.com/racing/bike-racings-newest-frontier-as-gravel-racing-defines-itself-these-riders-are-leading-the-charge

Outsports. (2021a, August 25). *Cyclist clay Davies comes out, calls out his sport for homophobia*. Outsports. https://www.outsports.com/homophobia/2021/8/25/22641481/clay-davies-british-cycling-gay-homophobia

Outsports. (2021b, January 8). *Gay cyclist Justin Laevens is one of first pro male riders to come out*. Outsports. https://www.outsports.com/2021/1/8/22220390/justin-laevens-cyclist-gay-belgium

Park, R. E. (1915). The conflict and fusion of cultures with special reference to the negro. *The Journal of Negro History, 4*(2), 111–133.

Parry, K. D., Storr, R., Kavanagh, E. J., & Anderson, E. (2021). Conceptualising organisational cultural lag: Marriage equality and Australian sport. *Journal of Sociology, 57*(4), 986–1008.

Parry, K., White, A. J., Cleland, J., Hardwicke, J., Batten, J., Piggin, J., & Howarth, N. (2022). Masculinities, media and the rugby mind: An analysis of stakeholder views on the relationship between rugby union, the media, masculine-influenced views on injury, and concussion. *Communication & Sport, 10*(3), 564–586.

Pearson, K. (1977). *Surfing subcultures: A comparative analysis of surf life saving and surfboard riding in Australia and New Zealand*. University of New England.

Petroczi, A., & Haugen, K. (2012). The doping self-reporting game: The paradox of a 'false-telling' mechanism and its potential research and policy implications. *Sport Management Review, 15*, 513–517.

Pfister, G. (2010). Women in sport – Gender relations and future perspectives. *Sport in Society, 13*(2), 234–248.

Philip, S. (2018). *A city of men? An ethnographic enquiry into cultures of youth masculinities in urban India*. (Doctoral dissertation, University of Oxford).

Pinker, S. (2012). *The better angels of our nature: Why violence has declined* (Illustrated ed.). Penguin Books.

Plummer, D. C. (2001). The quest for modern manhood: Masculine stereotypes, peer culture and the social significance of homophobia. *Journal of Adolescence, 24*(1), 15–23.

Polsky, N. (1969). *Hustlers, beats, and others*. Routledge.

Powell, D., Stiles, B., Haff, G., & Kilgore, L. (2005). The notion of masculinity in male collegiate road cyclists. *Creative Sociology, 33*(2), 153. https://ojs.library.okstate.edu/osu/index.php/FICS/article/view/1558

202 REFERENCES

Price, J. (2022, August 16). *Focusing on diversity and inclusion, gravel bike racing welcomes all to this sport.* NPR.org. https://www.npr.org/2022/08/16/1117440946/gravel-bike-racing-welcomes-everyone-to-fast-growing-sport

Pringle, R., & Markula, P. (2005). No pain is sane after all: A Foucauldian analysis of masculinities and men's rugby experiences of fear, pain, and pleasure. *Sociology of Sport Journal, 22*(4), 472–497.

Pro Cycling Statistics, Results and Rankings|ProCyclingStats.com. Pro Cycling Stats. 2022. Available online: https://www.procyclingstats.com/ (accessed on 15 December 2021).

Pronger, B. (1990). *The arena of masculinity: Sports, homosexuality, and the meaning of sex.* Macmillan.

Ravensbergen, L., Buliung, R., & Laliberté, N. (2019). Toward feminist geographies of cycling. *Geography Compass, 1.* https://doi.org/10.1111/gec3.12461

Rawlings, S., Takechi, R., & Lavender, A. P. (2020). Effects of sub-concussion on neuropsychological performance and its potential mechanisms: A narrative review. *Brain Research Bulletin, 165,* 56–62.

Reed, K. (2013). Beyond hegemonic masculinity: The role of family genetic history in Men's accounts of health. *Sociology, 47*(5), 906–920. https://doi.org/10.1177/0038038513494505

Rees, A., Gibbons, T., & Dixon, K. (2014). The surveillance of racing cyclists in training: A bourdieusian perspective. *Surveillance & Society, 11*(4), 466–480.

Reid, C. (2018, December 6). *Time-warp lunching at the World's oldest, poshest and Most eccentric bicycle Club.* Forbes. https://www.forbes.com/sites/carltonreid/2018/12/06/time-warp-lunching-at-the-worlds-oldest-poshest-and-most-eccentric-bicycle-club/

Reimer, A. (2021, August 25). *Cyclist clay Davies comes out, calls out his sport for homophobia.* Outsports. https://www.outsports.com/homophobia/2021/8/25/22641481/clay-davies-british-cycling-gay-homophobia

Riebl, S. K., Subudhi, A. W., Broker, J. P., Schenck, K., & Berning, J. R. (2007). The prevalence of subclinical eating disorders among male cyclists. *Journal of the American Dietetic Association, 107*(7), 1214–1217. https://doi.org/10.1016/j.jada.2007.04.017

Ripley, M., Anderson, E., McCormack, M., Adams, A., & Pitts, R. (2011). The decreasing significance of stigma in the lives of bisexual men: Keynote address, bisexual research convention, London. *Journal of Bisexuality, 11*(2–3), 195–206.

Ritchie, A. (1975). *King of the road.* Wildwood House.

Ritchie. (1988). Bearings, US. Andrew, Major Taylor, Bicycle Books, US, 1988.

Ritchie, A. (1999). The origins of bicycle racing in England: Technology, entertainment, sponsorship and advertising in the early history of the sport. *Journal of Sport History, 26*(3), 489–520.

Ritchie, A. (2018). *Early bicycles and the quest for speed: A history, 1868–1903*. McFarland.

Road CC. (2020, September 13). Team boss lauds Romain Bardet's "admirable courage" – But should someone have stopped Frenchman riding to stage finish with concussion? road.cc. https://road.cc/content/news/bardet-diagnosed-concussion-after-battling-finish-277217

Roberts, S. (2013). Boys will be boys... won't they? Change and continuities in contemporary young working-class masculinities. *Sociology, 47*(4), 671–686.

Roberts, S. (2018). *Young working-class men in transition*. Routledge.

Roberts, S. (2020). *Young working-class men in transition (critical studies of men and masculinities)* (1st ed.). Routledge.

Roberts, S., Anderson, E., & Magrath, R. (2017). Continuity, change and complexity in the performance of masculinity among elite young footballers in England. *The British Journal of Sociology, 68*(2), 336–357. https://doi.org/10.1111/1468-4446.12237

Roberts, C. J., Hurst, H. T., & Hardwicke, J. (2022). Eating disorders and disordered eating in competitive Cycling: A scoping review. *Behavioral Sciences, 12*(12), 490.

Robidoux, M. A. (2001). *Men at play: A working understanding of professional hockey*. McGill-Queen's Press-MQUP.

Robinson, V. (2008). *Everyday masculinities and extreme sport: Male identity and rock climbing*. Berg.

Robinson, S., & Anderson, E. (2022). *Bromance: Male friendship, love and sport*. Springer International Publishing.

Robinson, S., White, A., & Anderson, E. (2019). Privileging the bromance: A critical appraisal of romantic and bromantic relationships. *Men and Masculinities, 22*(5), 850–871.

Roderick, M. (2006). Adding insult to injury: Workplace injury in English professional football. *Sociology of Health & Illness, 28*(1), 76–97.

Rooney, D., Sarriegui, I., & Heron, N. (2020). 'As easy as riding a bike': A systematic review of injuries and illness in road cycling. *BMJ Open Sport & Exercise Medicine, 6*(1), e000840. https://doi.org/10.1136/bmjsem-2020-000840

Roper, E. A., & Halloran, E. (2007). Attitudes toward gay men and lesbians among heterosexual male and female student-athletes. *Sex Roles, 57*(11), 919–928.

Rotundo, A. E. (1993). *American manhood: Transformations in masculinity from the revolution to the modern era* (Reprint ed.). Basic Books.

Rouler. (2021). *Cycling's #MeToo moment*. Rouleur. https://www.rouleur.cc/blogs/the-rouleur-journal/cycling-s-metoo-moment-part-one

Rubinstein, D. (1977). Cycling in the 1890s. *Victorian Studies, 21*(1), 47–71.

Ryder, S., McLachlan, F., & McDonald, B. (2021). Riding in a Man's world: Gendered struggles in professional Women's Road Cycling. In *The Professionalisation of Women's Sport*. Emerald Publishing Limited.

Sabo, D. (2009). Sports injury, the pain principle, and the promise of reform. *Journal of Intercollegiate Sport, 2*(1), 145–152.

Sabo, D., Heywood, L., Miller, K. E., & Melnick, M. J. (2004). *Her life depends on it: Sport, physical activity and the health and well-being of American girls.* Women's Sports Foundation.

Sabo, D., & Panepinto, J. (1990). Football ritual and the social reproduction of masculinity. In *Sport, men, and the gender order: Critical feminist perspectives* (pp. 115–126). Human Kinetics.

Safai, P. (2003). Healing the body in the "culture of risk": Examining the negotiation of treatment between sport medicine clinicians and injured athletes in Canadian intercollegiate sport. *Sociology of Sport Journal, 20*(2), 127–146.

Sanchis-Gomar, F., Olaso-Gonzalez, G., Corella, D., Gomez-Cabrera, M. C., & Vina, J. (2011). Increased average longevity among the "tour de France" cyclists. *International Journal of Sports Medicine, 32*(08), 644–647. https://doi.org/10.1055/s-0031-1271711

Sanday, P. R. (1992). *Fraternity gang rape: Sex, brotherhood, and privilege on campus.* NYU Press.

Sanderson, J., Weathers, M., Snedaker, K., & Gramlich, K. (2016). "I Was Able to Still Do My Job on the Field and Keep Playing": An Investigation of Female and Male Athletes' Experiences With (Not) Reporting Concussions. *Communication & Sport, 5*(3), 267–287. https://doi.org/10.1177/2167479515623455

Sanderson, J., Weathers, M., Snedaker, K., & Gramlich, K. (2017). "I was able to still do my job on the Field and keep playing": An investigation of female and male athletes' experiences with (not) reporting concussions. *Communication & Sport, 5*(3), 267–287. https://doi.org/10.1177/2167479515623455

Schacht, S. P. (1996). Misogyny on and off the "pitch" the gendered world of male rugby players. *Gender & Society, 10*(5), 550–565.

Schlosser, A. J. (2016). *Concussion knowledge and attitudes: The impact of hegemonic masculinity.* The University of North Dakota.

Scott, M. (1968). *The racing game.* Aldine.

Scott, S. D., & Austin, M. (2016). Edgework, fun, and identification in a recreational subculture: Street BMX riders. *Qualitative Sociology Research, 12*(4), 84–99.

Sherry, E. (2013). The vulnerable researcher: Facing the challenges of sensitive research. *Qualitative Research Journal, 13*(3), 278–288.

Sidwells, C. (2019). *The call of the Road: The history of cycle Road racing.* William Collins.

Silberman, M. (2013). Bicycling injuries. *Current Sports Medicine Reports, 12*(5), 337–345. https://doi.org/10.1249/JSR.0b013e3182a4bab7

Simpson, C. S. (2007). Capitalising on curiosity: women's professional cycle racing in the late-nineteenth century. In *Cycling and society* (pp. 47–65). Ashgate Publishing.

REFERENCES 205

Slappendel, J. (2018, May 12). Op-Ed: The institutional sexism in cycling needs to end. Outside Online. https://www.outsideonline.com/culture/opinion/op-ed-institutional-sexism-cycling-needs-end/.

Smart, B. (2018). Consuming Olympism: Consumer culture, sport star sponsorship and the commercialisation of the Olympics. *Journal of Consumer Culture, 18*(2), 241–260. https://doi.org/10.1177/1469540517747146

Smith, M. (1983). *Violence in sport*. Butterworths.

Smith, C. (2015). Tour du dopage: Confessions of doping professional cyclists in a modern work environment. *International Review for the Sociology of Sport, 52*(1), 97–111.

Smith, B., & McGannon, K. R. (2018). Developing rigor in qualitative research: Problems and opportunities within sport and exercise psychology. *International Review of Sport and Exercise Psychology, 11*(1), 101–121.

Spencer, C. (1995). *Homosexuality a history* (0th ed.). Fourth Estate Ltd.

Sporting Cyclist, UK. (1967, October), p. 12.

Spring, J. H. (1974). Mass culture and school sports. *History of Education Quarterly, 14*, 483–499.

Stebbins, R. A. (1992). *Amateurs, professionals, and serious leisure*. McGill-Queen's University Press. http://www.jstor.org/stable/j.ctt81ccj

Stick, M. (2021). Conflicts in sporting masculinity: The beliefs and behaviors of Canadian male athletes. *The Journal of Men's Studies, 29*(3), 315–334.

Strange, L. S. (2002). The bicycle, women s rights, and Elizabeth cady Stanton. *Women's Studies, 31*(5), 609–626.

Taghdiri, F., Multani, N., Tarazi, A., Naeimi, S. A., Khodadadi, M., Esopenko, C., Green, R., Colella, B., Wennberg, R., Mikulis, D., Davis, K. D., Goswami, R., Tator, C., Levine, B., & Tartaglia, M. C. (2019). Elevated cerebrospinal fluid total tau in former professional athletes with multiple concussions. *Neurology, 92*(23), e2717–e2726. https://doi.org/10.1212/wnl.0000000000007608

Taylor, M. (2013). *The association game: A history of British football*. Routledge.

Taylor, T., Fujak, H., Hanlon, C., & O'Connor, D. (2022). A balancing act: Women players in a new semi-professional team sport league. *European Sport Management Quarterly, 22*(4), 527–547.

The Bristol Bicycle and Tricycle Club Monthly Gazette. (1897, January–December).

The British Continental. (2021a, July 29). *Clay Davies interview: Free spirit*. The British Continental. https://thebritishcontinental.co.uk/2021/07/23/clay-davies-interview-free-spirit/

The British Continental. (2021b, July 31). *Being gay in cycle sport: A junior rider's experience*. The British Continental. https://thebritishcontinental.co.uk/2021/07/29/being-gay-in-cycle-sport-a-junior-riders-experience/

Theberge, N. (1985). Toward a feminist alternative to sport as a male preserve. *Quest, 37*(2), 193–202.

Theberge, N. (2000). Gender and sport. In *Handbook of sports studies* (pp. 322–333). Sage.

Thornton, S. (1995). *Club cultures: Music, media, and subcultural capital.* Wesleyan University Press.

Thrasher, F. M. (1927). *The gang: A study of 1313 gangs in Chicago.* The University of Chicago Press.

Tosh, J. (2005). Masculinities in an industrializing society: Britain, 1800–1914. *Journal of British Studies, 44*(2), 330–342.

Trek. (2022). *The beginners guide to racing gravel.* Retrieved form https://blog. trekbikes.com/en_UK/2022/03/20/the-beginners-guide-to-racing-gravel/

Twenge, J. M., Sherman, R. A., & Wells, B. E. (2016). Changes in American adults' reported same-sex sexual experiences and attitudes, 1973–2014. *Archives of Sexual Behavior, 45*(7), 1713–1730.

USA Cycling. (2015, December 16). *Diversity, equity, & inclusion.* USA Cycling. https://usacycling.org/diversity-equity-inclusion

Vamplew, W. (2013). Theories and typologies: A historical exploration of the sports club in Britain. *The International Journal of the History of Sport, 30*(14), 1569–1585.

Velominati, T. (2014). *The rules: The Way of the Cycling disciple (illustrated).* W. W. Norton & Company.

Velominati. (2017). *The hardmen – Legends and lessons from the Cycling gods.* Pegasus.

Velominati – Keepers of the Cog. (2022, June 25). https://www.velominati.com/

Venkatesh, S. A. (2008). *Gang leader for a day: A rogue sociologist takes to the streets.* Penguin.

Vertinsky, P. A. (1990). *The eternally wounded woman: Women, doctors, and exercise in the late nineteenth century.* Manchester University Press.

Vilanova, A., Soler, S., & Anderson, E. (2020). Examining the experiences of the first openly gay male team sport athlete in Spain. *International Review for the Sociology of Sport, 55*(1), 22–37.

Waddington, I. (2000). Sport and health: A sociological perspective. In *Handbook of sports studies* (pp. 408–421). Sage.

Waddington, I. (2005). Changing patterns of drug use in British sport from the 1960s. *Sport in History, 25*(3), 472–496.

Waddington, I., & Gleyse, J. (2005). Le dopage sportif: la responsabilité des praticiens médicaux. Doping in sport: The responsibilities of medical practitioners. *Staps, 4,* 9–23.

Wadler, G. I., & Hainline, B. (1989). *Drugs and the athlete.* FA David.

Wagner, K. (2022, July 13). The sport of cycling fixates on pain too much. Bicycling. https://www.bicycling.com/tour-de-france/a40578977/sport-of-cycling-fixates-pain/

REFERENCES 207

Waldron, J. J., & Kowalski, C. L. (2009). Crossing the line: Rites of passage, team aspects, and ambiguity of hazing. *Research Quarterly for Exercise and Sport, 80*(2), 291–302.

Waldron, J. J., & Krane, V. (2005). Motivational climate and goal orientation in adolescent female softball players. *Journal of Sport Behavior, 28*(4), 378.

Waters, C. (1981). Badges of half-formed, inarticulate radicalism: A critique of recent trends in the study of working class youth culture. *International Labor and Working-Class History, 19*, 23–38.

Way, N., Cressen, J., Bodian, S., Preston, J., Nelson, J., & Hughes, D. (2014). "It might be nice to be a girl... Then you wouldn't have to be emotionless": Boys' resistance to norms of masculinity during adolescence. *Psychology of Men & Masculinity, 15*(3), 241.

Weinberg, S. K., & Arond, H. (1952). The occupational culture of the boxer. *American Journal of Sociology, 57*(5), 460–469.

Wellard, I. (2010). Men, sport, body performance and the maintenance of 'exclusive masculinity'. *Leisure Studies, 21*(3–4), 235–247. https://doi.org/10.1080/0261436022000030641

Wheaton, B. (2007). After sport culture: Rethinking sport and post-subcultural theory. *Journal of Sport and Social Issues, 31*(3), 283–307.

White, A., & Hobson, M. (2017). Teachers' stories: Physical education teachers' constructions and experiences of masculinity within secondary school physical education. *Sport, Education and Society, 22*(8), 905–918.

White, A. J., Magrath, R., & Emilio Morales, L. (2021). Gay male athletes' coming-out stories on Outsports.com. *International Review for the Sociology of Sport, 56*(7), 1017–1034.

White, A. J., Parry, K. D., Humphries, C., Phelan, S., Batten, J., & Magrath, R. (2020). Duty of Karius: Media framing of concussion following the 2018 UEFA champions league final. *Communication & Sport.* https://doi.org/10.1177/2167479520948048

White, P. G., & Vagi, A. B. (1990). "Rugby in the 19th-century British boarding-school system: A feminist psychoanalytic perspective." pp. 67–78 in Sport, Men, and the Gender Order, ed. Michael Messner and Don Sabo. Champaign, IL: Human Kinetics. Whitehead, N. J., & Hendry, L. B. (1976). Teaching Physical Education.

Wignall, L., Scoats, R., Anderson, E., & Morales, L. (2020). A qualitative study of heterosexual men's attitudes toward and practices of receiving anal stimulation. *Culture, Health & Sexuality, 22*(6), 675–689.

Wijlhuizen, G., van Gent, P., & Stipdonk, H. (2016). Sport Cycling crashes among males on public roads, the influence of bunch riding, experience and competitiveness. *Safety, 2*(2), 11. https://doi.org/10.3390/safety2020011

Williams, R. (1977). *Marxism and literature* (Vol. 392). Oxford Paperbacks.

Williams, R. (1983). *Culture and society, 1780–1950*. Columbia University Press.

Williams, T. (1989). Sport, hegemony and subcultural reproduction: The process of accommodation in bicycle road racing. *International Review for the Sociology of Sport, 24*(4), 315–333.

Wilson, B. (2006). *Fight, flight, or chill: Subcultures, youth, and rave into the 21st century*. McGill-Queen's University Press.

Wilson, L., Stewart, W., Dams-O'Connor, K., et al. (2017). The chronic and evolving neurological consequences of traumatic brain injury. *The Lancet Neurology, 16*(10), 813–825. https://doi.org/10.1016/s1474-4422(17)30279-x

Wittenberg, M. (2005). *Industrialisation and surplus labour: A general equilibrium model of sleep, work and leisure*. School of Economics, University of Cape Town.

Woog, D. (1998). *Jocks: True stories of America's gay male athletes*. Alyson.

Yesalis, C. E. (2002). History of doping in sport. In M. S. Bahrke & C. E. Yesalis (Eds.), *Performance enhancing substances in sport and exercise* (pp. 1–20). Human Kinetics.

Yinger, J. M. (1960). Contraculture and subculture. *American Sociological Review, 25*(5), 625–635.

YouGov. (2016, May 13). *Only 2% of young men feel completely masculine (compared to 56% of over 65s)*. https://yougov.co.uk/topics/politics/articles-reports/2016/05/13/low-young-masculinity-britain

Young, K. (1988). Performance, control, and public image of behavior in a deviant subculture: The case of rugby. *Deviant Behavior, 9*(3), 275–293.

Young, K. (2019). *Sport, violence and society* (2nd ed.). Routledge.

Young, K. A., & Atkinson, M. (Eds.). (2008). *Tribal play: Subcultural journeys through sport*. Emerald Group Publishing.

Young, K., McTeer, W., & White, P. (1994). Body talk: Male athletes reflect on sport, injury, and pain. *Sociology of Sport Journal, 11*(2), 175–194. https://doi.org/10.1123/ssj.11.2.175

Young, K., & White, P. (1995). Sport, physical danger, and injury: The experiences of elite women athletes. *Journal of Sport and Social Issues, 19*(1), 45–61.

Zheng, Y., Ma, Y., & Cheng, J. (2020). Cycling anger in China: The relationship with gender roles, cycling-related experience, risky and aggressive riding. *Transportation Research Part F: Traffic Psychology and Behaviour, 68*, 52–66. https://doi.org/10.1016/j.trf.2019.12.002

INDEX

A
Auto-ethnography, 10, 13

B
Bourgeoisie, 45, 48, 49
British Cycling, 3, 6, 110, 145, 146, 163, 166
British Sociological Association, 9

C
Cavalier masculinity, 49
Competitive sport, 7, 14, 15, 27–29, 42, 45–47, 50, 55, 68, 81, 104, 105, 110, 114, 124–129, 141–143, 147, 148, 153, 154, 160, 161, 167, 177
Cultural capital, 85, 86
Cultural lag, 15, 16, 29, 30, 69, 71, 153, 174, 178

Culture of risk, 15, 77, 93–95, 97, 98, 129, 133, 175
Cycling clubs, 48, 51–56, 84, 87

D
Dominant, Residual and Emergent culture, 29

E
Ethnographic, 8, 27, 87, 104, 105

G
Gazettes, 51–53

H
Hegemonic masculinity, 4, 23, 24, 31, 32, 34, 159

© The Author(s), under exclusive license to Springer Nature
Switzerland AG 2023
J. Hardwicke, *Masculinities and the Culture of Competitive Cycling*,
Palgrave Studies in Masculinity, Sport and Exercise,
https://doi.org/10.1007/978-3-031-26975-2

210 INDEX

Hegemonic Masculinity Theory (HMT), 23, 24, 26, 31
Homohysteria, 5, 25–27, 33, 68
Homophobia, 4, 5, 23–26, 66, 68, 70, 141, 143, 144, 146, 153, 154, 175
Host, 31, 178
Hypermasculine, 29, 49, 70, 160
Hyper subjectivity, 11, 12

I
Identity, 9, 11, 12, 15, 25, 26, 32, 44, 45, 48, 51, 65–68, 70, 80, 83–85, 91–93, 96, 98, 106, 114, 126, 136, 150, 168, 175, 178
Inclusive Masculinity Theory (IMT), 5, 9, 22, 24, 25, 27, 31–34, 69, 153, 174
Industrial Era, 28, 53, 56, 61, 105, 161
Injury, 2–4, 9, 15, 34, 45, 49, 53–55, 62, 63, 65, 69, 70, 86, 93–96, 103–116, 128–130, 133, 135, 136, 147, 161, 173, 175–178
Insider, 12, 14
Interactionist, 8, 133
Interview, 9, 10, 12, 13, 68, 90, 94, 95, 111, 113, 133, 143, 145

L
LGBTQ+, 4, 147, 148, 150, 151, 153

M
Macho, 61–65, 143–145, 174
Macro culture, 28, 29, 33, 65, 69
Male preserve, 21, 47, 159
Masculine hierarchy, 21, 27, 116

Membership, 3, 6, 9, 51, 52, 79, 80, 83–86, 89, 94, 110, 114, 115, 175
Military, 46, 52, 105, 125

N
Normalisation, 95–97

O
Objectivity, 12, 13
Orthodox masculinity, 8, 16, 22, 28–33, 50, 56, 68–70, 77, 90, 92, 115, 116, 125, 127, 128, 132, 135, 153, 154, 159–168, 173–176, 178

P
Physical capital, 90, 91

Q
Qualitative, 4, 9, 13, 79, 110, 154, 177
Quantitative, 4, 9, 110

R
Reflexivity, 12–14
Research method, 9
Rover Safety bicycle, 48, 49, 162

S
Sacrifice, 3, 28, 63–65, 80, 82, 88, 93, 104, 105, 136
Scorchers, 49
Self-report survey, 13, 65, 110, 147

INDEX 211

Serious leisure, 7, 84, 85, 92, 98, 148, 153, 175
Sexuality, 16, 43, 44, 62, 63, 141–144, 146, 148, 149
Sexual minorities, 3, 9, 16, 26, 70, 141–154, 159, 173, 175–177
Social capital, 27, 49, 53, 82, 83, 90
Social context, 4, 21, 22, 34, 51, 88, 137, 142, 176
Social institutions, 27, 31, 143, 144, 160
Socialisation, 44, 46, 47, 83, 88, 89
Social norms, 22, 78, 105, 136
Social world, 2, 11, 78, 82, 86–88
Socio-cultural, 3, 4, 7, 8, 21, 25, 85, 86, 114, 124, 126, 129, 132, 134, 137, 176–178
Sociology, 5, 12, 15, 77–81, 83, 143, 159
Sport ethic, 63, 104, 129, 135, 136, 175
Sport-related concussion (SRC), 108–111
Subcultural capital, 86, 116, 135
Subculture, 15, 28, 30, 31, 34, 69, 77–94, 96–98, 103, 112–116, 135–137, 154, 160, 167, 173–178

Subjectivity, 11–13

T
Tour de France, 63, 64, 108, 130, 131, 134, 163
Tradition, 13, 54, 77, 81, 126, 130, 176
Traditional sport, 161, 164

U
United Kingdom (UK), 3, 5, 6, 10, 12, 24, 25, 29, 66, 78, 109, 110, 112, 130, 135, 145, 148, 163

V
Velominati, T., 62, 63, 86
Victorian Britain, 7, 34, 41–56, 130, 174

W
Weekend warrior, 7, 9
Western culture, 22, 81, 83, 110
Winning at all costs, 116, 123–137, 175